WHEN FOOTBALL
CAME TO KETTERING

The history of
Kettering Town Football Club
Part 1: 1872 - 1900

&

The origins of
Kettering Rugby Football Club

Uppingham rules - rugby union - association football

Mel Hopkins & Bob Brown

To Lynne Hopkins & Linda Brown
For their patience

When Football Came to Kettering

ISBN 978-0-9567327-0-5

Researched, written & published by
Mel Hopkins & Bob Brown
November 2010

mel.hopkins@tiscali.co.uk

15 Welland Court
Burton Latimer
Kettering
NN15 5ST

Design/layout BBD&P
Printed and bound in England

Any profit made by the publishers through the sale
of this book will be donated to Cransley Hospice
(registered charity number 1052867)

Contents

Illustrations (With Acknowledgements)

Bibliography

Primary newspaper sources between 1862 and 1900 (in approximate order of publication):

The Field	*Northampton Weekly Reporter*
Northampton Mercury	*Kettering Observer*
Northampton Herald	*Kettering Guardian*
Northampton Albion	*Northampton Daily Reporter*
Northampton Albion & Wellingborough	*Kettering Leader*
& Kettering Chronicle	*Kettering Leader & Observer*
Northamptonshire Guardian	*Kettering Evening Telegraph*
Wellingborough & Kettering News	*Kettering Football Telegraph*
Northampton Mercury Daily Reporter	*Northampton Football Echo*

Kettering Parish and Uppingham School magazines of the 1870s

Books and booklets:

The Football Annual, Charles W. Alcock, Virtue, issues 1868-1889

The Book of Football: A Complete History and Record of the Association and Rugby Games The Amalgamated Press, 1906

Northamptonshire in the Twentieth Century: Contemporary Biographies, W.T. Pike, 1908

'Kettering Town Football Club Handbook 1957/58', Reg Abbott, Supporters' Club Committee, 1957

A History of British Football, Percy M. Young, Stanley Paul, 1968

'Kettering Rugby Football Club 1875-1975', Tony Hewitt, 1975

'Kettering Town Centenary Handbook', David Buckby & Mick Ward, Kettering Town Football Supporters' Association, 1976

'Physical Education at Thring's Uppingham', Malcolm Tozer, Uppingham School, 1976

'A Century of Cricket at Kettering 1885-1985', John & Peter Larcombe, 1985

Old Kettering – A View From the 1930s (Books 1-6), Tony Ireson, 1988, 1990, 1992, 1994, 1997, 1999

The Official History of the Football Association, Bryon Butler, Queen Anne Press, 1991

'The Royal Kettering Troop of the Northamptonshire Yeomanry', Vic Lawrence & Peter Hill, 1994

Denied F.C.: The Football League Election Struggles, Dave Twydell, Yore Publications, 2001

A History of Kettering, R.L. Greenall, Phillimore, 2003

England: The Official Rugby Football Union History, Virgin Books, 2004

Acknowledgements

It was back in 1982 – yes, that long ago! – while researching a book I was to write on the village of Geddington (my birthplace), that I came across an article in a *Northampton Mercury* newspaper published one hundred and ten years earlier, on 9 November 1872, hinting at the day when football came to Kettering: "A football club has recently been established in this town..."

Having attended the game to mark Kettering Town's centenary, a 3-1 victory over West Bromwich Albion, on 21 December *1976*, it was clear that something did not add up. Could it be that the club had been formed earlier than previously thought? The *Mercury* article set me on a quest to find out more about the Poppies (a nickname that can be traced back to October 1907, when it was coined by the local *Pink-un*, reflecting on the colour of the team's poppy-red strip).

For the next twenty years I copied by hand everything I could find regarding Kettering (Town) Football Club ('Town' would not officially become part of the title until the 1920s, despite numerous references to the 'town club' prior to this). I recorded the teams and goal scorers (see appendices), all the gossip about players, where they came from and where they went to.

The majority of information contained within this book was gleaned from contemporary newspaper articles. For their assistance in this task I must thank the staff – past and present – at the *Evening Telegraph* offices in Kettering and Rushden, and at the public libraries in Kettering and Northampton. Reference was also made to contemporary magazines, in particular those of Kettering Parish and Uppingham School, and my thanks are extended to the staff at the school, especially the librarian Harry Spry-Leverton.

Uppingham School is significant because it provided Kettering's first ever opponents, as well as the rules of football to which the club originally (albeit briefly) adhered. It is also interesting to note the role a member of Uppingham's staff – J.C. Thring – played in the development of the game during the years leading up to the formation of the Football Association in 1863.

Only after I transferred my notes to an Amstrad computer that subsequently became obsolete, thus necessitating a huge amount of rewriting, did I realise how much data I had accumulated over two decades, and that it would be all but impossible to encompass a complete history of the club in a single volume without glossing over details.

It was around this time that I received a letter from Bob Brown offering to get involved in the project. As I was becoming tired of the running question, *when is the book coming out?* I accepted his offer, and what you hold in your hands is the result – the beginning of the story, an account of the Poppies' formative years. A time when the sportsmen of Kettering enjoyed games of football played to rules quite different to those we know today.

Mel Hopkins

There have been, so far as I am aware, three previously published accounts of the early days of football in Kettering. Firstly, the late Reg Abbott laid out the results of his research in the Poppies' 1957-58 handbook. I had the privilege of meeting Reg to talk about his labours in October 2005, when he recalled how he spent around nine months sifting through the newspaper archives at the *Evening Telegraph* offices in Dryland Street, seeking out snippets of association football news amidst a plethora of rugby union match reports.

Mick Groom also spent time delving into the archives before writing his piece 'The Early Professional Days' for the club's 'Centenary Handbook', published in 1976 (that year again!) I am indebted to Mick for the loan of his extensive notes.

The third account I have seen is Tony Hewitt's booklet celebrating another centenary – that of Kettering Rugby Football Club, published in 1975(!) Obviously not intentionally written as an account of the football club's doings, it is only in the light of Mel Hopkins' research that it becomes quite reasonable to propose that the origins of the town's senior football and rugby clubs can both be traced to the same day in 1872.

No doubt one day *this* book will be superseded as new information comes to light. In fact a certain amount of material was added after Jim Welch 'rescued' a significant number of old newspapers dating back to the 1880s from a house-clearance skip, and immediately donated them to the Kettering Town (Poppies) Supporters Trust, which is steadily building an important collection of club memorabilia. I am extremely grateful to Jim and the Trust for the loan of his find.

Victorian newspaper and magazine pieces have been reproduced in the pages that follow in the manner in which they were published, with the result that what might be considered grammatical errors still remain within the text. Articles set out in the grey boxes are not *direct* copies because the antiquity of the paper on which they were printed would not allow it. They are, however, as close to the originals as possible.

Special mention has to be made of Alf Althorpe, guardian of his late uncle Fred Moore's collection of photographs. The image of association football being played at Eldred's Field (on the cover and page 67) has been reproduced by Alf's kind permission. It is, without doubt, one of the most remarkable photographs I have seen.

The credit for other images used in the book can be found on page iv. Thank you to everyone who contributed. Pictures not otherwise credited have been collected over the years either by myself or Mel. Many are of generally poor quality, being grainy newspaper reproductions of originals that were captured over a hundred years ago by photographers whose names are unknown. Phil Brigden has done his best to smooth out the imperfections, for which I am grateful.

The National Football Museum (and Peter Holm), the Manchester United Museum (and Brian Landamore), Burton Latimer Heritage Society and the staff within the Museum of Rugby at Twickenham were all very helpful. Mention must also be made of Dave Dunham, Paul Cooke, Bev Roberts (Ken Hall Footwear) and my father Clifford Brown for their assistance in various matters.

Finally, my sincere thanks go to Mel for allowing me to become involved in his project.

Bob Brown

One

From the Village to the Town

Origins of a Football Club

"As I think the present generation of football players in Kettering and district may not be aware of what they owe to the late Mr. G.W. Roughton (whose lamented death was recorded in your last issue) for the introduction of football, I venture to send you these few notes. Previous to 1872 the thud of the football, except for a scratch game now and again at Barton Seagrave under the present Rector, had hardly ever been heard in the town or neighbourhood. In the autumn of that year Mr. George Roughton and others formed a club, and I believe that the Kettering Club can boast of being the oldest in the county."

Origins of a Football Club

In the early spring of 1868, the Reverend and Honourable John Marsham walked beneath the crudely decorated tympanum and into the Norman church of St Botolph's. The second son of the third Earl of Romney and a grandson of the Duke of Buccleuch, Marsham was Barton Seagrave's new rector, a post he would hold for the next 40 years. Many Victorian clergymen played a role in the growth of sport throughout the Empire, believing exercise to be an important part of a young man's spiritual wellbeing, and this priest was no exception. A prominent cricketer, he promoted the sound of leather on willow in Barton, represented Northamptonshire's Northern Division and took a lead in efforts to form a county-level cricket club. But the Reverend was not just an exponent of the summer pastime, he also brought with him to the district knowledge of a somewhat rougher winter game – football.

Educated at Eton, Cambridge and Oxford, the new rector was acquainted with organised football played to rules and, at some time in the late 1860s or early 1870s (probably 1869), he set about arranging an annual match around the Christmas period, along the lines of the game he had learned at Eton.

Having identified a few budding footballers from in and around the village and explained the basics to them, Marsham had the nucleus of a side, including Jack Eayres, Charlie Maycock and James Robinson. However, there were insufficient numbers to play a full game so he issued an invitation to the young men of Kettering, beginning with the cricketers, to come to Barton and play football. The scratch team that came from the town included representatives from the families of Gotch, Lindsay, Mobbs, Roughton and Wilson. The Reverend provided the ball and posts for goals and set out the playing area in the first field on the left going from Barton to Warkton. He later recalled: "Barton was then too good for Kettering, and they sent them home sorely smitten." (*Kettering Leader & Guardian*, 9 October 1908.)

The number of contests that took place on a cold winter's day in the vicinity of Warkton Lane (?) is not recorded, but it is possible to sketch out the rudiments of the game most likely played. At every restart the forwards on each side would come together to form a 'bully' – something akin to a present-day rugby scrum – manoeuvring the football with their feet whilst pushing and shoving until the bully disintegrated, whereupon those still standing would chase the loose ball and dribble or kick it with the ultimate aim of sending it between their opponents' goalposts.

Whether or not rules other than Eton's were incorporated into the games is open to debate. The real significance of the Barton Seagrave matches lies in the fact that many of the participants, including the Reverend, would subsequently become members of a new football club in Kettering. One player in particular stands out, the gentleman most credited with establishing that club – George Woodford Roughton.

A plaque at the entrance to the western driveway leading up to the imposing Parish Church of St Peter and St Paul pays tribute to the Roughton family in Kettering, residents of the town from 1487 to 1933. Farmers at first, they later served the community as doctors, father and son, for five generations. Indeed, George's father, Dr James John Roughton, was a very influential and respected man of the period, responsible for all manner of improvements to local services.

The *Northampton Mercury* credits W. Shrives (of whom little is known) as a co-founder of the club, and it is apparent that Nathaniel Newman, referred to by his contemporaries as 'The Father of Kettering Football', also took an active role. And no doubt others did, too. But the importance of George Roughton's place in the history of football in Kettering may be gleaned from an article entitled 'The Late Mr. G.W. Roughton', published in the *Kettering Guardian* on 7 April 1899:

> Mr. Geo. Woodford Roughton, whose death from dysentery was recorded in our last issue upon the news becoming known by means of a cablegram from Bombay [Roughton died in March 1899, aged 48], is best known to the older people in Kettering as a keen supporter of local sports. The Town Football Club was practically started by him. In Bombay he was well known. He had lived there for the last 19 years, and in 1896 was made chairman of the Chamber of Commerce. He has for many years been Commanding Officer of the Bombay Volunteer Artillery, and only last month received the appointment of A.D.C. to the Viceroy, in recognition of his services. He has also been very active as Visiting Justice under the Plague Commission since the outbreak of the plague, and there is little doubt that his death in the prime of life is to be attributed largely to that. He always enjoyed remarkably good health for a European, and was of fine physique.
>
> An original member of the Kettering Football Club writes to us:– "As I think the present generation of football players in Kettering and district may not be aware of what they owe to the late Mr. G.W. Roughton (whose lamented death was recorded in your last issue) for the introduction of football, I venture to send you these few notes. Previous to 1872 the thud of the football, except for a scratch game now and again at Barton Seagrave under the present Rector, had hardly ever been heard in the town or neighbourhood. In the autumn of that year Mr. George Roughton and others formed a club, and I believe that the Kettering Club can boast of being the oldest in the county [it is quite possible that football was played in Wellingborough in the late 1860s, but Kettering Town is the oldest football club in Northamptonshire to have been in continuous existence]... Mr. Roughton was a brilliant player himself, being a good kick and very fast on his legs, and having complete control of his side, made an ideal captain."

After Rev Marsham had introduced the sport in the village, it must have seemed a logical next step for those involved to start a club in the town; not only had a number of potential players honed their skills in a field in Barton, but Kettering was expanding and the growing population would increasingly be drawn to taking part and watching as respite from the grind of everyday life. Even so, the code of football that Roughton and company initially elected to master – Uppingham rules – is, on the face of it, an obscure choice that requires some explanation.

By the middle of the 19th century, many of the public, proprietary and endowed grammar schools had developed different versions of an outdoor game played with a ball. Attempts to agree a common standard – enabling the ex-pupils of these establishments to compete against one another in a game they all understood – began at Cambridge University in 1846, when former Shrewsbury schoolboys John Charles Thring and Henry de Winton persuaded some Old Etonians to join them in forming a football club. A few matches took place but the club did not last long. Undeterred, Thring and de Winton arranged a meeting at Trinity College in October 1848. Here, a set of general football principles was agreed. The rules were printed and posted up on Parker's Piece (an area of grassland in Cambridge). Despite this progress, the schools themselves were far from ready to embrace a unified game, and the 1850s came and went without any further advances.

On 14 December 1861, *The Field*, 'The Country Gentleman's Newspaper', asked: "What happens when a game of football is proposed at Christmas among a party of young men assembled from different schools? Unless the public schools will combine and draw up a code of rules under which football can be played by all classes, we despair of seeing it take place." The question posed set in motion a debate that would culminate in the formation of the Football Association two years later. Major contributors to that debate would be *The Field*'s John Dyer Cartwright, and J.C. Thring (as John Charles is almost universally referred to today), who published 'The Simplest Game', his own set of ten 'simple and universal' rules, in January 1862.

As was the case in the majority of games played at the time, Thring's rules allowed everyone on the field to handle the ball to some degree (even the embryonic FA would permit a 'fair catch'); there was a detailed definition of a player being 'out of play' – 'offside', in modern parlance; and in an enlightened move away from the traditional 'hacking' and general violence considered part and parcel of many codes – particularly those influenced by the game played at Rugby School – Thring outlawed tripping up and the kicking of an opponent's heels.

1. A goal is scored whenever the ball is forced through the goal and under the bar, except it be thrown by the hand.

2. Hands may be used only to stop a ball and place it on the ground before the feet.

3. Kicks must be aimed only at the ball.

4. A player may not kick the ball whilst in the air.

5. No tripping up or heel kicking allowed.

6. Whenever a ball is kicked beyond the side flags, it must be returned by the player who kicked it, from the spot it passed the flag-line, in a straight line towards the middle of the ground.

7. When a ball is kicked behind the line of goal, it shall be kicked off from that line by one of the side whose goal it is.

8. No player may stand within six paces of the kicker when he is kicking off.

9. A player is out of play immediately he is in front of the ball, and must return behind the ball as soon as possible. If the ball is kicked by his own side past a player, he may not touch it, or advance, until one of the other side has first kicked it, or one of his own side, having followed it up, has been able, when in front of him, to kick it.

10. No charging is allowed when a player is out of play – i.e. immediately the ball is behind him.

'The Simplest Game', published in 1862 by John Charles Thring.

Born at Alford, Somerset on 29 November 1821, (the Reverend) Thring matriculated at St John's College, Cambridge in 1843. Whilst at Cambridge, he gained a BA, was a curate until 1855 – and became an early proponent of a unified game of football. Thring joined the staff at Uppingham School in 1859, and his ideas on football continued to flourish through 'The Simplest Game' and 'Football, the Winter Game' (16 rules, published in 1863). He led the call for goalkeepers, coloured marks to distinguish between the players of opposing teams, and the use of some form of crossbar (not included in the FA's original set of rules) to prevent goals being scored at any height between the posts.

Considering the merits of football over cricket, Thring wrote:

It is cheaper, a fair level field – say, 200 by 100 yards is required; four poles 11 feet long, and two cross-bars 15 feet long; eighteen flags on short sticks; these are all that are wanted: a round leather ball, mind you, of fair dimensions and tolerable weight – not a light thing, which like a piece of misshapen India-rubber, bounds any way but that which it ought to do; and an hour and a half is quite enough for the enjoyment of the game; and one player to stand between the goal posts to guard against the ball passing through.

The debate in *The Field* came to a head in October 1863. On the 10th, Thring announced: "There will probably be a meeting in London shortly, in order to draw up a code of laws." The newspaper was less optimistic: "No school will ever adopt the games of another, any more than they would its colours, its customs, its slang, or its constitutions." A fortnight later, Cartwright was close to despair: "Two years ago, in the hope of effecting an improvement, we published the rules of the game as played at the chief schools. Neither the amalgamation of which our correspondents spoke, nor the formation of a new universal set of laws, took place; and the game is now surrounded by as foggy an atmosphere as ever."

But things were about to become a little clearer. Two days after Cartwright's piece, on Monday, 26 October 1863, representatives from a handful of clubs met at the Freemason's Tavern in London, where Messrs Morley and McKenzie respectively proposed and seconded the resolution: "That it is advisable that a football association should be formed for the purpose of settling a code of rules for the regulation of the game of football." The FA was born, but it would take another half-dozen meetings to finalise the rules under which its members would play.

A number of Thring's ideas (on offside and pitch size, for example) were taken up at these meetings. It is even possible that association football – as it would become known – might have been based entirely on his vision, but in the end it was the rules that had evolved at Cambridge University – the Cambridge rules (which he and de Winton had laid the foundations of some 15 years earlier) – that provided more of a template, largely because a committee of gentlemen who had been at the leading public schools had put their names to the most contemporary version.

Thring, who had been on the staff at Uppingham School since 1859, had indicated to the FA that the school was desirous of becoming a member, but the Association's leaning towards the Cambridge rules resulted in the exclusion of the bully from their game, prompting him to write in *The Field*: "I think an unfair prejudice against it must exist. I therefore cannot join those who object to it and wish for its total abolition."

Thring and Uppingham were not the only ones to turn their back on the new organisation.

Nine years after the FA's formation, Wanderers beat the Royal Engineers by a goal to nil in the very first FA Cup final and England drew 0-0 with Scotland in Glasgow in the first officially recognised international fixture. But despite these notable matches, in 1872 the Association was still struggling to assert its rules over numerous regional variations. Association football had not yet caught the public's imagination – nor would it in Northamptonshire for at least another decade. Consequently, the influence of a young man's education proved greater than that of any sporting body and, for a short time, Kettering adopted the game played by the boys at Uppingham School.

George Roughton had studied at Uppingham. And in his footsteps followed two of his brothers, James and Quintus, who would both take part (one on each side) in Kettering's first arranged fixture – versus a team from the school. Even Uppingham's captain on what would be a wet December afternoon, Harry Marryatt Lindsay, was a local lad who had played in the games at Barton Seagrave and would later turn out for his home-town club. Christened Henry but popularly known as Harry, he was the eldest son of Canon Henry Lindsay, Rector of Kettering between 1863 and 1892 (in whose honour Canon and Lindsay Streets are named).

Football had been played at the school since the appointment in September 1853 of Edward Thring, a former student of Eaton and King's College, Cambridge – and brother of J.C. Thring. When the first Committee of Games was convened four years later, amongst the rules it published was a set that governed football at Uppingham (along with a resolution that at least one match a week should take place). It was a game which bore similarities to that played at Eton (the 'field game'), with additional elements 'borrowed' from Rugby School, and a few quirks all of its own. Played on an oval pitch with a goal at each end, the objective was to drive the ball through your opponents' goal. The ball could be kicked, or handled – and then kicked, but not passed – if caught cleanly or off the first bounce. Long fly-kicks followed by prolonged bullies were the game's notable features.

During the five years J.C. Thring spent at the school, he would clearly have had an influence on the way football evolved at Uppingham (and perhaps the boys helped shape his own ideas for 'The Simplest Game'). He moved on in 1864, the year before George Roughton enrolled. When Roughton completed his studies in 1869, the code of football he had been taught was now defined by around 25 rules – with the dimensions of the goals set at seven feet high and 40 feet wide!

By the autumn of 1872, according to an article to be found in an issue of the school's magazine that year, the game at Uppingham had become a neat blend of association football and rugby union:

> It is the most happy combination of the two rules that could possibly have been conceived. There is just enough running to give additional excitement and pleasure, there is no more handball than is absolutely necessary, while there is as large a scope as there is in the Association game for a display of science and skill in the subtle art of dribbling. One more word; it is harder work than either of the two other games, and that this has much to do with making it the most enjoyable is the full belief of 'One who has played all three.' The great evil of the Association game is there is really no off-side; instead of 'backing up' the Associates 'pass on' the ball to one of their own side, who, by the rules of the Rugby Union and our game, is off-side.

A follow-up piece in the magazine's next issue explains why 'the subtle art of dribbling' would have been difficult in practice: "Everybody will admit that dribbling, not running and heaving, is the point in which the school wishes to excel. Why, then, is the Rugby oval ball used in our game? By using the Association round ball, the dribbling of the School would be far more perfect..."

Footballs at Uppingham (and elsewhere) were originally made from sections of cow hide stitched together and turned inside out. A pig's bladder was inserted into the cavity and blown up through a pipe, the neck of the bladder tied and the opening into which it had been inserted then laced. The result was more a plum- or egg-shaped ball, similar to a modern rugby ball but with more rounded ends. Even after the introduction of vulcanised indiarubber bladders (and pumps), facilitating the mass-production of completely round balls for those games that required one, Uppingham's boys continued to use one that would not roll in a straight line.

And so it was that when Kettering's footballers first took to a field in the town – in an era when long pants were *de rigueur* and the rules were upheld by gentlemanly captains – it was for a game that involved both kicking and handling an oval ball, on a (possibly oval) pitch whose boundaries might have been marked out with flags or sticks (if anything at all), with a goal at each end formed by a rope 'crossbar' strung between two wooden posts. This was raw sport. Played for its own sake.

This was football, and it had come to Kettering.

Two

A Game in George Eldred's Field

1872 - 1874

"The sides were evenly matched, the heavier weights of the Kettering club being fully counter balanced by the greater experience of the Uppingham players. No advantage was gained by either party until the sides were changed, though the school had a hard try at goal, and doubtless would have got it had the ropes been tightly drawn, as it was the ball went over. The sides having been changed, Kettering played up more together, keeping the ball well down to their opponents' goal, and very shortly a long heave by C. Maycock sent the ball through goal. After this no further advantage was obtained by either side."

35 years into the reign of Queen Victoria, when Gladstone held the office of Prime Minister; 13 years after the publication of Darwin's *On the Origin of Species* and seven years before the birth of Einstein; in the decade of war with the Zulus, the invention of the telephone and the adventurer Stanley stumbling across the 'lost' missionary Dr Livingstone; whilst the Impressionists were changing the face of art and the cricketer W.G. Grace was in his prime, the town of Kettering was booming. The number of footwear manufacturers had increased threefold since the end of the 1860s, mostly in the wake of French Government orders for army boots to fight the Franco-Prussian War. The Kettering Industrial Co-operative Society was by now established and starting to expand, the Midland Railway brought new faces to the town daily and its population of 7,000 was set to quadruple over the next 30 years.

Meanwhile, on an expanse of green still removed from Kettering's Industrial Revolution, the sound of townsmen kicking a ball could be heard...

The earliest reference to a football club in Kettering is to be found tucked away in the pages of the *Northampton Mercury* of Saturday, 9 November 1872:

A football club has recently been established in this town through the instrumentality of Messrs G.W. Roughton and W. Shrives. The want of an out-door amusement on Saturday afternoons, to take the place in winter that cricket holds in summer, has long been felt, which this club will no doubt satisfy. Upwards of 30 members have already joined, and the first game is to take place this afternoon in a field kindly lent by George Eldred.

Businessman, philanthropist, churchwarden and Sunday-school teacher, Mr Eldred was a well known figure in Kettering. His field (or 'Home Close') ran adjacent to London Road and Green Lane. Present-day St Peter's Avenue and York Road roughly complete its boundaries, with Tennyson Road running through an area where the pitch must once have been. Cricket had been played on the site since at least the 1860s.

The object of that November afternoon was to give the new club's members some practice. There were those who had played at Barton Seagrave but there would have been others who might never have seen a football before. One of the original members later recalled how poorly prepared some of his fellows were for the rough-and-tumble of Victorian sport: "It may cause some amusement when I mention that at the first practice game of the newly-formed club one or two of the players turned up to play in canvas shoes." (*Kettering Guardian*, 7 April 1899.)

Nevertheless, just a few weeks later, on Thursday, 19 December, 17 members of the Kettering Football Club were ready for their first 'competitive' match, versus a team from Uppingham School. (Nowadays the fixture would be termed a 'friendly', as would the rest of the club's games during the 1870s and the majority of those played throughout the 1880s, before leagues and cups were competed for on a regular basis.) George Eldred's field was again the venue.

It might seem unlikely that the fledgling club could compete with a side from the school that had given its name to the game being played, but Kettering did hold some advantages. They had an extra man – 17 to Uppingham's 16 (ironically, Uppingham rules football was supposed to be 15-a-side!) Added to this, the most accomplished of the visitors would have played against the school's Old Boys just 24 hours earlier (the last day of term), whilst the rest were probably some way below first XV standards. In truth, Kettering were not up against the best team Uppingham could have mustered.

KETTERING	UPPINGHAM SCHOOL
George Roughton (captain, aged 21)	Harry Marryatt Lindsay (captain, aged 16, from Kettering)
James Roughton (20)	Edgar Atlee Hunt (18, London)
Henry Roughton (14)	George Robert Irwin (17, Tynan)
Charles Bayes (age unknown)	William Price James (18, Cardiff)
Fred East (18)	John Gale Thring (18, the headmaster's son)
D. Gotch (age unknown)	Edward William Mitchell (18, Lyme Regis)
Harry Hanger (16)	Walter St. John Field (17, Tunbridge Wells)
John Hanger (23)	Wilfred Dryden Grant (18, Litchborough)
Frank Mobbs (17)	Arthur Shadwell (18, Ilford)
Nat Newman (35)	Arthur A. Williams (17, Bristol)
James Robinson (24)	Thomas George Styan (16, London)
Charlie Smith (18)	Quintus Ernest Roughton (17, Kettering)
George Wilson (29)	Arthur L. Lloyd (15, Sutton Coldfield)
Thomas 'Miller' Wilson (27)	Harry Butler Mallam (17, Oxford)
F. Lamb (age unknown)	Charles Marten Powell (17, Guildford)
Charlie Maycock (26)	F. St. John Pym (17, Bedford)
C. Wright (age unknown)	

Kettering's 17 players and the 16 from Uppingham School who faced one another across George Eldred's field on 19 December 1872. (Pieced together from various contemporary sources.)

All of which made for a close contest, as evidenced by a short report in the *Northampton Mercury*:

> The sides were evenly matched [except for the extra Kettering player!], the heavier weights of the Kettering club being fully counter balanced by the greater experience of the Uppingham players. No advantage was gained by either party until the sides were changed [half-time], though the school had a hard try at goal, and doubtless would have got it had the ropes been tightly drawn [between the goalposts], as it was the ball went over. The sides having been changed, Kettering played up more together, keeping the ball well down to their opponents' goal, and very shortly a long heave by C. Maycock sent the ball through goal. After this no further advantage was obtained by either side.

Thus, the 17 men of Kettering emerged triumphant and Charlie Maycock, encouraged to play football by Rev John Marsham at Barton Seagrave, earned the right to be known as the scorer of the club's first goal, albeit in a game far removed from the one we know today.

Another match took place on Boxing Day, when a George Roughton XV provided the opposition. This time the venue was John Turner Stockburn's field (later to become the original home of the town's cricket club), next to the Gas Works at the bottom of what is now Meadow Road (formerly Gas Street and, before that, Goose Pasture Lane). After an hour and a quarter the game ended in a 0-0 draw.

The club's first venture out of town was to play the Leicester Athletic Society on Saturday, 22 February 1873. Between 1806 and 1883, horse racing took place on a piece of land not far from the site of Leicester's railway station; it was also a venue for team sports and Kettering's match on the 22nd was played here, as were many of their subsequent games in Leicester. Known locally as Victoria Park or the Racecourse, the land would officially be opened as a public park in 1882.

The usual custom was for the home side to dictate by which set of rules the match should be played – and the Athletic Society chose to play rugby.

Rugby School's game had existed alongside all the other variations of football without being viewed as particularly different, until the birth of the Football Association in 1863. Initially, it was quite possible that one unified game of football would arise because the FA had only two problems with Rugby's rules: carrying the ball in one's hand for any distance, and stopping an opponent by means of hacking him down. Some compromise might have been reached on carrying the ball, but there was a great divide between those members for, and those against, hacking. Blackheath

Football Club's delegate at the meetings to shape the FA's direction considered hacking to be an essential element of football, arguing that if it were done away with the physical element of the game would disappear. In the event, the milder views of others won the day and Blackheath withdrew from the Association, paving the way for the gradual evolution of two distinct types of sport.

The split between the round and oval ball codes passed the point of no return when representatives from 21 clubs met at the Pall Mall restaurant in London on 26 January 1871 to form the Rugby Football Union – formally establishing a separate game based on the Rugby School model "to promote the interests of Rugby Football as well as a greater amount of sociability and good fellowship between the various Clubs comprising the Rugby Football Union." (1873 edition of the *Football Annual*, a publication edited for many years by Charles W. Alcock, FA Honorary Secretary.)

And so, just over two years after the formation of the RFU, Kettering's footballers played, and lost, their first game of rugby union. One source gives the score as two rouges and three touch-downs to three touch-downs, another (which suggests the contest actually took place on 8 March) shows the margin of defeat to be three rouges and five touch-downs to two touch-downs. A confusion perhaps stemming from the fact that, at the time, the RFU's game was defined by the grand total of 59 rules (association football was based on just ten). And the term 'rouge' would certainly have upset the administrators in London, according to an extract from 'The Rugby Game' that appeared in the 1873 *Football Annual*:

It is to be regretted that "rouges" and other inapplicable terms still crop up in the accounts of Rugby football published in the sporting papers. The term "rouge" has no existence either at Rugby [School] or in the Union code: why will clubs belonging to the Union persist in using it? A *touch-down* occurs when the defending side are compelled to touch the ball down in their own goal. When the attacking side touch the ball down in their opponents' goal, they gain a *try* or *punt-out*, according to whichever means they adopt with a view to obtaining a goal. [Rugby in the 1870s was all about scoring goals – a single goal was worth more than any combination of tries, punt-outs, posters, touches-in-goal, touch-downs or any other means of 'scoring'. Indeed, purists might argue that Kettering's first game of rugby should be viewed as a draw rather than a defeat, as neither side actually kicked a goal.] These definitions are simple enough, and if secretaries of clubs following the Union rules would remember them, their accounts of matches would be intelligible to others besides themselves.

Whatever the final score really was, it was not to be Kettering's last game of rugby – not by a long chalk!

Below and opposite: Two photographs that show 13 of the players (names in capitals) who were present in George Eldred's field for Kettering Football Club's first fixture – versus Uppingham School – 19 December 1872.

Uppingham School XV, 1872.

From left to right: W.St.J. FIELD, E.W MITCHELL, G.R. IRWIN, A. Hassall, W.M. Cameron, P.H.N. Lake, W.H. Charsley, E.C. Hamley, H.T. Luddington, R.B. Faulkner, C.L. Brook, F.B. Champion, W.D. GRANT, W.P. JAMES, H.M. LINDSAY.

Uppingham's colours were red jerseys with blue trim and white trousers. In the centre of the picture is a flimsy-looking goalpost with rope (or tape) forming a crossbar. The tall gentleman on the far right is Harry Lindsay, who regularly brought a team of schoolboys to Kettering to play Uppingham rules football. An excellent all-round sportsman, he also represented the school at cricket and in his final year won the accolade of Athlete Champion. Alcock's 1873 Football Annual *describes Lindsay as "a very useful player in and out of bullies..." He would turn out for Kettering FC during the 1873-74 season.*

Kettering FC, 1873-74.

Back row: Alf Wykes, Billy Parker, JAMES ROBINSON, Walter East, MILLER WILSON, Bill Cattell, HARRY HANGER, John Saddington, CHARLES BAYES, CHARLIE SMITH. Front row: Teddy Smith, Trooby (some references have 'Truby') Newman, GEORGE ROUGHTON (captain), FRANK MOBBS, Jack Eayres.

There is no record of Kettering's players having worn a uniform colour for their first match in 1872. However, by the time the above photograph was taken during the 1873-74 season, they had adopted navy-blue and white hooped jerseys and socks, and white knickerbockers. Probably taken prior to a game in the town, it is the earliest known image of the Kettering club and the only one discovered to date to include George Roughton in the line-up. Reminiscing in the Kettering Leader & Guardian *more than 50 years later, Henry Raby, who worked in the offices of Messrs Lamb and Stringer with the club's co-founder, commented: "The team owed much of its success to the efforts and popularity of its captain, Mr. George Roughton, who, coming straight from a public school, introduced the Uppingham game with great enthusiasm."*

On 4 October 1873, the *Northampton Herald* reported: "The Kettering Football Club which made so successful a beginning last year is making active preparations for the coming season. The first practice takes place to-day. The members have adopted a uniform colour for jerseys etc."

Writing in the *Kettering Leader* in 1921, Harry Mobbs, who played for the club in its early days and went on to captain the rugby side, states: "The costume selected was a blue and white striped jersey, and cap and stockings, white flannel trousers which eventually gave place to blue knickers." Contemporary photographs show the 'stripes' to be horizontal, more usually referred to as 'hoops', and Alcock's 1874 *Football Annual* further defines the colour as "navy"-blue. There is no mention of anything approaching red – now considered to be Kettering's traditional colour – until 1886, when deep crimson shirts would be worn for the first time. Mobbs goes on to describe the players' footwear: "Low shoes, elastic web side springs, bluchers, and a variety of laced boots." Apparently, it was not until later that 'knobs' and 'bars on the sole' came into use.

For those who made the team, it was an acknowledged honour to receive a polite note from George Roughton, advising of selection. Later, for those who earned it, there was a badge of merit to be sewn onto the holder's jersey. This was prized beyond measure. The first badge was cut from the old scarlet Kettering Yeomanry coat of James Fisher Mobbs, the father of a number of Mobbs brothers who would play for the club. The Northamptonshire Yeomanry had been formed in 1794, with Kettering providing one of the original troops. On 12 November 1844, Queen Victoria and Prince Albert passed through the town, stopping at the White Heart Inn (later renamed the Royal Hotel), before being escorted on the road to Stamford by a troop of cavalry – thereafter known as the Royal Kettering Yeomanry Cavalry. The Kettering Yeomanry was disbanded in 1873, which would explain why members of the football club were able to cut up at least one old Yeomanry coat (and presumably more followed). It is not clear what the actual design of the club's badge of merit was (the badge of the Northamptonshire Yeomanry depicted the White Horse of Hanover). A grainy photograph taken at the end of the decade appears to show a cross (possibly red) on the left side of the jerseys worn by some Kettering players, but earlier images indicate an indistinct (circular) badge more to the centre.

A year to the day after the club's first game against Uppingham, Harry Lindsay once more brought a team from the school. On this occasion it was 20-a-side and the venue was Mr Lamb's field (off Gipsy Lane). Again Kettering came out on top, this time by two goals to nil.

On 17 January 1874, Bedford Britannia provided the opposition for a match played in William Goosey's field (somewhere in the region of Broadway). That the contest ended in a draw is known, the score or the rules used are not.

A week later, playing Uppingham's code of football in front of an estimated 700 spectators (around ten per cent of Kettering's population!) the club avenged the previous season's rugby defeat at the hands of the Leicester Athletic Society, and the *Northampton Mercury* once again carried a brief piece on the occasion:

> Kettering scored the first and only goal got in the match about ten minutes before change, the ball being bullied through the Leicester goal after a long and exciting struggle ['bullied through' suggests the football being driven between the posts by the momentum of the Kettering men gathered around it, leaving the visitors sprawled in the mud]. Ends were changed ... but the fortune of the day remained the same, although several good tries were made at goal by both sides, the ball actually once being kicked against the Leicester goal post, and rebounding into play again.

The game lasted a full 90 minutes and the reporter considered the large crowd "a striking proof of the popularity which the best of winter games has attained in the town of Kettering."

The side that day was George Roughton (captain), Harry Lindsay, J. Mobbs, Charles Bayes, Jack Eayres, Walter East, Bill Cattell, Teddy Smith, Trooby Newman, Charlie Smith, Harry Hanger, James Robinson, Billy Parker, Alf Wykes and Teddy Woolston.

The return match, played between teams of 20 on the Victoria Park, took place on 21 February and Kettering won what was almost certainly a game of rugby. George Roughton (captain), Frank Mobbs, Walter East, Bill Cattell, Teddy Smith, Charlie Smith, Nat Newman, Trooby Newman, M. Noble, F. Patrick, Teddy Woolston, Billy Parker, Harry Hanger, James Robinson, Alf Wykes, Charles Bayes, Jack Eayres, W. Sculthorpe, John Saddington and C. Wright were the men who secured the club's first known away win – and possibly the first victory in a contest played under Union rules.

The following Saturday, in Mr Panther's field (location unknown), Kettering beat their neighbours Wellingborough by one goal to nil in a 12-a-side game of rugby. Beginning a sporting rivalry between the two towns that would become quite acrimonious over the next few decades. The weather that afternoon was very pleasant and the contest drew several hundred spectators. Details of the club's forthcoming fixtures were being posted by Henry Raby outside Joseph Rain's hairdresser shop in the High Street, and it appears that the growing local workforce was taking more than a passing interest in Kettering's matches.

On 14 March, Northampton's Abington School was defeated 1-0 in yet another game of rugby, this time played on a neutral ground in Wellingborough.

The close of the club's second season was celebrated on the evening of Thursday, 9 April at Mrs Miller's Peacock Inn on Lower Street. Between 30 and 40 members sat down to supper, at the end of which the chair was taken by George Roughton – captain, secretary and treasurer – who recounted that of the 12 matches played over the past six months (a record of all 12 has not yet been unearthed), five had been won, two lost and five drawn.

This was almost the end of Roughton's involvement with the football club he had done so much to lay the foundations of. His career was set to take him south, to London, and then east, to India. So far as is known, he would never again take to the field wearing the distinctive blue and white hoops, although he would regularly return to Kettering, and on at least one occasion get together a side to play against his former team-mates. This certainly did not mark the end of the Roughton family's connections with the club, but it was farewell to a gentleman who had helped put the town well and truly on the sporting map.

Plaque paying tribute to the Roughton family in Kettering, to be found at the entrance to the western driveway leading up to the Parish Church of St Peter and St Paul.

And 4,500 miles to the east, by the entrance door to St Thomas Cathedral, Mumbai (formerly Bombay), India, there is an inscription dedicated to the memory of George Roughton himself, detailing the posts he held within that city before his death on 26 March 1899.

Three

Barbarians in a Swamp

1874 - 1879

"After the play on Saturday one would suppose the members of the Kettering F.C. had had quite enough of the Rugby rules, and if they have not, pray let them, in the cause of humanity, abandon them and cease behaving like barbarians in a swamp. Let them consider the number injured and be satisfied."

With very few local sides playing association football, and even fewer prepared to try Uppingham's rules (most of the school's fixtures were internal affairs), the winter sport in Kettering was fast becoming rugby union. Interest in rugby was growing throughout the region as clubs favouring the Union's oval ball handling code emerged in the larger towns of Coventry, Leicester and Northampton; towns where the Association's game had failed to take a hold.

It will no doubt come as something of a surprise to the majority of today's supporters of the football club to learn of its rugby-playing past. But Kettering is by no means alone in this respect; many clubs founded prior to the 1880s experimented with two (or more) codes. Football was football, and whether it was played to the FA's rules or the RFU's (or a variation of either) really didn't seem to matter all that much.

The 1875 *Football Annual* lists the club as a member of the Rugby Football Union (at a time when the RFU had a membership of just over 100 – slightly more than that of the FA). The publication honours Kettering with a place amongst 'The Principal Clubs', coupled with a complete set of the season's fixtures and results:

1874.
Oct. 24, at Kettering,– *v.* Stony Stratford. Drawn; 1 goal, 2 tries and 4 touch-downs to 1 goal, 1 try and 7 touch-downs.
Nov. 7, at Bedford,– *v.* Britannia Club. Lost; 1 goal to 2 goals.
Nov. 21, at Kettering,– *v.* Leicester Athletic Society. Won; 1 goal, 1 try, 1 touch-in-goal and 5 touch-downs to nothing.
1875.
Jan. 13, at Kettering,– *v.* Mr. H.M. Lindsay's Team. Won; 2 goals to nothing.
Jan. 23, at Stony Stratford,– *v.* Stony Stratford. Lost; 4 touch-downs to 1 goal, 1 try and 2 touch-downs.
Jan. 30, at Kettering,– *v.* Britannia Club. Won; 1 goal, 2 tries, 1 punt-out, 3 touches-in-goal and 10 touch-downs to 1 touch-down.

The 1875 *Football Annual* also provides a first record of the club fielding a second XV, which played nine matches; winning six, drawing one and losing two, with 12 goals kicked for and four against.

Despite playing ever more rugby, the fixture at Bedford Britannia on 7 November is, so far as is known, the club's first game of association football (although it is possible that a game was played the previous season). Britannia, who were members of the FA, won the round ball contest on home soil but were soundly beaten at rugby when they travelled to Kettering in January, as noted by the *Northampton Herald*:

The return match was played in Mr. Roughton's field [the field belonged to Dr J.J. Roughton, George Roughton's father], on Saturday last, and was witnessed by an unusually large number of people. Kettering Club won the toss, and Farrar kicked off for Bedford at three p.m. [considering this was the end of January, it must have been quite gloomy just an hour or so later]. The home team, who had been well selected, soon forced their opponents before them; and, after a strong scrimmage, the ball was kicked over the goal. The ball was prettily touched down by Gotch, which eventually resulted in a goal. Ends were then changed, and the Bedford men were driven home again, and several touch-towns were scored by the Kettering men, who had the whole of the game in their hands. When time was called the Kettering side had scored one goal, two tries, one punt out, three touches in goal, and ten touch-downs against one touch-down.

The newspaper also recorded the Kettering team – with positions played: Jack Eayres and Alf Wykes (backs); Trooby Newman (three-quarter); Billy Parker and Charles Henson (half-backs); Frank Mobbs (captain), Charles Bayes, Walter East, Harry Gotch, Harry Hanger, Fred Henson, George Hawks, James Robinson, Tom Spencer and John Saddington (forwards).

Under the auspices of the RFU, rugby was now generally a 15-a-side game (it had been 20). Matches continued to be decided in favour of the team scoring the most goals – a goal being registered when the ball was kicked between the posts and over the crossbar of the H-shaped frame. A try, which is now the most highly rewarded method of scoring in the game, then only resulted in a 'try at goal'. A points system, giving value to tries (etc.) would not be introduced before 1886. Much of the play was taken up by large scrummages or 'scrimmages' – a disorderly struggle – and there was very little passing between players, many of whom considered it 'poor form' to rid themselves of the ball before being tackled, better to be brought crashing to the ground still clutching it.

Another game to have taken place in Dr Roughton's field was the fixture on 13 January, played under Uppingham rules against a side assembled by Harry Lindsay. Lindsay had left Uppingham the previous June and his team, which included no less than three Roughtons, was probably a mixture of current and old boys of the school, along with some Kettering members. 12 of the side that would later beat Bedford at rugby were involved in the match, ten of them in the Kettering XV and two on Lindsay's side. The *Northampton Herald* commented: "The match was well contested, the town team proving the stronger, and obtaining two goals to their opponents nothing. One goal was prettily kicked by D. Clark, and the other was 'bullied.'"

Roughton's field was off London Road, near what is now Silverwood Road and opposite what was then a brickyard. Overall, the location was considered to be poor, being wet and uneven, with a barn for a dressing pavilion. But it was cheap and served the purpose. Until a permanent home could be found, the goalposts, flags and other paraphernalia had to be moved from field to field before each game.

On 29 March 1875, the Royal Hotel was the venue for what had become referred to as the 'Annual Supper' – a regular end-of-season event. Members and their friends sat down to an excellent repast provided by the proprietor Mr T. Richardson. After the cloth was drawn and a loyal toast drunk, the club captain Frank Mobbs proposed the health of his predecessor George Roughton, who was with them that evening, and presented him with a silver flask the members had purchased as a token of their respect and good feeling towards him.

Among the toasts that followed was one to the health of those gentlemen who had kindly favoured the club with fields to play in. This was responded to by Mr C. Bayes, who said that he was very much interested in the game and would do all he could to find another suitable field. This he did; his being in the area of Northfield Avenue (which did not exist in 1875), near the bridge under which the road to Rothwell passed, between the railway and the Slade brook.

Kettering FC, 1874-75.

Back row: Edward Quincey, Frank Henson, Goss Clarke, Joe Spence, Harry Bayes, John Saddington, Tom Spencer, Alexander Henson, Alf Wykes, Fred Henson, Charlie Mobbs, George Hawkes, Charles Henson. Middle row: Fred East, Nat Newman, Frank Mobbs (captain), Walter East, Teddy Smith, Charles Bayes, Harry Hanger. Front row: Tom Quincey, Charlie Dixon, Trooby Newman, James Robinson, Owen Spence, W. Sculthorpe, Harry Mobbs, Jack Eayres, Billy Parker.

Bayes' Field.

The photograph reproduced in this old postcard was probably taken around the turn of the 20th century, looking southeast across Kettering from the railway embankment close to the bridge that carries trains over Rothwell Road. In the distance is the spire of the parish church and in the centre stands T.H. Geary's factory on Lower Street. Bayes' Field is to the lower-left of the picture – muddy host to Buffalo Bill's Wild West Show in 1903, and Kettering FC almost 30 years earlier.

Eldred's Field would eventually become the football club's first acknowledged home ground. Exactly when this happened is unclear, but it was almost certainly at some point during the latter half of the 1870s, after the death of George Eldred in November 1875, when possession of the land passed to his son – also called George. Until then, Mr Bayes' was one of perhaps a half-dozen different fields in and around town used by the club to stage games.

The Bayes family were sportsmen, too, with the name appearing twice amongst the team group opposite.

1. The maximum LENGTH OF THE GROUND shall be 200 yards, the maximum BREADTH shall be 100 yards, the length and breadth shall be marked off with flags; and the goals shall be upright posts, 8 yards apart, with a tape across them, 8 feet from the ground.

2. The winners of the toss shall have the option of kick off or choice of goals. The game shall be commenced by a place-kick from the centre of the ground; the other side shall not approach within ten yards of the ball until it is kicked off.

3. After a goal is won ends shall be changed, and the losing side shall kick off. In the event, however, of no goal having fallen to either side at the lapse of half the allotted time, ends shall then be changed. After the change of ends at half-time, ends shall not again be changed.

4. A goal shall be won when the ball passes between the goal posts under the tape, not being thrown, knocked on, or carried. The ball hitting one or other of the boundary posts and rebounding into play, is considered in play.

5. When the ball is in touch, a player of the opposite side to that which has kicked it out, shall throw it from the point on the boundary line where it left the ground in a direction at right angles with the boundary line, at least six yards, and it shall not be in play until it has touched the ground, and the player throwing it in shall not play it until it has been played by another player.

6. When a player kicks the ball, any one of the same side who, at such moment of kicking, is nearer to the opponents' goal-line is out of play, and may not touch the ball himself, nor in any way whatever prevent any other player from doing so until the ball has been played, unless there are at least three of his opponents nearer their own goal-line; but no player is out of play when the ball is kicked from the goal-line.

7. When the ball is kicked behind the goal-line by one of the opposite side, it shall be kicked off by any one of the players behind whose goal-line it went, within six yards of the nearest goal-post; but if kicked behind by any one of the side whose goal-line it is, a player of the opposite side shall kick it from the nearest corner flag-post. In either case no other player shall be allowed within six yards of the ball until kicked off.

8. No player shall carry or knock on the ball, and handling the ball, under any pretence whatever, shall be prohibited, except in the case of the goal-keeper, who shall be allowed to use his hands, but shall not carry the ball. In the event of any infringement of this rule, a free kick shall be forfeited to the opposite side from the spot where the infringement took place, but in no case shall a goal be scored from such free kick.

9. Neither tripping nor hacking shall be allowed, and no player shall use his hands to hold or push his adversary, nor charge him from behind.

10. No player shall wear any nails, excepting such as have their heads driven in flush with the leather, iron plates, or gutta-percha, on the soles or heels of his boots.

MEM.– Handling is understood to be playing the ball with the hand or arm.

DEFINITION OF TERMS.

A PLACE KICK is a kick at the ball while it is on the ground, in any position in which the kicker may choose to place it.

HACKING is kicking an adversary intentionally.

TRIPPING is throwing an adversary by the use of the legs.

KNOCKING ON is when a player strikes or propels the ball with his hands or arms.

HOLDING includes the obstruction of a player by the hand or any part of the arm below the elbow.

TOUCH is that part of the field, on either side of the ground, which is beyond the line of flags.

A FREE KICK is a kick at the ball in any way the kicker pleases, when it is lying on the ground: none of the kicker's opponents being allowed within six yards of the ball, but in no case can a player be forced to stand behind his own goal-line.

Above: The ten rules (or laws) of association football as they appeared in Alcock's 1873 Football Annual.

Opposite and following two pages: The 59 rules of rugby union as they appeared in the same publication. (The idea, under 'PLAN OF THE FIELD', that perimeter lines be cut out of the turf was short-lived – it was too easy for players to twist an ankle!)

Quite why the more complicated of the two games was so much more popular at the time is an interesting question. Perhaps it was simply more fun to play.

1. A DROP KICK or DROP is made by letting the ball fall from the hands, and kicking it the *very instant* it rises.

2. A PLACE KICK or PLACE is made by kicking the ball after it has been placed in a nick made in the ground for the purpose of keeping it at rest.

3. A PUNT is made by letting the ball fall from the hands and kicking it *before* it touches the ground.

4. EACH GOAL shall be composed of two upright posts, exceeding 11 feet in height from the ground, and placed 18 feet 6 inches apart, with a cross-bar 10 feet from the ground.

5. A GOAL can only be obtained by kicking the ball from the field of play direct (*i.e.*, without touching the ground or the dress or person of any player of either side) over the cross-bar of the opponents' goal, whether it touch such cross-bar, or the posts, or not; but if the ball goes directly over either of the goal posts it is called a *poster*, and is not a goal.

6. A goal may be obtained by any kind of kick except a *punt*.

7. A match shall be decided by a majority of goals only.

8. The ball is *dead* when it rests absolutely motionless on the ground.

9. A TOUCH DOWN is when a player, putting his hand upon the ball on the ground in touch or in goal, stops it so that it remains dead, or fairly so.

10. A TACKLE is when the holder of the ball is held by one or more players of the opposite side.

11. A SCRUMMAGE takes place when the holder of the ball, being in the field of play, puts it down on the ground in front of him, and all who have closed round on their respective sides endeavour to push their opponents back, and, by kicking the ball, to drive it in the direction of the opposite goal line.

12. A player may *take up* the ball whenever it is rolling or bounding, except in a scrummage.

13. It is not lawful to take up the ball when dead (except in order to bring it out after it has been touched down in touch or in goal) for any purpose whatever; whenever the ball shall have been so unlawfully taken up it shall at once be brought back to where it was so taken up and there put down.

14. In a scrummage it is not lawful to touch the ball with the hand under any circumstances whatever.

15. It is lawful for any player who has the ball to run with it, and if he does so, it is called a RUN. If a player runs with the ball until he gets behind his opponents' goal line, and there touches it down, it is called a RUN IN.

16. It is lawful to *run in* anywhere across the goal line.

17. The goal line is in goal, and the touch line is in touch.

18. In the event of any player holding or running with the ball being tackled, and the ball fairly held, he must at once cry *down*, and there put it down.

19. A MAUL IN GOAL is when the holder of the ball is tackled inside goal line, or being tackled immediately outside, is carried or pushed across it, and he or the opposite side, or both, endeavour to touch the ball down. In all cases the ball, when so touched down, shall belong to the players of the side who first had possession of it before the maul commenced, unless the opposite side have gained entire possession of it.

20. In case of a *maul in goal*, those players only who are touching the ball with their hands when it crosses the goal line, may continue in the maul in goal, and when a player has once released his hold of the ball after it is inside the goal line, he may not again join in the maul, and if he attempts to do so he may be dragged out by the opposite side. But if a player when *running in* is tackled inside the goal line, then only the player who first tackled him, or if two or more tackle him *simultaneously*, they only, may join in the maul.

21. TOUCH IN GOAL (see plan). Immediately the ball, whether in the hands of a player (except for the purpose of a *punt out* – see Rule 29) or not, goes into touch in goal, it is at once *dead* and out of the game, and must be brought out as provided by Rules 41 and 42.

22. Every player is ON SIDE, but is put OFF SIDE if he enters a scrummage from his opponents' side, or being in a scrummage, gets in front of the ball, or when the ball has been kicked, touched, or is being run with by any of his own side behind him (*i.e.*, between himself and his goal line.) No player can be off side in his own goal.

23. Every player when *off side* is out of the game and shall not touch the ball in any case whatever, either in or out of touch or goal, or in any way interrupt or obstruct any player, until he is again *on side*.

24. A player being *off side* is put *on side* when the ball has been run five yards with, or kicked by, or has touched the dress or person of any player of the opposite side, or when one of his own side has run in front of him either with the ball or having kicked it when behind him.

25. When a player has the ball, none of his opponents who at the time are *off side* may commence or attempt to run, tackle or otherwise interrupt such player until he has run five yards.

26. THROWING BACK. It is lawful for any player who has the ball to throw it back towards his own goal, or to pass it back to any player of his own side who is at the time behind him, in accordance with the rules of *on side*.

27. KNOCKING ON, *i.e.*, deliberately hitting the ball with the hand, and THROWING FORWARD, *i.e.*, throwing the ball in the direction of the opponents' goal line, are not lawful. If the ball be either *knocked on* or *thrown forward* the captain of the opposite side may (unless a fair catch has been made as provided by the next rule), require to have it brought back to the spot where it was so *knocked* or *thrown on*, and there put down.

28. A FAIR CATCH is a catch made direct from a kick or a *throw forward*, or a *knock on* by one of the opposite side, or from a *punt out* or a *punt on* (see Rules 29 and 30), provided the catcher makes a mark with his heel at the spot where he has made the catch, and no other of his own side touch the ball. (See Rules 43 and 44.)

29. A PUNT OUT is a *punt* made after a touch down, by a player from behind his opponents' goal line, and from touch in goal if necessary, towards his own side, who must stand *outside* the goal line and endeavour to make a fair catch, or to get the ball and *run in* or *drop* a goal. (See Rules 49 and 51.)

30. A PUNT ON is a *punt* made in a manner similar to a *punt out*, and from touch if necessary, by a player who has made a fair catch from a *punt out*, or another *punt on*.

PLAN OF THE FIELD.

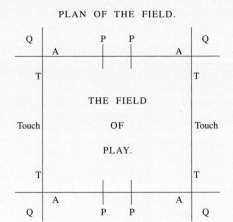

AA. AA. Goal lines.   *PP. PP.* Goal Posts.
TT. TT. Touch Lines.   *QQ. QQ.* Touch in Goal.

The Touch Lines and Goal Lines should be cut out of the Turf.

31. TOUCH. (See plan). If the ball goes into *touch*, the first player on his side who touches it down must bring it to the spot where it crossed the touch line; or if a player when running with the ball cross or put any part of either foot across the touch line, he must return with the ball to the spot where the line was so crossed; and thence return it into the field of play in one of the modes provided by the following rule.

32. He must then himself or by one of his own side, either (i.) bound the ball in the field of play, and then run with it, kick it, or throw it back to his own side; or, (ii.) throw it out at right angles to the touch line; or, (iii.) walk out with it at right angles to the touch line, any distance not less than *five* nor more than *fifteen* yards, and there put it down, first declaring how far he intends to walk out.

33. If two or more players holding the ball are pushed into *touch*, the ball shall belong *in touch* to the player who first had hold of it in the field of play, and has not released his hold of it.

34. If the ball when thrown out of *touch* be not thrown out at right angles to the touch line, the captain of either side may at once claim to have it thrown out again.

35. A catch made when the ball is thrown out of touch is not a *fair catch*.

36. KICK OFF is a place kick from the centre of the field of play, and cannot count as a goal. The opposite side must stand at least *ten yards* in front of the ball until it has been kicked.

37. The ball shall be *kicked off* (i.) at the commencement of the game, (ii.) after a goal has been obtained.

38. The sides shall change goals as often as and whenever a goal is obtained, unless it has been otherwise agreed by the captains before the commencement of the match.

39. The captains of the respective sides shall toss up before commencement of the match, the winner of the toss shall have the option of choice of goals, or the kick off.

40. Whenever a goal shall have been obtained, the side which has lost the goal shall then kick off.

41. KICK OUT is a drop kick by one of the players of the side which has had to touch the ball down in their own goal or into whose touch in goal the ball has gone, (Rule 21,) and is the mode of bringing the ball again into play, and cannot count as a goal.

42. KICK OUT must be a *drop kick*, and from not more than *twenty-five yards* outside the kicker's goal line: if the ball when kicked out pitch it touch, it must be taken back and kicked out again. The kicker's side must be behind the ball when kicked out.

43. A player who has made and claimed a *fair catch*, shall thereupon either take a *drop kick* or a *punt*, or *place* the ball for a place kick.

44. After a *fair catch* has been made, the opposite side may come up to the catcher's mark, and (except in cases under Rule 50), the catcher's side retiring, the ball shall be kicked from such mark, or from a spot any distance behind it.

45. A player may touch the ball down in his goal at any time.

46. A side having touched the ball down in their opponents' goal, shall *try at goal* either by a *place kick* or a *punt out*.

47. If a TRY AT GOAL be made by a *place kick*, a player of the side which has touched the ball down shall bring it up to the goal line (subject to Rule 48), in a straight line from and opposite to the spot where the ball was touched down, and there make a mark on the goal line, and thence walk straight out with it at right angles to the goal line, such distance as he thinks proper, and there place it for another of his side to kick. The kicker's side must be behind the ball when it is kicked, and the opposite side must remain behind their goal line until the ball has been placed on the ground. (See Rules 54 and 55).

48. If the ball has been touched down between the goal posts, it may be brought out in a straight line from either of such posts; but if brought out from between them, the opposite side may *charge* at once. (See Rule 54).

49. If the *try at goal* be by a *punt out* (see Rule 29), a player of the side which has touched the ball down shall bring it straight up to the goal line opposite to the spot where it was touched down, and there make a mark on the goal line and then *punt out* from touch in goal, if necessary, or from any part behind the goal line not nearer to the goal post than such mark, beyond which mark it is not lawful for the opposite side (who must keep behind their goal line) to pass until the ball has been kicked. (See Rules 54 and 55).

50. If a *fair catch* be made from a *punt out* or a *punt on*, the catcher may either proceed as provided by Rules 43 and 44, or himself take a *punt on*, in which case the mark made on making the fair catch, shall be regarded (for the purpose of determining as well the position of the player who makes the *punt on* as of the other players of both sides,) as the mark made on the goal line in the case of a *punt out*.

51. A catch made in touch from a *punt out* or a *punt on* is not a fair catch; the ball must then be taken or thrown out of touch as provided by Rule 32; but if the catch be made in touch in goal, the ball is at once dead, and must be *kicked out* as provided by Rules 41 and 42.

52. When the ball has been touched down in the opponents' goal, none of the side in whose goal it has been so touched down shall touch it, or in any way displace it, or interfere with the player of the other side who may be taking it up or out.

53. The ball is *dead* whenever a goal has been obtained: but if a *try at goal* be not successful the kick shall be considered as only an ordinary kick in the course of the game.

54. CHARGING, *i.e.*, rushing forward to kick the ball or tackle a player, is lawful for the opposite side in all cases of a *place kick* after a *fair catch* or upon a *try at goal*, immediately the ball touches or is placed on the ground; and in cases of a *drop kick* or *punt* after a *fair catch*, as soon as the player, having the ball, commences to run or offers to kick, or the ball has touched the ground; but he may always draw back, and unless he has dropped the ball or actually touched it with his foot, they must again retire to his mark (see Rule 56). The opposite side in the case of a *punt out* or a *punt on*, and the kicker's side in *all* cases may not *charge* until the ball has been kicked.

55. If a player, having the ball when about to *punt it out*, goes outside the goal line, or when about to *punt on*, advances nearer to his own goal line than his mark, made on making the fair catch, or if after the ball has been touched down in the opponents' goal or a fair catch has been made, more than one player of the side which has so touched it down or made the fair catch, touch the ball before it is again kicked, the opposite side may *charge* at once.

56. In cases of a *fair catch*, the opposite side may come up to and *charge* from anywhere on or behind a line drawn through the mark made by the player who has made the catch and parallel to their own goal line; but in the case of a *fair catch* from a *punt out* or a *punt on*, they may not advance further in the direction of the touch line nearest to such mark than a line drawn through such mark to their goal line and parallel to such touch line. In all cases (except a *punt out* and a *punt on*) the kicker's side must be behind the ball when it is kicked, but may not *charge* until it has been kicked.

57. NO HACKING, or HACKING OVER, or tripping up, shall be allowed under any circumstances.

58. No one wearing projecting nails, iron plates, or gutta percha on any part of his boots or shoes shall be allowed to play in a match.

59. The Captains of the respective sides shall be the sole arbiters of all disputes.

As the club became ever more established, an 'Annual Meeting' was held prior to the commencement of every new season so that the necessary arrangements could be made, a committee formed and a captain chosen. It was the committee – including a secretary and treasurer – that effectively ran things. There was no owner or team manager (Kettering would not appoint a manager as such until 1920) and it is likely that the gentlemen of the committee had a big say in the selection of players for any given match. Funds for the club were raised through the subscriptions paid by its members, of whom there were now around 50.

At the meeting on 20 September 1875, Frank Mobbs once more accepted the honour and responsibility of the captaincy. The formalities that Monday evening were conducted at the Boys National School, which had opened two-and-a-half years earlier on an area of land in the centre of Horsemarket and was a regular venue for club get-togethers in the early days. (The school, or at least the building that originally housed it, was demolished in 1970.)

Kettering all but disappears from the *Football Annual* and is no longer listed as a member of the RFU. This might have been an oversight during the compilation of Alcock's latest volume, or perhaps any benefits to be gained from rejoining the Union had to be weighed against the fact that the annual subscription had been raised from five to 21 shillings at the end of the previous season. Either way, the majority of fixtures were still contested under the Union's rules.

The club remained unbeaten throughout the 1875-76 campaign, with six matches known to have been played. The first, versus Stony Stratford on 25 October, was drawn, and the rest were all won: versus Bedford Britannia on 6 November, a George Roughton team on 27 December, Northampton Scorpions on 30 December, Stony Stratford on 5 February and, finally, Bedford Britannia again on 26 February. Of the Britannia encounters, the November fixture was a game of rugby played somewhere in Kettering and the return match at Bedford is the club's first recorded victory in a game of association football (although the actual score is unknown).

On 6 May, the *Northampton Mercury* shed some light on why the committee was struggling to increase the number of fixtures: "It was announced at the Annual Supper that the Club has again passed a most successful season, though few matches have been played partly owing to the weather being unfavourable, but more especially to the inability to get clubs strong enough to accept challenges from them."

Kettering was gaining a reputation!

Local newspapers carried very little information about football at this time, and Kettering's only mention was on 7 April 1877, when the *Northampton Herald* reported: "Owing to the strength and good play of the team who won the first matches of the season, clubs who had fixtures with them, excused themselves from playing when they saw they were sure to be defeated; and when the Club had been out and beaten others they would refuse to play the return match at Kettering." Consequently, games were again much scarcer than would have been hoped for. Of the ten that did take place – again under the captaincy of Frank Mobbs – Kettering won six, drew three and lost one (making just one defeat in 16 games over two seasons).

In 1928, Frank Mobbs's brother Charlie, who played for the club for almost a decade from the mid-1870s, wrote an article for the *Kettering Leader & Guardian*, reflecting on Kettering's rugby exploits of the 1870s and 80s:

In those days Kettering possessed a very powerful Rugby team (all amateurs). First class teams only were played, and to do this we had to travel some long and awkward journeys such as to Rugby town, Leicester, Moseley Harriers (Birmingham), Stony Stratford, Marlborough Nomads, Oundle School, and many others...

The Kettering Rugby F.C. [whether or not 'Rugby' was ever a part of the club's name is a moot point – contemporary *Football Annuals* and newspapers refer simply to Kettering Football Club; only in pieces written many years later is the word added] had a lot of members, and so many being of equal merit, the team was constantly varied to give the better men a match game. The players were told off so many each week to carry and place the heavy Rugger goalposts, and set out the field, as often we had to play in Roughton's Field, nearly opposite the London-road brickyard, Gipsy-lane, and the now much debated Bayes' Field, if not waterlogged, as it frequently was even in those days.

Without being egotistical, let me say the players were very keen indeed. Jack Saddington (a dashing forward) invariably had a bleeding nose. On one day at Market Harborough Miller Wilson, in order to gain a try, jumped into a brook in his keen interest. In those days no limit was marked out behind the touch-line as there is nowadays [in fact there were no markings on the pitch at all, in either the Union's or the Association's game – the corners of the playing area were almost certainly indicated by flags and possibly the halfway point was as well, but an actual halfway-*line*, drawn across the pitch, would not appear until the latter half of the 1880s].

The four Henson brothers were powerful heavy men in the forward line, also the late Mr. Fred East, Sam Bell (a local farmer) and others. The back players, such as Charlie Dixon (Hapworth), Goss Clarke, Teddy Woolstone [some correspondents omit the 'e' to give Woolston] and others were very swift runners.

Charlie and Frank Mobbs would be joined by their brothers Harry and Septimus in wearing the club's colours. The four of them, along with their father James, were musicians and performed as a quintet. Harry (whose name can be found on a plaque inside Kettering Library commemorating the generosity of the five gentlemen who gave the land upon which the building now stands) was known as a fine violinist, and Septimus (destined to become the Mayor of Watford) as a flute and piccolo player with few equals. How often did these burley footballers sit in the corner of a room gently making music at a Victorian social gathering in the town? They were businessmen, too; between them starting up Mobbs Bros. and Mobbs & Lewis (both associated with the footwear industry).

Frank was a cellist in his father's quintet and held a number of sporting and civic offices to boot. A participant in the club's first game back in 1872, he would tour Australia and New Zealand with the British team of bowlers shortly before he passed away in 1927. Part of a generation that did so much to improve the quality of life in Kettering, many column inches were dedicated to the achievements of Frank Mobbs after he died, including his chairmanship of the Urban Council:

THRICE "MAYOR" OF KETTERING.

For about 34 years Mr. Mobbs has been prominent in public life. Elected about the year 1893 as one of the Liberal members of the Kettering Board of Guardians, he gained experience in public life during the two years he held that office, which stood him in good stead in after years when he served in various other public capacities...

The present Urban Council [forerunner of Kettering Borough Council] came into existence in 1894, and he served thereon continuously until 1907 – a total period of 14 years – since which time, owing to increasing business demands he did not contest a seat.

Thrice he passed through the chair of the Urban Council, having been unanimously elected to that important office in 1899, 1904, and 1905, and he discharged the duties with distinct credit to himself and the town generally. [It is uncertain which newspaper carried this article.]

Another well-known Kettering family touched on in Charlie Mobbs's *Kettering Leader & Guardian* article is the Hensons. Brothers Alexander, Charles, Frank and Fred all turned out for the club during the 1870s. Alexander served in the fire brigade for a time, whilst Charles and Fred were part of the Henson family building business, responsible for many notable landmarks across the town – factories, shops, banks, homes, schools, etc. Another footballer-musician, Charles was a skilled handbell ringer of national repute.

Four rugby fixtures are known to have been arranged this season: versus Oundle School, Luton, Rugby and Leicester St Margaret's – Kettering winning the latter away from home by a goal to nil. It is unlikely the team participated in any more games of Uppingham rules football beyond this point, but the FA's code was not completely ignored and a 'Club versus Gentlemen' match was played in the town under Association rules on 5 January 1878.

It is apparent that the railway was very much a deciding factor in planning fixtures. Destinations such as Luton and Leicester were easily reached by train in an era when the network linked far more local towns and villages than it does now. A station had opened in Kettering in 1857, and by 1872 the Midland Railway had become the most popular in England, running third class coaches on all trains – so that even the working class could visit the capital at an affordable price!

Wherever the venue and whoever the opposition, Kettering continued to enjoy success, but it has to be said that not everyone appreciated the club's bruising rugby encounters, as illustrated by a letter that appeared in the *Wellingborough & Kettering News* on 2 February: "After the play on Saturday one would suppose the members of the Kettering F.C. had had quite enough of the Rugby rules, and if they have not, pray let them, in the cause of humanity, abandon them and cease behaving like barbarians in a swamp. Let them consider the number injured and be satisfied." Suffice it to say that, for the time being, the writer's plea fell on deaf ears!

On 23 February, Kettering's final match of the season resulted in a 2-0 victory at Coalville, in a game reportedly played under Sheffield rules. To all intents and purposes this would have been a game of association football because a year earlier the Sheffield FA had agreed to come under the umbrella of the 'London' FA. Clubs affiliated to the Sheffield Association (formed in 1867) had played their own version of football until February 1877, but by the beginning of the 1877-78 season the rules of the round ball dribbling game – association football – had been standardised throughout England. The FA was now a truly national governing body.

And other countries were following suit. Associations had sprung up in Scotland (1873) and Wales (1876), and in 1880 the Irish FA would emerge in Belfast, paving the way for the creation of the British Home Championship – the first international tournament – and the International Football Association Board, whose task was to ensure unity of the rules across the British Isles. (It would be 1904 before FIFA was conceived in Paris as a 'world governing body'.)

Once again, information concerning the club is sparse and only two matches are known to have taken place, both ending in draws away from home and most likely games of rugby. The first was played at Bedford on 9 November 1878 when, under the captaincy of Bill Cattell, Kettering's team is recorded as Cattell and Harry Mobbs (backs); Charlie Mobbs and Charlie Dixon (three-quarters); Billy Parker and Trooby Newman (half-backs); Charles Bayes, Harry Bailey, Charles Denton, James Driscall, Arthur Foulds, Septimus Mobbs, Charlie Smith, Teddy Woolston and Jack Woolston (forwards). The second match was versus Leicester Amateurs on the Victoria Park.

Intriguingly, there are echoes of the 1870s still to be found today in the blue and white jerseys donned during the winter months at Waverley Road, home of the rugby union game in Kettering (just a long punt from where the grass in Dr J.J. Roughton's field once grew).

Anyone who has read the booklet celebrating the centenary of Kettering Rugby Football Club (edited by Tony Hewitt, published in 1975) will already have recognised many of the names and venues in *this* narrative. Although KRFC did not evolve *directly* from the club formed in 1872 – between 1889 (when Kettering FC would cease to play any games of rugby) and 1921 an oval ball was barely seen in the town – it is not unreasonable to suggest that Kettering's football and rugby clubs share a common origin.

The links between the two can be traced back to day one, when a 17-year-old Frank Mobbs stepped on to George Eldred's field to play his part in the victory over Uppingham School. Later, after George Roughton's departure, Mobbs captained the team throughout a period during which the Union code enjoyed great popularity. Then, on 3 March 1921, he would chair the meeting at the Royal Hotel at which the present-day rugby club was formed (or, perhaps, *re*-formed, depending on one's point of view), and the honour of becoming its inaugural president was bestowed upon him. And the colours the new club would eventually adopt? None other than a version of the blue and white hoops first worn by the Victorian footballers of Mobbs's youth.

So why would the oval ball game all but disappear from the town for the best part of 32 years at the end of the 1880s? For a number of reasons no doubt, but a major factor in Kettering FC's gradual transition to wholly association football was the influence of a man of God, who would join the club in time for the 1879-80 season.

Four

The Trouble With Umpires

1879 - 1883

"Now that the football season may be said to have commenced, I shall feel much obliged if you will allow me a small space in your paper to call attention to a question of some importance in connection with the Kettering F.C.; namely, the desirability of having a person fully qualified to undertake the responsible position of umpire. I should say that as a rule half the number of matches played are brought to an abrupt end, either through the umpires being unable to agree when appealed to for a decision, or else through some player or players challenging the umpire's decision, which always ought to be final. One has even heard of a free fight being the result in such a case."

Almost a century before the club would grace the pitch beneath (old) Wembley's Twin Towers its members made their first serious concerted effort to play association football, arranging three games against scratch teams (two of which were won and one drawn) and appointing a captain specifically for the round ball game – the Reverend George Thurston.

Having studied at Eton and Oxford and been ordained a deacon in Peterborough Cathedral, the Reverend became a curate at Kettering Parish Church in January 1877. A churchman and sportsman in the mould of Barton Seagrave's Rev John Marsham, Thurston is generally regarded as the main instigator of association football in the town. Every bit a leader, he would captain Kettering's footballers for four seasons and later captain the town's cricketers after forwarding the proposal leading to the formation of Kettering Town Cricket Club on the evening of 19 March 1885.

Despite Thurston's influence, the focus for now was still on rugby and ten matches were arranged: versus Bedford County Schools, Irthlingborough Hawks (twice), Leicester Amateurs (twice), Leicester Athletic Society (twice), Oundle and Rushden (twice). Kettering won all ten without conceding a goal. At the end of the season the question was raised as to why the club had not played against the best side Northampton had to offer, the answer came back that no one could compel them to play, they had been asked and their refusal could only mean they were frightened to take on Kettering! Indeed, it was widely accepted throughout the county that there was no better rugby team than Kettering's.

It having been decided that the club would field teams under both Union and Association codes, the overlap between the two can be seen after the *Northampton Mercury* named the Kettering side that beat Wellingborough Britons by a goal to nil – playing association football – on 20 November 1880: Charles Denton, Rev George Thurston (captain), Bill Cattell, Charlie Dixon, Trooby Newman, J. Dixon, Arthur Foulds, Harry Mobbs, Billy Parker, Charlie Smith and Jack Woolston. The majority of these men regularly participated in the oval ball game.

The return match was played at Wellingborough on 18 December. The team that day was Bill Cattell (captain), Charlie Dixon, Trooby Newman, Jack Woolston, Billy Parker, Septimus Mobbs, Harry Mobbs, W. James, C. Cooch, James Driscall and Goss Clarke. Kettering won 2-1 and the goal scorers are recorded as Mobbs and Parker – the first instance of the club's scorers being named in this code of football, although it is not known whether it was Harry or Septimus Mobbs.

On 26 March 1881, the club suffered its only round ball defeat of the campaign, losing 6-1 to Wellingborough Grammar School. Having been formed the previous season, the school team would become one of the top sides playing association football throughout Northamptonshire and the neighbouring counties over the next decade. Unlike Kettering, the students were not hindered by rugby commitments. F. Dixon (goal); Bill Cattell and Harry Mobbs (backs); Jack Woolston and W. James (half-backs); Arthur Foulds, James Driscall, Charlie Smith, Charlie Mobbs, William Slow and Billy Parker (forwards) represented Kettering – the earliest known account of the positions they played under Association rules. Once again, Parker scored for Kettering.

Opposite: Kettering FC, 1879-80.

Back row: Charles Denton (forward), Charles Bayes (forward), Harry Bailey (forward), Harry Mobbs (back), Septimus Mobbs (forward), Arthur Foulds (forward). Front row: Goss Clarke (three-quarter), C. Cooch (forward), Trooby Newman (half-back), Billy Parker (half-back), Bill Cattell (three-quarter), Charlie Mobbs (forward), Charlie Dixon (three-quarter), unknown player (possibly Teddy Woolston), Charlie Smith (forward).

This is a team ready for a game of rugby (15-a-side). The positions these men favoured playing the Union code this season (as recalled by Mr Joseph Sumpter more than 50 years later) have been noted, and it is possible to compare these with the positions they adopted under Association rules (see the side that lost to Wellingborough Grammar School in 1881).

On 8 October 1881, the *Wellingborough & Kettering News* printed a letter drawing attention to the standard of officiating at Kettering's games:

> Now that the football season may be said to have commenced, I shall feel much obliged if you will allow me a small space in your paper to call attention to a question of some importance in connection with the Kettering F.C.; namely, the desirability of having a person fully qualified to undertake the responsible position of umpire. I should say that as a rule half the number of matches played are brought to an abrupt end, either through the umpires being unable to agree when appealed to for a decision, or else through some player or players challenging the umpire's decision, which always ought to be final. One has even heard of a free fight being the result in such a case. All this kind of thing is, of course, most disagreeable to an onlooker, and considering the amount of rivalry which exists between the Kettering club and neighbouring clubs, it seems a pity that no real estimate of their doings can be formed simply through this one neglected rule. A gentleman is needed as umpire who knows the rules of the game, and who is both determined and impartial in his decisions. Disputes, such as have happened of late years, never occurred in the days of the club's infancy when under the careful management of Mr. G.W. Roughton. Trusting then that some improvement in this respect may be forthcoming during the season just commenced.

With regard to the Association game, it would be another decade before a referee, assisted by two linesmen on the sidelines, enforced the FA's laws on the pitch. Until then, standards were upheld by two umpires – one provided by each team – occasionally aided by a referee outside the field of play whose functions included time-keeping, watching for violent conduct and adjudicating in disagreements between the umpires. (It is unlikely that many of Kettering's early games – of any code – were policed by a referee.) Each umpire stuck to the half of the field nearest the goal defended by the party nominating him, generally only intervening if appealed to by the captain of the opposing side.

Originally, of course, when the game was played for the game's sake, disputes were settled quite amicably by the two opposing captains. But those days were long gone and in 1888 a local scribe would be moved to pen a tongue-in-cheek description (source uncertain) of umpires that was probably not far from the truth:

> This is the usual way of making an umpire. A member or follower of the club is found, to him goes the captain: "I say, old man, will you umpire for us?" (mark the 'for us'). "Don't think I can, old fellow, I've never umpired before." "Never mind that, old chappie, hold up your stick every time we claim anything, and you'll be all right." And so the umpire goes onto the field, and meets the umpire of the other side, whose method

of working is identically the same, and each becomes the mouthpiece of his side, and the new umpire is now a qualified man for future occasions. If there is a referee, he will decide; if there is not, there are squabbles and rows through the game.

Only four matches were reported in the newspapers regarding the club this season. Playing rugby, Kettering lost at Moseley Harriers in the first round of the Midland Counties Football Union Challenge Cup – almost certainly the first cup competition the club had entered and therefore its first truly 'competitive' fixture. The MCFU had been formed in 1879 by rugby-playing clubs from the Shires, and Moseley was by far its strongest member. A journey to Victoria Park also ended in defeat at the hands of Leicester Football Club – formed the previous season by the amalgamation of three clubs and known today as Leicester Tigers – one of the giants of domestic rugby union.

And Kettering fared no better in the two games of association football known to have taken place: losing 4-2 at Wellingborough on 14 January 1882, and going down by two goals to nil after 'time' was called 10 minutes early in the return match on 11 March.

FOOTBALL.– MOSELEY v. KETTERING (Midland Counties Challenge Cup, 1st round) – This match was played at Moseley on Saturday, in miserable weather, the ground being very heavy, and the ball hard to pick up. Moseley, losing the toss, started the ball up-hill and against the wind. During the first half the game was very even, Moseley touching down twice and Kettering once in self-defence. On change of ends Moseley had matters pretty well their own way, and in two minutes Gibson obtained the first try, but the place did not come off. Soon after P. Lea obtained the second try, from which Smith kicked a goal. Williamson obtained the third and fourth tries, Smith placing a goal from the first. Here for a little variation Smith dropped a goal very neatly with his left foot. Shortly before "no side" Milner obtained the last try, Smith converting it into a goal. Kettering also touched down six times. Victory thus rested with Moseley by 4 goals, 2 tries, 7 touches, to 2 touches. Teams – Moseley: G. B. Jones (back), A. Smith (captain), G. Fowler, H. V. Hasluck (three-quarter backs), W. Hasluck, F. Reeve (half backs), D. Gibson, W. Breedon, A. J. Oster, F. Fowler, R. Williamson, C. N. Milner, A. Marlow, H. Everill, and P. Lea (forwards); umpire, J. S. Chandler. Kettering: H. W. Mobbs (captain), J. Woolston (backs), C. Dixon, J. Althorpe (three-quarter backs), W. Parker, W. Newman (half backs), C. Bayes, H. Bayes, W. Slow, F. Hanger, S. Marsh, C. Smith, G. Spence, A. Mitton, and C. Cooch (forwards); umpire, C. F. Mobbs.

The Northampton Herald'*s report of what was more than likely Kettering's first cup tie – a game of rugby played at Moseley on 22 October 1881.*

Kettering FC, 1882-83.

A round ball and 11 players indicate the above photograph was taken prior to a game of association football. H.E. Dixon, nephew of Charlie Dixon and regular reserve team player, later recorded the names of those in the picture and added some detail:

From left to right: Frank York, a goalkeeper; Ernest Thompson, later resident of the off-licence and grocer shop on the corner of Wood Street and Wilson Terrace; Charlie Dixon, one of Kettering's fastest runners who excelled at both rugby and the Association game, popularly known as 'Hap'orth'; Charlie Mobbs, one of the famous Mobbs brothers; Jack Woolston, a foreman clicker at Messrs Abbott and Bird's shoe factory, which overlooked Eldred's Field and now dominates Green Lane; George Brains, a solo cornet player of some repute and member of the Kettering Rifle Band; Trooby Newman, one of the smallest and 'trickiest' of players to have mastered both codes, he was apt to turn somersaults when he scored; Septimus Mobbs, who later left his brothers and went into business in Watford, where he became the town's mayor; Billy Parker, of Parker and Charlton, shoe manufacturers; William Spence, better known as 'Buff' and probably Kettering's first regular goalkeeper; Lew Lindsay, another of Canon Lindsay's sons, tall, fast and very powerful, he would later join George Roughton in India, where he too would pass away.

The gentleman sitting in front of the group is Nat Newman. Often referred to as 'The Father of Kettering Football', he played in the club's first game and was its first president. He was also associated with Newman Bros., the boot and shoe manufacturers who built the factory still standing today at the end of Newman Street (currently Ken Hall Footwear).

On 28 October 1882, following on from the previous season's disquiet regarding umpires, a piece that paints a far from 'gentlemanly' picture of sport – on or off the pitch – appeared in the *Northampton Herald*:

> At a football match (Rugby rules) played in connection with the Midland Counties Union Challenge Cup at Kettering on October 21 between Kettering and Leamington, some questions were raised as to the validity of a victory which the Kettering men claimed, and ultimately it was decided to refer the disputed point to the committee of the M.C.U. At the meeting of that body it was decided that the match should be played over again, but the Leamington team openly declined to re-visit Kettering on account of the hostile attitude of the spectators on the previous Saturday. One member stated that after his experience on that day he rather questioned whether he and his comrades would all come home safe in the event of their beating the local team, and ultimately it was decided that the match should be played upon entirely neutral ground. That love of fair play which Englishmen like to pride themselves upon seems to be on the decline where football is concerned.

A week later, the newspaper printed an irate response from a gentleman by the name of Thomas Heighton:

> Sir, I was favoured with a seat at one of the windows in the terrace which commands a view of the whole ground [Eldred's Field]. I saw one of the players pull one of the Kettering players down by the back hair of his head, and another of the same players had his pants torn completely from the moorings, showing the callice lining. But play went on, none of these irregularities being reported. When play was over and Leamington fairly beaten, the umpires compared notes, and appeared quite satisfied. I was most indignant when I heard the Leamington players had so lowered themselves as to make such dastardly, cowardly, and untruthful statements. The play was witnessed by about a thousand spectators, besides the many ticket-holders who availed themselves of seats at the windows.

The protest that Leamington took to the MCFU committee was that they had scored tries on three occasions but were unable to kick for goal on account of the 'roughs' and 'blackguards' – referring to rowdy spectators – at the edge of the pitch. Kettering refused to replay the match at a neutral venue and the tie was awarded to Leamington.

Overleaf: the Kettering Guardian's *report on the Leamington game, followed by captain Harry Mobbs's account of proceedings, published in the* Kettering Observer *on 3 November 1882.*

FOOTBALL.

KETTERING v. LEAMINGTON ROVERS.

This match was one in the first round of contests under the management of the Midland Counties Football Union for the Midland Counties Challenge Cup, and was looked forward to with much interest and expectation by the football players of the town and district, as it was well-known that the Leamington team was one of the best in the Midlands, having won all their matches last year with the exception of one, namely, the Moseley Harriers Football Club. The time for the commencement of the game was ushered in by a shower, and then the weather was all that could be desired, which helped to put players and spectators in the best of spirits for an enjoyable game. Leamington won the toss and elected to play with the wind and sun in their favour, Kettering starting the ball, which was well followed up by them, and play commenced in the visitors' ground, the usual scrimmage and run progression not being interrupted until Kettering allowed the visitors to press them on goal line and were forced to touch-down twice in self-defence, when from the kick off at quarter flag the Leamington backs displayed their passing and running to the advantage of their side and managed to get a run in and a try was obtained, but free kick proved a failure. From this part of the game the home team seemed endued with fresh life, and, by brilliant forward play fought yard by yard successfully into close quarters of the Leamington goal, whereupon several splendid runs brought the ball to the side of the flag, where the ball was burst. The men were started with a fresh ball which went rolling to the visitors' end; and, after several unsuccessful attempts Brains kicked a goal from the field of play. Soon after ends were changed, and the same well-matched game was played, in the course of which Leamington had two touch-downs, and Kettering three times. Nothing further was scored except a fair catch just in front of the visitors' goal, by C. Bayes, which was not allowed, and the game ended thus:– Kettering, 1 goal, 1 try to 1 try and 6 touch-downs.

The following are the names of the players:– Leamington – E. A. Clarke (back); R. Bullock, C. E. Chapman, L. Richardson, H. Bedford (three-quarter back); G. Gill, H. Bellot (half-back); Rawlinson, Rose, Haywood, Gascoigne, Dunne, Green, Wayte, and Winterton (forwards). Kettering:– C. Bayes, F. Hanger, S. L. Marsh, A. Mitton, S. G. Mobbs, C. Smith, G. Spence, W. Slow (forwards); C. Dixon, W. Newman (half-back); G. Brains, J. Woolston, R. Spence (three-quarter back); F. Loasby, H. W. Mobbs, capt. (back).

FOOTBALL.

KETTERING *v.* LEAMINGTON.– Mr. H. W. Mobbs, the captain of the Kettering team writes:– "There is a paragraph going the round of the papers to the effect that at the above match played at Kettering, the spectators were so far beyond control that the visitors obtained several points in the game which they durst not claim, for fear of being molested. This being false, as you personally know, I hope, in justice to the Kettering Football Club, and the spectators of that match, you will give some publicity to the following:– By the omission of the Midland Counties' Football Union to send (according to their rules) a referee for the match *v.* Leamington, the umpires were entire managers of the game, and did their task fairly and well. At the end of the game, which was conducted without any noticeable dispute, the umpires jointly and after comparing notes, mutually gave the score to you as follows:– Kettering, one goal, one touch down; to Leamington, one try, seven touchdowns; the former being duly declared winners of the match. At a meeting of the Midland Counties' Football Union, to receive the result of the first round of matches, Leamington claimed to have scored three tries, adding that the spectators, who were composed of *roughs* and *blackguards*, interfered with the players, would not let them have their free kicks at goal, and so frightened them that under fear of their life the Leamington team dare not maintain their rights. THIS YOU KNOW TO BE FALSE. Well, upon the evidence of the Leamington representatives, which was stoutly denied, cross-examined and exposed (where wrong) by the Kettering delegates, the M. C. F. U. summarily decided (without reference to the umpires or a disinterested party) that the match was void, and must be played again, on neutral ground. This of course the Kettering players unanimously refused to do, as the match was fairly won, and thus the Union have given the match to Leamington." [We think the Kettering team have done right in refusing to play again. The allegations as to the conduct of the spectators are utterly without foundation, and unworthy of those who call themselves gentlemen. But we suppose, as they had been backing themselves to win, laying £12 to £2 on themselves, they could not afford to lose. They talked loudly about Rugby rules, but the deliberate pushing of the ball along the ground at the hands of one of the Rovers, was only one of several infringements of the rules. ED. *Observer.*]

In 1882 association football began to take off in the county with the advent of the Wellingborough & District FA. Kettering, for the time being, chose not to join the organisation, preferring to continue concentrating more on rugby. Even so, after losing 4-1 at home to Wellingborough, the club's members decided to have some more practice at the round ball game, with the result that Kettering thrashed their neighbours 6-1 in the return match and won every other game they played under Association rules this campaign: defeating the Church Institute and Wesleyans (both Kettering clubs), Oakham, a Rev Thurston team (twice) and Uppingham (home and away).

Despite the formation of a local Football Association, rugby remained the principal sport in the county and the club would continue to play it until the end of the decade. However, under the guidance of Rev Thurston, the pendulum was slowly starting to swing the way of association football; a fact acknowledged in a *Kettering Observer* match report following the defeat of Uppingham on 2 December: "The Association game has apparently in the past been looked upon by the Kettering people with little or no interest, they having been very enthusiastic for the Rugby Union game, in which no doubt Kettering has gained a wide fame. But we have no hesitation in predicting that in the future ... there is no doubt the Association game will have a greater share of their patronage and support."

And the *Kettering Guardian* was no less enthusiastic in its appraisal of the game played against a team captained by the Reverend on 6 January 1883:

This match was decided on Saturday last, upon the club ground, under the Association Rules, being one of a series of matches contested annually, the sides being the Kettering Football Club versus a team of gentlemen home for the holidays, which team in not a few cases comprises some of the most skilful and best players of the day. It was this year captained by the Rev. G. Thurston, and being generally a very interesting game, many spectators were induced to attend, amongst whom were noticed many of the old school of players. The ball was kicked off at 2.45, and with the best of weather, a game commenced which for excitement and skilful play has never before been witnessed in Kettering under the above rules. Instead of being a win for the scratch team, which has often been the case, a most brilliant success for the club was the result. Woolston scored two goals, one of which was from a tight scrimmage; Parrish one, and Parker one; and after some excellent work by C. Dixon, W. Newman, and S.G. Mobbs, H.W. Mobbs scored two goals, which were not allowed, leaving a total of four goals by the club to nil. For the club:– H.W. Mobbs (captain), G. Brains, C. Dixon, S.L. Marsh, S.G. Mobbs, W. Newman, F. Newman, W. Parker, H. Parish, E.R. Quincey, C. Smith, G. Spence, E. Thompson, and J. Woolston [presumably the game was 14-a-side].

At the Corn Exchange in early May, the end of the season was celebrated in some style judging by the words of one local correspondent:

> On Tuesday evening last, at the Corn Exchange, we had the pleasure of "assisting" at the annual *soirée* of the Kettering Football Club. It was one of the pleasantest parties that we have had the pleasure of attending. All were hail fellows well met, and if anyone felt strange it was his own fault. The seniors were Mr. N. Newman (the president), Rev. G. Thurston (association captain), Mr. F. Henson, and one or two others. Then there was a large gathering of young men, prominent amongst whom were the Spences, the Mobbses, the Newmans, the Bayes', the Loasbys, and other well-known names who have sustained the reputation of our town in many a toughly-contested game. Some 60 or more sat down to a first-class collation of meat tea, supplied by Mr. W. Palmer, the Coffee Tavern Company's manager...

After a report from the secretary and treasurer G.W. Spence – which revealed that the highest gate receipts had yielded £4-16s-9d (against Leicester) and the lowest just eleven pence (opposition unknown) – Harry Mobbs gave his assessment of the club's rugby doings; not surprisingly focussing on the 'shady' dealings of the Leamington 'gentlemen', but also highlighting the greatest triumph of the season – the defeat of Leicester by a goal to nil.

Towards the end of the evening – which was enlivened by music and songs from the members – it fell to Rev Thurston to say a few words on the games that had been played with a round ball. He began by congratulating the club on its success and prosperity, the number of matches won (22 out of 26 played under both codes), its financial position (the accounts were in the black to the tune of £1-3s-5d) and the number of members, which continued to rise. Some people, he said, considered the Association game to be quite 'tame', but this was not his experience – and there were plenty of opportunities for 'hard knocks' in the sport if anyone so desired! He hoped it would not be thought that because he did not join in the Union game he did not appreciate it; but he supposed he preferred the other because it was the code he had learned at school. Finally, he told his audience they should congratulate themselves on having made considerable progress in the way of playing association football, particularly in displaying an 'unselfishness' when it came to the art of passing the ball.

1882.			Where played.	result	Goals made	Goals lost
Oct. 7	Leicester	R	Leicester	lost	0	1
” 14	36 All Comers	R	Kettering	won	1	0
” 21	Leamington	R	Kettering	won	1	0
” 28	Wellingborough	A	Kettering	lost	1	4
Nov. 10	Loughborough	R	Kettering	won	6	0
” 18	Church Institute	A	Kettering	won	2	0
” 25	Wesleyans'	R	Kettering	won	2	0
” 25	36 All Comers re.	R	Kettering	won	1	0
Dec. 2	Uppingham	A	Kettering	won	1	0
” 9	Loughborough	R	Loughbro'	won	1	0
” 16	Wesleyans'	A	Kettering	won	1	0
” 28	Northampton	R	Kettering	won	4	0
” 29	Wesleyans'	R	Kettering	won	0	0
” 30	Rothwell	R	Rothwell	won	1	0
1883.						
Jan. 6	Mr. Thurston's Team	A	Kettering	won	4	0
” 20	Stamford	R	Stamford	won	0	0
” 27	Wellingborough	A	Wellingborough	won	6	1
Feb. 10	Uppingham	A	Uppingham	won	7	3
” 10	Irthlingborough	R	Kettering	lost	0	0
” 24	Leicester Second Team	R	Leicester	won	0	0
” 24	Oakham	A	Oakham	won	3	0
Mar. 3	Leicester	R	Kettering	won	1	0
” 3	Rothwell	R	Kettering	won	3	0
” 17	Irthlingborough	R	Irthlingborough	lost	0	1
” 24	Vice - Captain's Team	R	Kettering	won	0	0
” 31	Mr. Thurston's Team	A	Kettering	won	3	1

Matches played, 26; won, 22; lost, 4.

The 1882-83 fixtures and results as submitted at the end-of-season meeting and published in the local press. 'R' refers to games of rugby union, 'A' to games of association football. Whilst in both codes the number of goals scored was the most important factor in determining a winner, tries etc. have obviously been taken into consideration in the case of a rugby match finishing 0-0. Interestingly, the infamous Leamington cup tie is stubbornly recorded as 'won'!

Five

Cup Winners!

1883 - 1888

"The final match in the Wellingborough and District Challenge Cup competition was played on the Wellingborough Cricket Ground, on Saturday, the contesting Clubs being Kettering and Wellingborough Town. Although the weather was wet, a heavy shower falling during the first half-hour's play, there was a large attendance of spectators, including a great number from Kettering, who evinced a lively interest in the game. Three-thirty was fixed for a start, but it was a quarter of an hour after that time before Wellingborough, who won the toss, kicked off with a slight wind in their favour."

In 1871, in an attempt to further the appeal of association football, the FA's secretary, Charles Alcock, had proposed: "That it is desirable that a Challenge Cup should be established in connection with the Association, for which all clubs belonging to the Association should be invited to compete." A knockout competition, along the lines of that played at Alcock's old school, Harrow, where the school houses competed for the honour of being the 'Cock House', was duly approved and £20 secured a fitting trophy from Messrs Martin, Hall & Co. 15 clubs entered (of which only 12 actually competed), the majority from the London area and one from Scotland (Queen's Park). The FA Challenge Cup was up and running. What would become the world's most famous competition for domestic clubs had introduced the principle of competitive football to the public. Gradually, local competitions were established and interest in the round ball game began to grow. Even in Northamptonshire.

In 1882, with the founding of the Wellingborough & District FA, came the Wellingborough & District Challenge Cup – today known as the Hillier Senior Cup. Now that Kettering's players had really got the hang of the game, the club joined their local Football Association and entered its knockout competition, which this season comprised eight other teams: Earls Barton, Higham Ferrers, Rushden Wanderers, Wellingborough Revellers, Wellingborough Town and – from outside the county – Bedford, Market Harborough and Newport Pagnell (holders of the cup, having been the competition's first winners).

Prior to Kettering's first round game at home to Wellingborough Revellers on 20 October 1883, the *Kettering Observer* felt the need to provide a brief description of what those spectators more used to rugby could expect to see: "The Rugby game is played with an oval ball but the Association game is played with a round one. You must not handle the ball but you can bring it down using your head or your chest. The object of the game is to kick the ball through the posts and under the cord [fixed crossbars were still not yet widely in use]."

Kettering beat the Revellers 2-0 and were handed a bye in the second round. In the semi-final, played at Wellingborough on 22 March 1883, Kettering were held to a 1-1 draw by Higham Ferrers, but had no trouble in winning the replay 3-0 a week later. It was back to Wellingborough again for the third time in a fortnight for the final on Saturday, 5 April; and the *Northampton Daily Reporter* printed an account of the club's first cup final:

WELLINGBOROUGH AND DISTRICT CHALLENGE CUP.
KETTERING V. WELLINGBOROUGH. – The final match in the Wellingborough and District Challenge Cup competition was played on the Wellingborough Cricket

Ground, on Saturday, the contesting Clubs being Kettering and Wellingborough Town. Although the weather was wet, a heavy shower falling during the first half-hour's play, there was a large attendance of spectators, including a great number from Kettering, who evinced a lively interest in the game. Three-thirty was fixed for a start, but it was a quarter of an hour after that time before Wellingborough, who won the toss, kicked off with a slight wind in their favour. The ball was well returned and after a few minutes play hands were claimed by Kettering, but nothing resulted from the free kick. Kettering played up well and the leather was kept in the ground of their opponents and a corner was secured. The kick, however, proved fruitless and some good play on both sides followed, the partisans of Kettering being very demonstrative, as in fact they were throughout the game. Kettering again pressed their opponents and looked like securing a goal, when hands were called for Wellingborough and the ball was taken into the visitors' territory. It did not remain there long, however, as it was speedily kicked up the ground, and H. Mobbs getting possession of the ball, did a splendid piece of dribbling, and passing the leather to Dickson [Dixon] a short distance from the goal, the latter cleverly managed to get it through the posts, amid loud applause. The goal was objected to by Wellingborough on the ground of off-side, but the judges decided in favour of Kettering. On the ball being restarted, the home team exerted themselves to the utmost, and their opponents' goal was several times in danger, thanks to the good play of Parkinson, Southern, and Marriott. Hands was called just in front of the Kettering goal, and a corner kick was also obtained by Wellingborough, but no good came from either, although it must be admitted the home team had rather bad luck. This put Kettering on their metal, and the ball was soon transferred from one side of the ground to the other, and through the instrumentality of Dickson and R. Lindsay a corner was secured, but this time the ball was badly kicked out by the Rev. G. Thurston, and Wellingborough successfully defended their goal. Immediately afterwards the ball was brought up by Parker, and Woolston kicked a goal, but it was not allowed on account of hands. Wellingborough then showed better form, and about this time the Rev. G. Thurston did his side good service by his splendid kicking, which was conspicuous throughout. When half-time was called no further advantage had been gained by either sides. On changing ends Wellingborough pressed their opponents, and the Rev. R.E. Goldingham made a good kick for goal, the ball passing only a few inches on the wrong side; and then a good attempt was made by Wellingborough, and a corner followed, but still Kettering held their own. Dickson now relieved his side by taking the ball into his opponents' territory, but owing to the excellent play of Brazier and Southern it was quickly returned. The latter made a splendid kick for goal, but the Kettering goal [keeper] cleverly kept the ball out. H. Mobbs came to the rescue, and the leather was again in close proximity to the Wellingborough goal. It, however, passed the goal line, and this enabled the home team to send it to the other side of the ground, and a corner was scored. Kettering admirably defended their fortress, and also managed to follow this up by adding another corner to their credit. From this, too, a second goal was made. The Rev. G. Thurston kicked the ball in splendid style, and it was cleverly put through the posts amid hearty applause from the Kettering spectators. About 20 minutes more time remained, and the game became fast and very exciting. Through the exertions of the Rev. R.E. Goldingham the leather was taken into the Kettering ground, and about three yards before the goal hands was claimed by Wellingborough [resulting in a free kick – penalty kicks would not be introduced before 1891]. The rev. gentleman lifted the ball up with his foot, and, by a well-directed effort, Brazier sent it through the posts with his head. This called forth the applause of the supporters of the Wellingborough team. After this the home players did their utmost to secure another goal, and the ball was kept nearly all the time in their opponents' ground. They had two or three excellent chances of scoring but failed. Wellingborough had two corners and hands close to their opponents' goal in a very short time, but their anxiety to score appeared to interfere with their success, and when time was called Kettering was declared the winners of the cup by two goals to one. The cup was won last year by Newport Pagnell. We are inclined to think that the best team won on Saturday. The Kettering forwards seemed to play together much better than their opponents who held that position, and the Kettering back men were superior to the Wellingborough backs, the Rev. G. Thurston being an extraordinarily good kick and back man.

The team that wet spring afternoon is recorded as William Spence (goalkeeper); Lew Lindsay (back); Rev George Thurston (captain and three-quarter-back – a rugby term!); Trooby Newman and Harry Mobbs (half-backs); Jack Woolston, Charlie Dixon, Septimus Mobbs, William Hart, R. Lindsay and Billy Parker (forwards).

With victory, Kettering became the first Northamptonshire club to win the competition. Despite Newport Pagnell's reluctance to hand back the cup they had held for a year – numerous letters were sent by the Wellingborough & District Association before it was returned by post – the trophy was eventually brought to Kettering where it was proudly displayed for all to see in the window of Mr Baxter's Furnishing Warehouse, 48 & 49 High Street.

Five friendlies brought the total number of games played under Association rules this season to nine; seven won and two drawn. 13 games of rugby resulted in eight wins, three draws and two defeats. Off the pitch, a total of £25-9s-6d was taken in gate money, and the club more or less broke even. The biggest item of expenditure was travel to away matches: £11-16s-4d; whilst just over £9 was spent on 'ground improvements' – flags, fences, posts and ropes were all repaired or put in place – as the public, through the columns of the local press, began to voice an opinion that conditions for spectating ought to be made better:

In view of the big [rugby] match [Northants v Marlborough Nomads – county fixtures were often played at Eldred's Field at this time] coming off next week on the Kettering ground, I wish to put forward the following suggestions to the committee with regards to the 6d reserve. First of all that the Green-lane side with its shelter from the north wind, is certainly the best side for watching the game, and should therefore form the reserve space, and secondly that a plan almost universally adopted elsewhere, should be tried, namely of providing those who pay more, with boards to stand on. I may mention that the last time I paid reserved price, I could positively see nothing, and was obliged to cross to the other side. [*Kettering Guardian*, 21 December 1883.]

Eldred's Field.

By now the club was firmly established at Eldred's Field, which appears to the right of this photograph taken from the spire of the parish church looking northeast across Kettering (circa 1886). London Road runs diagonally through the picture from right to left until it becomes Horsemarket (with the Boys National School in the centre) and then Dalkeith Place. Although there are no signs yet of any spectator comforts, in its heyday – the early 1890s – the centrepiece of the ground would be a large grandstand, the playing-area would be roped off and the paying public provided with wooden planks to stand on.

The members formed a harriers club this season, the first run being arranged for a late September evening. After journeying through Weekley, Warkton and Barton Seagrave, a gentleman by the name of Needs reached the Coffee Tavern in town first, in a time of 58 minutes. Mr Robinson come in second and the others, about 20 in total, were close behind. They all ran in their new 'football costumes' purchased from Jenkinson & Towndrow (there is no evidence to suggest the colours were anything other than blue and white hoops, after a proposal at the Annual Meeting three weeks earlier to switch to a white jersey with a black band was rejected).

Unfortunately, the club was about to lose the services of two very influential players: Rev Thurston, who had done so much to help develop the Association game at Kettering, and Lew Lindsay, who had played alongside Thurston in the team that won the Wellingborough & District Cup and was also a first-class exponent of the rugby game, being captain of both club and county.

Lindsay was due to leave the town at the turn of the year to take up an appointment with the Madras Mounted Police in India. Such was his standing within the community that two gatherings were arranged to mark his departure. On the evening of Monday, 15 December 1884, the Great and the Good of Kettering held a farewell dinner in his honour at the George Hotel; and 24 hours later, at the same venue, his footballing colleagues said their goodbyes and Nat Newman presented him with a set of gold studs and links, along with a testimonial (neatly written on vellum, to which more than 80 names were appended) bearing the words: "The members of the Kettering Football Club in asking Mr. L.J. Lindsay's acceptance of a small token of their regard and appreciation of his services to the club, hope that it may remind him of his many friends in Kettering, whose earnest wish is that there may be a prosperous and successful career before him in the country for which he is leaving."

After the presentation, Lindsay rose and spoke of the county and Kettering rugby sides, making reference to how the game was changing. Three days later, the *Kettering Observer* carried his speech:

Mr. Newman and Gentlemen, I thank you all most heartily, first of all for the kind vote of thanks you have passed in recognition of my services to the Kettering Football Club... When I first joined the club as a member, I changed from forward to back, the real reason being, I am afraid, that I was rather idle and did not want much to do. (Laughter.) As to my connection with the county club, though last year we were not very successful, anyone could tell who saw the matches that we had some good players, and there was great promise for the future. (Hear, hear.) Last year we lost the first match by two goals and a try, but after that we showed better form, though the result was against us, and this year, as you know, we have opened with a victory – (cheers) – and it is a very gratifying thing to me to be the captain of a county club that has won a victory. As regards the present, it is a great pleasure to me to accept it, for though our acquaintance has been short, I think I have managed to make friends with everyone in the club. (Applause.) Mr. Newman said he had some good forwards in the Kettering team, and I may say they are among the best in the county. (Applause.) I am quite certain we might take all the forwards to represent the county out of the Kettering club alone, and that they would do credit to town and county. (Applause.) We have some good backs, too, but I am afraid they have not had the opportunity of distinguishing themselves. The character of the game, as most of you know, has greatly changed within the last few years. In the old days it was all scrummaging, and everyone did the best he could for himself, but now it is quite different, and a man, if he wishes to do the best he can for his club, must be unselfish and must pass, and unless he does he is not in it. I am afraid, as a club, we have hardly mastered the art of passing yet – (hear, hear) – but I trust it will not be long before we do. We have good men for it, as I am sure we could not have better three-quarter backs and half backs, who only want more training. The object of the latter should be to get on to the backs as soon as the ball is out of the scrummage, passing as soon as there is a favourable opportunity. (Hear, hear.)

In the first round of the Wellingborough & District Cup, Kettering again beat Wellingborough Revellers, this time by two goals to one, but lost 2-0 to Rushden Wanderers in the semi-final. Just four other matches are known to have been played under Association rules this season – all defeats: Wellingborough Grammar School twice (3-0 and 5-0), Wellingborough Town (3-1) and Higham Ferrers (2-0). Kettering were certainly a poorer side without the skills of Lindsay and the Reverend.

Overleaf: The Kettering Guardian*'s report of the club's Annual Meeting, published on 5 September 1884, followed by an account of the club's Annual Dinner (or Supper), which appeared in the* Kettering Observer *on 22 May 1885.*

The two articles serve to illustrate the workings of Kettering FC at the time; the formal election of officials and captains pre-season, and a review of finances and footballing matters when the campaign had ended. Whilst it is recorded that there was 'a growing interest' in the Association game, it appears that the Kettering public was still more inclined to turn up to watch a rugby match in the mid-1880s.

KETTERING FOOTBALL CLUB.

The annual meeting of the Kettering Football Club was held at the Boys' National School, on Tuesday evening, when there was a good number present. The Rev. G. Thurston having been voted to the chair, in the absence of the president (Mr. N. Newman), it was agreed that they secure the same field if possible in which to play, as heretofore – Mr. Eldred's.– Mr. Eli Robinson proposed, and Mr. L. J. Lindsay seconded, that the club colours remain the same as last year.– Mr. S. Marsh moved as an amendment that they change the colours from last year, suggesting a white jersey with a black sash.– This was seconded by Mr. C. Robinson, but was lost by a large majority. It was then resolved that they play the same rules as last year, both Rugby and Association; and that they subscribe to the County Club as before, and also to the Wellingborough and District Association.– Mr. C. Robinson spoke as to the advisability of having a few more second team matches, with a separate committee and captain. He contended that by so doing they would "bring out" some good players for the first team matches; and thought that last year the younger ones had comparatively little opportunity of becoming experts, as the matches allotted to them were not confined to second team men.– The Chairman having spoken as to the need of a second captain out of the 60 or 70 members of the club, Mr. H. W. Mobbs pointed out that of the 22 matches played last season, five were cup matches and nine were first team, leaving eight for the second team, who, he thought, had an equal opportunity of becoming better players.– Mr. Hart thought it was a question as to whether the expenses would allow for the proposal to be carried out; but this did not seem to be the opinion of the majority of those present, and after some further discussion Mr. C. Robinson proposed, and it was seconded by Mr. G. Abbott, that during the next season there shall be a captain for the second team, which was agreed to.– Mr. G. W. Spence then read the following names of clubs who had arranged with the officers of that club to play matches at Kettering during the forthcoming season: Rushden Football Club, Raunds second team, Northampton Unity first and second, Leicester first and second, Rothwell second, Burton-on-Trent first, Bedford first, Coventry first, Rugby first, Wellingborough, Wellingborough Grammar School, Higham Ferrers, Earl's Barton, Uppingham, Bedford Association, Oakham, North v. South, on October 4th.– It was agreed that they ask the Marlborough Nomads to play them on Boxing Day at Kettering, and also the Wellingborough Grammar School.– The Chairman mentioned that they had entered for the football contest at Finedon, on the 23rd inst.– The selection of officers for the ensuing year was then proceeded with. Mr. N. Newman was unanimously re-appointed president; and Mr. Eli Robinson proposed that the Rev. Geo. Thurston be re-elected Association captain.– Mr. Thurston said he was sorry to say he could not accept that office during the coming year, as he should not be able to take such an active part in football as he had done.– After some discussion, several of the members expressing their sorrow that Mr. Thurston had declined, Mr. W. H. Parker was elected. Mr. L. J. Lindsay was appointed captain of the Rugby team, Mr. W. H. Mobbs vice-captain, and Mr. Chas. Robinson captain of the second team. The following committee were elected:– Messrs. H. Bayes, F. Hanger, C. Dixon, J. Woolston, J. W. Greasley, E. R. Quincey and W. Newman.– Mr. G. W. Spence was then re-appointed secretary, and Mr. J. Hutchen, treasurer, and a vote of thanks to the Chairman terminated the meeting.

KETTERING FOOTBALL CLUB.

The annual dinner of the members was held last Monday evening at the George Hotel, being preceded by a short business meeting, when a report and statement of accounts was presented.

Mr. G. W. Spence (secretary) explained that owing to the journal not being made up he could not give a complete report, but would do so in a few days. He read the minutes of the last annual meeting, and stated that two of the most important out-of-town matches, those with Rugby and Coventry, fell through, involving a loss to the club. They had not been so fortunate with association matches, which were fewer, while the second team was an expensive though a necessary luxury, as from that the best players were chosen. Year by year the work of the Secretary seemed to grow, as he had written 403 letters, 199 post cards, and sent nine telegrams.

The President (Mr. N. Newman) said that he thought there was a growing interest in the Association game, and it would increase when the public saw such play as that shown by the East Midland team.

Mr. Hanger said the fact remained that while they could always make sure of a good gate at a Rugby match, it was not so in the case of Association matches.

After some conversation as to the letting of the ground for Association play, Mr. Spence moved and Mr. C. Bayes seconded that an adjourned meeting be held shortly to make a list of fixtures and transact other business, and it was agreed to.

Mr. Hutchen (treasurer) submitted a comprehensive financial statement, from which it appeared that the expenditure had been unusually heavy, owing to the erection of new goal posts, new posts for fencing off the ground, &c., while the failure of two clubs to play the return matches had helped to place the balance on the wrong side. This as it stood was about £16, but if the members in arrear paid their subscriptions, the balance would be reduced to £5 or £6. He gave the items in which there had been an increase, and showed that with economy, the probability was the balance would be on the right side at the close of the next season.

Mr. Hill proposed, and Mr. O. Spence seconded, a vote of thanks to the Treasurer and Secretary for their services, which was heartily carried, and the party adjourned for dinner. Mrs. Franklin made a capital spread, at what the French call a *Prix fixé*. Mr. N. Newman presided, with Mr. C. Bayes in the vice-chair, and the company included Messrs. F. Hanger (captain of the Rugby), W. H. Parker (captain of the Association), C. Dixon (vice-captain of the Rugby), C. Robinson (captain of the second team), H. Bayes, F. Goodall, G. C. Tomkins, O. Spence, W. Spence, G. W. Spence, J. Hawthorn, M. A. Patrick, A. Patrick, C. Lawrence, W. Cattell, G. Tunnicliffe, F. Miller, C. Hill, A. Mitton, J. Allen, W. Crane, E. Quincey, T. Quincey, G. Cooper, E. Loasby, G. Bailey, &c. A string band was engaged for the occasion, and rendered acceptable service after dinner. The only formal toast was "Success to the Football Club," proposed by Mr. Hill, who alluded to the magnificent Association match, East Midland v. Cambridge. Mr. Hanger for the Rugby team, and Mr. W. H. Parker for the Association, suitably responded.

A vote of thanks was passed to Mrs. Franklin for the excellent dinner and equally admirable attendance, and at the hour of closing the company broke up after having spent "a jolly evening."

It was reported that the club's new secretary, John James Driscall, died on 5 December 1885, two weeks after receiving a kick in the back 'whilst at play'. He was just 26. Whether or not the injury was sustained playing football is unclear, but shattered bones and occasional fatalities were not unheard of amongst those who participated in Victorian sport. His place as secretary was taken by Jack Hutchen (also known as John), who had been with the club for the past two years and already captained the reserves and acted as treasurer. A keen sportsman, Hutchen also played cricket for the town and was a founding member of the Kettering Cycling and Athletic Club. He later served with distinction in the Boer War (eventually settling in South Africa when hostilities ended).

In the Northants & District – formerly Wellingborough & District – Challenge Cup, Kettering beat Northampton Association 7-0 at Eldred's Field on Boxing Day, only for the club's interest in the competition to end at the semi-finals stage again with another 2-0 defeat to Rushden Wanderers (who went on to win the competition for the second year running). The Boxing Day game was watched by a crowd of around 700, which was no longer considered to be particularly large. The Kettering public had still not taken to the county knockout competition in any great numbers, and rugby continued to prove a more popular game. (Even so, two days after beating the Northampton club, more than 1,000 spectators turned up to see a novel 'Top Hat' match – black top hats versus white – which was presumably played under Association rules.)

Of 32 matches arranged at the beginning of the season, frost and rain ensured that only 18 were played; 11 games with an oval ball and seven with a round one (of which five were won).

Increasing numbers of young men were now taking up football and new clubs were regularly springing up across town: Alberts, Britons, Broadway Alma's, Church Institute, Excelsior, New Town, Revellers, Rovers, Star, Swifts, United Church Choirs and Wanderers all regularly fielded sides playing the RFU or FA's code (or even half a game of each if opponents could not agree on which to play!)

It was quite common to find a Kettering footballer turning out for another club when his services were not required; whilst the very fact that there *were* more clubs meant that the pool of players in the town was increasing, and those who stood out from the crowd had a good chance of finding their way into the Kettering team sooner or later.

At last it was time to set aside the blue and white hoops and Kettering adopted new colours: a deep crimson jersey, white knee-length shorts (still referred to as knickerbockers) and black stockings. On the heart of the jersey was a large badge bearing a cross keys emblem (the manorial sign of the Bishop of Peterborough) and the letters K-F-C embroidered in gold. The uniforms were provided by 'Chas' E. Towndrow – 'Athletic Clubs Outfitter and Uniform Contractor' – of 11 & 12 High Street, Kettering. (It appears that Messrs Jenkinson and Towndrow had gone their separate ways!)

There were changes, too, in the structure of county football. In March 1885, the Wellingborough & District FA had amended its name to Northamptonshire & District, which was fine, except for the fact that a 'rival' East Midland Counties Association also encouraged membership from Northants clubs. It was a situation that benefited neither organisation and, on the evening of Saturday, 25 September 1886, a meeting was held at the Hind Hotel in Wellingborough for the purpose of electing officers and amalgamating the two organisations into the Northamptonshire and Bedfordshire FA (membership of which was set at an annual cost of five shillings). It took just six months for the next change of name; in March 1887, 'Bedfordshire' was dropped from the title and Kettering became a member of the Northamptonshire Football Association – a name still in use today. But it was a relationship that was not destined to last. Storm clouds were already gathering on the horizon.

14 games of association football yielded four wins, four draws and six defeats (including a 4-2 reverse at home to Wellingborough Town in the first round of the Senior Cup). But the tide had turned – for the first time, the club would contest more matches during the season under Association rules than Union, with just nine games of rugby being played; five won, two drawn and two lost.

One rugby fixture eagerly anticipated in the town was Kettering's first encounter with the St James club from Northampton – forerunner of today's Northampton Saints. On 26 March 1887, a large crowd gathered at Eldred's Field, and the *Northampton Herald* considered it a game important enough to describe in some detail:

ST. JAMES'S F.C. v. KETTERING F.C.

This match, played at Kettering on Saturday last, produced much interest in local football circles, being, as it was, the first meeting of these two Rugby Clubs. Consequently a large number of spectators were present. Both teams have shown good form, Kettering especially, and as both clubs have defeated the Northampton Unity this season, a good game was anticipated. Up to half-time the match was splendidly contested, only one try being registered in favour of the home team, but in the final half the Kettering forwards showed their superiority by adding two goals and a try to their total. Albeit the game was not of the one-sided character that the score would indicate, the visitors on several occasions being within an ace of scoring. But still there is no denying the fact that the best team won. The home team got together the strongest team they have placed in the field this season. Norman, however, was absent through indisposition. The St. James's fifteen, although a representative team, was not the best the Club possessed, for York, Griffiths, Goodson and Blackwell were absentees. For the home team Phillips was a fair back. All the three-quarters played a good game, Panther showing prominently. The two halves were useful, while of an exceptionally good lot of forwards Mitton, Mercell, and Abrahams were most conspicuous. For the visitors Parr collared well, and made a few good runs. Dunkley was the pick of the three-quarters, making two or three brilliant runs. Orton made good use of the few chances given him, while Stanley collared beautifully, and put in a lot of useful kicks. Barker was a rattling half back, while Jesson was useful. Of the rather light lot of forwards (and it was in the packs that Kettering held the sway) Golding, Civil, and Stanley were the pick. Details:– Kettering won the toss, and chose to kick towards the church. Civil for St. James's kicked off, Panther returning, and the first scrimmage was formed in mid-field. After a few tight packs Orton got possession from a pass by Jesson, and ran to the home "25" flag before being floored by Panther. After more scrimmaging had been indulged in Panther got away, but was pushed into touch by Dunkley. Parr equalised by a run and punt, and more scrimmaging took place in the centre. Owen, however, handled, and took the oval close to the Northampton goal line; and although the home forwards made energetic attempts to get over, they were well met by the visitors' backs, and Dunkley, getting possession, ran to the centre before being "grassed" by Owen. The Kettering forwards, however, dribbled back again, and the ball being kicked behind, Joyce ran over and secured a try. Panther made a good attempt to score the major point [kick a goal], but the ball fell short of the uprights. From the kick-out Stanley put in a useful run, and finished up by dropping into touch. Dixon, however, brought it back, and kicking behind, Parr saved. Dunkley next was conspicuous by a splendid gallop into the centre. Here some stubbornly-contested scrimmages were formed, and the first half was brought to a conclusion by a neat run by Jesson. Dixon re-started with a dribble, and brought the ball close to the St. James' "25" flag. Parr, however, got it away by a run and punt. Abrahams here put in a neat run, and passed to Panther, who passed all the visitors' three-quarters, and looked certain of getting in until he was "collared" by Parr. Barker took the ball to the centre, and some very fast play was indulged in, Panther, Dixon, and Robinson being conspicuous for Kettering, while Bellchambers, Facer, and Civil were busy for St. James'. Joyce next got away, and passed to Mercell, who, amidst great applause, dropped a goal. There was a large amount of dispute with regard to the fairness of the goal, as it was alleged by the visitors' umpire that Joyce touched the ball dead before passing to Mercell. However, the referee gave his decision in favour of the home team. Civil re-started, and Panther (who was now playing full back) "mulling" the return, the leather was kept in the home "25" for some time. Stanley next made a plucky effort to get over, but was well tackled by Owen. Tunnicliffe equalised by a good run to the centre. The home forwards now came with a rush, and dribbled near the Northampton goal, and Mercell picking up got over. Panther took the kick, and obtained a splendid goal. Dunkley again distinguished himself by a sharp sprint into the home territory. Lewis, however, got away, but was "floored" by Parr close on the goal line. After a few tight scrimmages, Tunnicliffe secured a try, Panther failing at the place [kick]. From the drop out some fine kicking was indulged in by the backs of both sides. Barker, Stanley, and Jesson were instrumental in taking play near the Kettering uprights. Stanley and Dunkley made two energetic attempts to get over, and the latter had hard lines in not doing so. Dixon relieved the pressure by running to neutral territory. Some give-and-take play now took place, and Phillips kicking behind, Parr had again to "save." Civil and Bellchambers dribbled to the centre, and Abrahams getting possession put in a useful run, and finished up by kicking behind, the visitors having again to "save." "Time" was then called, leaving the home team victorious by two goals, two trys, and four touchdowns to *nil*. Teams:–

Kettering: J. Phillips, back; C. Dixon, A. Panther [actually Panter?], and G. Owen, three-quarter backs; W. Joyce and W. Crane, half-backs; A. Mitton, A.R. Mercell, C. Robinson, G. Tunnicliffe, J. Payne, J. Lewis, A. Abrahams, R. Abrahams, and A. Letts, forwards.

St. James: C. Parr, back; E. Dunkley, C. Stanley, and A. Orton, three-quarter backs; G. Barker and E. Jesson, half-backs; T. Stanley, A. Timms, F. Timms, J. Facer, G. Reynolds, J. Bellchambers, J. England, J. Golding, and H. Civil, forwards.

𝔉ootball.

An illustration that was used in the Kettering Observer *from the mid-1880s. It appeared above match reports, regardless of whether the contest was one played under Association or Union rules.*

The question of whether the club should continue to play under both Association and Union rules raised considerable discussion this season. Rugby was undoubtedly hampering the progress of association football at Kettering; there were several players who took part in both codes and when games of each were scheduled for the same day one of the teams, if not both, would take to the field below strength. However, it was thought that it would be a pity for the club to discontinue playing rugby because, when it could put its best side out, it was always a match for anyone in this part of the country – even Coventry. And so it was decided that Kettering would continue, for the time being, with both the round and oval ball games.

One gentleman who would have been a part of these discussions was John Winter Dryland, who now held the position of club president. Another of the town's 'Great Victorians' to be associated with its football team, Dryland was a doctor who worked tirelessly to control the infectious diseases that could decimate populations in the era in which he lived. He held many public offices and was held in high esteem by his fellow townsmen. He was ahead of his time, too, believing that footballers must be temperate in eating and drinking if they wished to become proficient. The good doctor is still remembered today in the Dryland Memorial outside the library and in Dryland Street in the town centre, which was named after him.

13 of the 19 matches that were played under Association rules this season were won: versus Higham Ferrers (twice), Leicester Fosse (twice), Leicestershire, Market Harborough (twice), Notts Bohemians, Oakham (twice), Raunds Unity, Rushden Wanderers and Wellingborough. Two games against Hugh Roughton's Cambridge University XI ended in draws, and defeats were recorded against Notts County, Raunds Unity, Rushden Wanderers (4-2 in the first round of the Senior Cup) and Wellingborough Grammar School. 61 goals were scored and 38 conceded. Just nine games of rugby were played, of which five were won and four lost.

On 11 May 1888, it was reported in the *Kettering Leader* that the club had made a decision to disconnect itself from the Northamptonshire Football Association. Furthermore, Kettering would be looking to join the national Association directly and enter *its* knockout competition. It was the opinion of the members (of which there were now well in excess of 100) that the club had not been fairly represented in county matches, whilst at meetings of the county FA, whose committee was said to be composed chiefly of Wellingborough and Rushden players, the suggestions of the Kettering representatives were regularly disregarded and the club itself decidedly snubbed. Indeed, there was an opinion in the town that 'Northamptonshire' might as well be amended back to 'Wellingborough & District'!

Six

Association Rules For Ever

1888 - 1890

"By defeating Leicester Fosse on Saturday, the Kettering Town Association Club has added another to a long list of successes this season. The game had been anticipated with a considerable amount of interest, and the special trains from Kimbolton and Market Harborough brought a number of visitors, there being close upon a thousand spectators on the Town Ground to watch the match. Leicester, with the exception of Vickers, brought their full strength, and Kettering were also thoroughly represented. From start to finish, and particularly in the second half, the game was very fast, grand form being shown by both teams, notably by the home backs."

The first winners of the FA Challenge Cup were Wanderers, a team of ex-public school and university players, captained by the man whose idea had led to the competition, the FA's Mr Alcock. In front of around 2,000 spectators, Wanderers defeated the Royal Engineers by a goal to nil in the final at the Oval on 16 March 1872 – the year of Kettering's formation.

The very first match in connection with the FA Cup – popularly known as the English Cup (or 'Little Tin Idol') – played on Northamptonshire soil took place in Kettering on Saturday, 6 October 1888, when the club lost 4-3 to Newark in the first qualifying round at Eldred's Field. The score stood at 2-2 at the end of 90 minutes, but to save the trouble and expense of a replay the game continued for another half-hour. The following Monday, the *Northampton Herald* carried a full report of this landmark occasion:

THE ENGLISH ASSOCIATION CHALLENGE CUP.
Newark v. Kettering.

For the first time in Northants football history an English Cup tie match under Association rules was contested in the county on Saturday afternoon. The opposing teams were Kettering and Newark, and the game was played on the ground of the former, in the presence of about 1,000 persons. Neither town was fully represented, Newark being without the services of McRae and Chattern, whilst the home men lacked the assistance of A.B. Panter, and W. Lilley amongst others. However, as was anticipated, the encounter was an exceedingly exciting one, Kettering eventually losing with three goals to their opponents' four. Had Kettering possessed better combination it is probable the result would have been favourable to them, as much of their individual play was decidedly superior to that of members of the Newark team. The visitors won the toss, and Kettering, with a slight wind in their faces, started the ball towards the church at 2.20. During the first three quarters of an hour matters were not so interesting as they later on proved. In the first fifteen minutes Newark had much the best of it, forcing Kettering several times back on to their lines, and at last, in spite of the wariness of Palmer, ... Grocock, assisted by H. Heppenstall, by a sharp shot scored goal one for his side. This initial success seemed to put Kettering on their mettle, and they made one or two assaults on the Newark goal, but all in vain. C. Piggott and C. Dixon were frequently conspicuously good in passing and dodging manoeuvres, and Roughton and Bates did much useful work at this period, both in kicking and dribbling. Palmer, who had been busy and smart in repulsing the "quick returns" of Newark, was, about ten minutes before half time, again beaten, on this occasion by Paling, who secured goal two for Newark, by a brilliant dash in conjunction with A. Heppenstall. Parlby, a well-known sprinter, was, later on, often to the fore with fine spurts on the Newark right, but was always well stopped by Wilson, or the Kettering half-backs. Jenkins in the meantime had a splendid chance of scoring, but failed to take advantage of it, and directly following this the Newark forwards carried play into the Kettering ... and hustled the ball between the posts. No point was allowed on an appeal for offside, and a similar objection was allowed once or twice subsequently. At half time Newark had two goals to *nil*, but on changing sides the Kettering general play noticeably improved. Brewer, Langford, Jenkins, Wilson, Bates, Wright and Tunnicliffe all in turn showed up well. The home team were within an ace of scoring repeatedly, and at length Jenkins fed Piggott, who managed very skilfully to plant the leather between Newark poles. This point, which was registered amidst applause, was quickly followed by another obtained by Jenkins, who put in a long shot rather too high up for the goal-keeper, who in trying to reach it made a "mull." There was no change in the relative positions at the call of time, and an additional quarter of an hour each way was played. At the conclusion of the first fifteen minutes Kettering, through the instrumentality of Wilson, had made one more goal, and were therefore that point ahead. When the teams crossed over for the last time Kettering's prospects were rosy, but succeeding events dispelled any hopes of winning which Kettering might have had. Newark speedily equalised matters, H. Heppenstall getting goal three, and just before the call of time A. Heppenstall was enabled to work another goal and win the match for Newark. Teams:–

Kettering.– F. Palmer, goal; A. Jenkins and M. Brewer, backs; G. Tunnicliffe (captain), G. Wright, and J. Langford, half-backs; H. Roughton and G. Wilson, left wing; C. Dixon and C. Piggott, right wing; G. Bates, centre.

Newark.– R. Foottit, goal; W. Morley and T. Paling, backs; J. Stennett, J. Tunbull, and W. Darcey, half-backs; R. Grocock and H. Heppenstall, left wing; E. Parlby and A. Heppenstall, right wing; A. Wilson, centre.

Umpires: [Tommy] Maycock (Kettering) and J.C. Hunt (secretary to Newark); referee, H.W. Proctor, of the Notts Association.

Prior to the match the Kettering Rifle Band paraded the town, and during the interval played a selection.

Entering the FA Cup was a big step for Kettering's footballers and there were serious questions to be asked about the club continuing to play rugby, even though the oval ball game remained popular with the spectating public. A fact illustrated when, just two days after losing to Newark, Kettering hosted Swinton – a prominent Lancashire rugby club that was on a tour of the country – in a fixture that drew an impressive Monday afternoon crowd of between 1,500 and 2,000.

Swinton were then a powerful side that included a number of county players and two England rugby union internationals: Sam Roberts and Jim Valentine. (Now known as Swinton Lions, the club would switch codes to rugby league in the latter half of the 1890s.) Three of the men who had played in Kettering's cup tie on the

Saturday took to the field again: Charlie Dixon (who captained the rugby XV), Hugh Roughton and George Tunnicliffe; they were joined by Fessor Lilley, who would almost certainly have played against Newark had he not been representing the county at rugby against the touring New Zealand Maoris on the same day. In the event, Swinton proved too strong and ran out winners by a goal, three tries and five touchdowns to one touchdown.

As a result of the previous season's split with the Northamptonshire FA, it had been decided to set up a competition to rival the established Senior Cup. This was a move that would require the official sanction of the game's governing body. So, on Monday, 24 September, in the week prior to the Newark game, Messrs H.T. Favell and C. Henson travelled to London (at a time when the city was awash with news of Jack the Ripper's grisly exploits in the East End) to put the club's case to a meeting of the Football Association Council at 51 Holborn Viaduct.

Originally placed fifth on the agenda, the council agreed to discuss the Kettering matter first and the club's representatives were accordingly asked to state their case as clearly and concisely as possible. Favell rose and presented the need for the proposed competition, produced a set of printed rules and explained why the club was disconnected with the county FA. At the conclusion of his address, several questions were asked by individual members of the council and these were answered to everyone's satisfaction. The chairman, Dr Morley (of Blackburn Rovers), then announced he would place the opposing side of the matter before the council and asked the secretary (Mr Alcock) to read the correspondence that had passed between the FA and Messrs C. Claridge (of Rushden) and H.E. Platt (of Wellingborough), officers of the Northamptonshire Association. This done, the Kettering deputation was asked to withdraw whilst the matter was discussed in private. After a lapse of six or seven minutes, Favell and Henson were called back into the room and Dr Morley said he was pleased to inform them that the competition had the approval of the council.

A few days later, as a result of further objections raised by Claridge and Platt, the FA advised the club to change the name of the competition from 'Challenge Cup' to 'Charity Cup'. This was done and, with the FA's blessing, the Kettering & District Football Charity Cup was born. (Given the hostility between the club and its neighbours, it is somewhat ironic that 1888 saw the introduction of a telephone line between the towns of Wellingborough and Kettering!)

Open to teams playing the Association's game within a 50-mile radius of the town, there was a splendid silver cup, valued at 30 guineas, and medals for the winners and runners-up (all of which were displayed in Mr Baxter's shop window on the High

Street). The gentlemen who promoted the competition and collected the voluntary subscriptions did so with the aim of 'assisting and encouraging the game in the district', and at the same time with a view to benefiting the Northampton Infirmary and Kettering Dispensary.

100 invitations were sent out and 12 clubs accepted. Along with Kettering, the competition's first entrants were Bedford, Cambridge Granta, Cambridge Swifts, Finedon Revellers, Grantham Town, Higham Rovers, Hitchin, Kettering Hawks, Leicester Mill Hill House, Loughborough Town, Wellingborough Town and Wolverton. (Wellingborough Grammar School and a team to represent the town of Rushden were notable absentees.) After a 3-1 victory over Wellingborough in the first round, Kettering lost by two goals to nil at home to Loughborough in the second. The first winners of the competition were Grantham, who beat Cambridge Granta by a goal to nil on 17 March at Eldred's Field, watched by a crowd of around 2,500. It would, in fact, be the Kettering Charity Cup, not the FA Cup – and certainly not the Senior Cup – that enticed large crowds to association football matches in the town and stimulated a greater interest throughout the county.

A NEW FOOTBALL BOOT. – The "Boot and Shoe Trades Journal" states that the Kettering Boot and Shoe Manufacturing Company have recently purchased the rights of manufacture of Howe's patent "Sure Kick" football boots. The special feature of this patent lies in the corrugation of the toes, which is accomplished by laying pieces of hard cord, in any suitable design, between the toe-cap and vamp, by pressing and stitching the leather down on either side, and otherwise hardening the toe. The sole at the toe is also corrugated, in order to prevent slipping from the toe when the ball is wet. For "dribbling" and long kicks, it is claimed to be invaluable. The uppers are cut from well selected russet hides, and in bottoming the sample is all that could be desired. With each pair of boots sent out is enclosed a neatly got up book containing the latest information as to the laws relating to football.

Whilst the club was making progress on the pitch, the factories of Kettering, famed for their shoemaking skills, were helping to ensure that football could be enjoyed by the masses. Kettering Observer, *14 December 1888.*

At the end of the season, Charlie 'Hap'orth' Dixon officially 'retired' (he would actually carry on playing for a couple more years and later act as a 'trainer'). His name first appears in connection with the club in 1874, and it was said that he never missed a game, other than through illness or other unavoidable cause. The epitome of those men who were able to master any code of football, Dixon captained both the round and oval ball sides, twice represented the county – versus Cambridgeshire (association football) and Cheshire (rugby union) – and was a member of the team that secured the Wellingborough and District Cup. Known as one of Kettering's fastest runners and described by a contemporary as a player who never minded 'getting into the ribs' of men much bigger than himself, Dixon generally played the Association game at inside-right and was a three-quarter when it came to rugby. He was the first retiring player in Northamptonshire to be awarded a benefit match, which took place at Eldred's Field on the first Saturday in April against Rushden Wanderers. It was a warm spring day and quite an occasion, with the Kettering Town Band parading the principal streets of the town prior to kick off and performing a selection of music at half-time.

After the game, which the visitors won by three goals to two, an adjournment was made to the Coffee Tavern for tea, followed by a few words from Nat Newman and a presentation by Mr Favell of a handsome silver watch (inscribed: "Presented to C. Dixon by the Kettering F.C. after 15 years service, 1889") and a purse containing six sovereigns.

Improvements were made to the club's surroundings when a strong door was constructed to replace the dilapidated 'pigeon-hole' that for many years had served as the entrance to Eldred's Field, and wooden planks were laid down for spectators to stand on, which was much appreciated. By now the club's membership had risen to 127 ordinary and 44 honorary members, and a most welcome balance in hand of over £13 was reported at the end of the campaign, which saw 23 matches played under Association rules: 11 won, two drawn and ten lost; and five games of rugby, resulting in one draw and four defeats.

The issue of Kettering continuing to play under both codes had come to a head back in February, when the president and chairman of the committee resigned following a vote of no confidence, brought about by those within the club who favoured the rugby game and felt it was being allowed to fade into the background. A week later the situation had calmed. Those who had stepped down were back in office, but the dual code 'problem' had not gone away.

Then, finally, on Friday, 10 May 1889, under the headline 'ASSOCIATION RULES FOR EVER', the *Kettering Observer* conveyed the news that at a meeting the previous Monday, the motion to drop rugby had been passed by a large majority. The club would now concentrate solely on association football. It was doubtless inevitable that this would happen sooner or later; the Association game was growing in popularity, whilst it was becoming increasingly difficult to find local rugby-playing opponents; just putting 15 men in the field capable of doing the club and the sport justice could no longer be taken for granted.

The report went on to reminisce about the position Kettering once occupied in the rugby world; a time when, as an old player at the meeting aptly put it: "Like Alexander the Great, they had to sit down because there was nobody else to conquer." Indeed, Kettering had competed against, and beaten, the senior rugby clubs from Northampton and (quite regularly) Leicester, and the *Kettering Observer* concluded: "It does really seem a pity that the old dashing code should become extinct in such a spot." Nevertheless, after 17 seasons, Kettering Football Club had severed its ties with the Union game.

Kettering FC, 1888-89.

Back row: H.T. Favell (secretary of the new Kettering Charity Cup competition), Tommy Maycock (umpire), H.D. Foster (captain), Fred Palmer, Fessor Lilley, Arthur Jenkins, George Wright, George Tunnicliffe, Billy Coltman (club secretary). Front row: Charlie Piggott, Charlie Dixon, George Bates, Jack Langford, George Wilson, Jack Hutchen (club treasurer).

The large badge introduced in 1886 can clearly be seen on the players' jerseys – which are distinctly white; quite when white came into use is uncertain, but the colour continues to appear on and off in team photographs into the early 1890s. Also noticeable are the knee-length shorts and the wearing of shinguards (outside the socks).

The Kettering Rugby team's visit to Leicester on Saturday, appears not to have been conducive of a pleasant game between the "crack" Rugby clubs. The Leicester club is well known to possess a first-class team, which for the last two seasons has been very successful in vanquishing most Rugby playing clubs of the Midlands. Kettering, however, have for nine seasons been completely their masters, winning all but one of the 18 matches they have played them. The nineteenth match, was also lost, owing doubtless to the manner in which the Rugby game has been allowed to fall off at Kettering, and the twentieth contest, which came off last Saturday, ended in an unsatisfactory draw. It was little thought by many that Kettering, with a weaker team than usual, would "get a look in," but to the surprise of a large number of supporters, who availed themselves of a cheap trip to the "Anti-vac town," and even to their own astonishment, they completely smothered their opponents' forwards by their fine play. "Fessor's" forward play was a distinctly noticeable feature in the game, and the Leicester men found for once their equal in tackling. It would, however, be invidious to particularise, as the visitors played a grand game throughout. The passing game Leicester played was far superior to that of the Kettering men, who scarcely ever passed the leather during the match. This selfishness was the only bad feature of the play, and indeed contributed in no small degree to their not pulling the game off.

A Kettering gentleman, well known in local football circles, writing to me under the *nom de plume* of "One who was there," anent the Leicester match, says:–

Such a result as Kettering drawing the game with Leicester clearly proves that there is still left a very good element of our old Rugby game, and it is a pity that playing both rules considerably hinders the progress of the team playing the one, and weakens the composition of the other. The Rugby team to me seems quite worthy of independent support, and no doubt if this were done it would be once again thoroughly able to hold its own against clubs from the neighbourhood, and also those from a distance. The men at present situated cannot reasonably be expected to play in anything like form after – as is sometimes the case – the interval of a month without a practice.

One of the last games of rugby that Kettering played in the Victorian era – against the club known today as Leicester Tigers, as reported in the Kettering Leader, *25 January 1889. (The 'Anti-vac town' comment is a reference to Leicester's reluctance to administer the smallpox vaccination.)*

This remarkable photograph captures a scene of association football being played at Eldred's Field about 120 years ago (the factory in the background can still be found today at the end of Newman Street). It cannot be said with 100% certainty that one of the teams is Kettering because games not involving the club were also played here. However, given that there is a reasonable crowd, and that a photographer has considered the occasion important enough to record, there is every likelihood that this is the oldest surviving image of Kettering in action (indeed, it is probably one of the oldest surviving images of the Association game being played anywhere). Although the picture's exact age is unknown, there are good reasons for believing it was taken in the late 1880s or early 1890s; certainly prior to the summer of 1893.

For the first time, trial matches were organised at the start of the season with the aim of assessing the form of the players. This was considered to be a 'capital idea', and it was hoped that 'better proportioned teams' would be the result. A brand new strip was purchased in recognition of the club playing only association football from now on. The jerseys being an interesting combination of chocolate brown and salmon pink in broad vertical stripes, worn for the first time on Saturday, 5 October 1889, at home to Notts County Reserves (a friendly, which County won 6-1).

RESERVE TEAM.

Date.		Club.	Where Played.
Oct.	12	Finedon	Away
"	19	Oakham Amateurs	Home
"	26	Northampton	Home
Nov.	2	Wolverton	Away
"	9	Irchester	Home
"	16	Wellingborough	Home
"	30	Rothwell	Away
Dec.	7	Wolverton	Home
"	14	Wellingborough	Away
"	28	Oakham Amateurs	Away
Jan.	4	Market Harborough	Home
"	11	Market Harborough	Away
"	18	Wellingborough All Saints	Home
"	25	Northampton	Away
Feb.	1	Wollaston Harriers	Home
"	8	Wellingborough All Saints	Away
"	15	Irthlingborough	Home
"	22	Rothwell	Home
Mar.	1	Wollaston	Away
"	15	Irthlingborough	Away
"	22	Finedon	Home
"	29	Irchester	Away

Above and opposite: In October 1889, the Kettering Observer *printed fixture lists for the club's senior and reserve sides – and for the first time there were no games of rugby included. (The fixtures appeared after the game with Notts County Reserves on the 5th.)*

FOOTBALL FIXTURES.

◆

KETTERING FOOTBALL CLUB.

SEASON 1889-90.

FIRST TEAM.

Date.		Club.	Where Played.
Oct.	12	Wolverton	Home
,,	19	Aston Villa (r)	Away
,,	26	English Cup, 2nd Round	
Nov.	2	Notts Forest	Home
,,	4	Kettering Hawks	Home
,,	9	Loughboro' Town	Away
,,	16	Wellingborough	Home
,,	23	Aston Villa (r)	Home
,,	30	Leicester Fosse	Home
Dec.	7	Newark	Away
,,	14	Mill Hill House	Home
,,	16	Mr. H. Roughton's XI	Home
,,	21	Sheepshed	Home
,,	26	Chatham (Box. Day)	Home
		Winners Kent County Badges,	
		1886-7-8. Kent County Cup, 1889.	
Dec.	28	Northampton	Home
Jan.	4	Wolverton	Away
,,	11	Notts Rangers	Home
,,	18	Sheepshed	Away
,,	25	Wellingborough	Home
Feb.	1	Leicester Schools	Home
,,	3	Kettering Hawks	Home
,,	8	Mill Hill House	Away
,,	15	Oakham Grammar School	Home
,,	22	Leicester Fosse	Away
Mar.	1	Loughboro' Town	Home
,,	8	Leicester Schools	Away
,,	15	Newark	Home
,,	22	Oakham Grammar School	Away
,,	29	Northampton	Away
Easter		Birmingham Victorias	Home
Monday		(Cup Holders.)	

After receiving a bye in the first qualifying round of the FA Cup, the club was drawn away to Gainsborough Trinity in the second. However, the tie was forfeited because of the difficulties associated with travelling at the time. (Leaving the town at around eight in the morning, the team would not have reached Trinity's ground before three o'clock at the earliest. This would have allowed just two hours for changing, playing the game and getting back to the station before the return train – scheduled to arrive in Kettering at midnight – departed Gainsborough at five.)

The Charity Cup had proved a big success and around 20 clubs entered this season, including Leicester Fosse and Luton Town. Kettering began well, beating Higham Ferrers 5-2 and then Bedford 8-1. In the third round, Leicester brought a strong team to Eldred's Field, only to be sent home with their tails between their legs, courtesy of a George Bates hat-trick:

KETTERING CHARITY CUP COMPETITION.
KETTERING *V.* LEICESTER FOSSE.

By defeating Leicester Fosse on Saturday [8 February 1890], the Kettering Town Association Club has added another to a long list of successes this season. The game had been anticipated with a considerable amount of interest, and the special trains from Kimbolton and Market Harborough brought a number of visitors, there being close upon a thousand spectators [other sources indicate 1,500] on the Town Ground to watch the match. Leicester, with the exception of Vickers, brought their full strength, and Kettering were also thoroughly represented. From start to finish, and particularly in the second half, the game was very fast, grand form being shown by both teams, notably by the home backs.

Kettering lost the toss and kicked off against a strong east wind, hostilities opening in the Fosse's right, who dribbled down to a dangerous point, when West grandly turned the ball in the opposite direction. Again it was brought down, a shot by Murdoch being well put out by Lilley, who was defending at the London-road end. Here Kettering were given hands, and later on obtained a corner, which was quickly followed by a second. An appeal for off-side was granted Kettering in the centre, and a minute or two afterwards Knight received from the right, but shot wide. Some determined and combined play by the Leicester forwards transferred the leather to the opposite end, and Webb made a dangerous shot, which passed over the bar. Kettering replied by a dribble down on the right, and being passed across there was a good opening for Knight, who failed to fully utilise it. Once more the ball was returned to the other end of the field, when Atter crossed to Johnson, who had what looked like a splendid chance, but again the Fosse were disappointed, the ball rising considerably above the bar. Kettering gave a corner, after which some capital play was witnessed in the centre, where the visitors were conceded hands. Subsequently Webb experienced hard lines, a beautiful angular shot, which quite beat Lilley, striking the upright and passing outwards. This seemed to rouse the home players, and Panter was loudly applauded for a grand kick which called out the Leicester goal-keeper. The visitors retaliated by a fine run on the right, which Bentley finished by an attempt, the ball touching the cross-bar [wooden crossbars were now in use] as it passed over. The leather was soon taken back, Panter exchanging to Bates, who tried to score but was frustrated by the goal-keeper. Before the latter, however, had time to recover, Dixon returned the ball and Bates put it through, the first point going to Kettering amidst great cheering. This was followed up by exciting play in the vicinity of the Fosse's head-quarters, until relief came from the right, and running down to the other end of the field Leicester claimed a corner, which was not improved upon. "Hands" were given against Kettering ten yards from their goal, and in the scrimmage a high shot by Atter dropped between Lilley's hands and the cross-bar, much to his astonishment, thus equalising matters just before half time. Play in the second half opened with a run up by the Fosse, and things looked serious for Kettering until Draper, by a clever kick over his head, relieved the position to the delight of the onlookers. Directly afterwards the home forwards swarmed round the Leicester goal, and although the visitors tried their best the town backs were always equal to any emergency. Kettering gained a corner, and "hands" were given off Dixon. Then followed a series of attempts on the part of Kettering to add another point, the visitors' goal-keeper being repeatedly called out. At length he was tempted too far, a low shot by Bates passing under his legs to the delight of the Kettering spectators. In the play that followed both goal-keepers' services were required, and corners were obtained by each team. Kettering were allowed an appeal for a foul. Another foul by the Leicester captain rather excited the indignation of those who witnessed the affair. This was near the Fosse posts, and in the scrimmage the ball struck the bar. Just on the moment of time Panter brought the leather down the ground and crossed to Bates, who, with a nicely-judged shot over the goal-keeper's head, registered the third goal to Kettering, the match ending amidst great enthusiasm in favour of the home team by three goals to one. Teams:–

Kettering Town.– W. Lilley, goal; H.D. Foster (capt.) and W. Draper, backs; J. Langford, G. West, and G. Wright, half backs; C. Dixon [who 'retired' the previous season!] and A.B. Panter, right wing; W. Knight, centre; G. Wilson and G. Bates, left wing.

Leicester Fosse.– W. Walker, goal; A. Knight and E. Davis, backs; J. Johnson, R. Perry, and S. Harris, half backs; E. Bentley and Murdoch, right wing; J. Atter and E. Johnson, left wing; Webb, centre.

Umpires, Messrs. G.T. Maycock and W. Cooper; referee, Mr. R. Marriott (Wellingborough). [*Kettering Observer*, 14 February 1890.]

Founded in 1884, Leicester Fosse were regular opponents for Kettering during the 1890s, even after their election to the Football League in 1894. Not long after the conclusion of the First World War, financial problems would result in the club going to the wall – only to be reincarnated shortly after as Leicester City.

The draw for the semi-finals of the Charity Cup paired Kettering with Luton Town at Eldred's Field (the venue for both semi-finals) on 8 March, but there was to be no cup final for the hosts as they bowed out of the competition with a 2-1 defeat. Even though the town's club was not involved, a crowd of over 4,000 turned up at Eldred's Field to watch Luton draw the final 1-1 with Grantham Rovers, resulting in gate receipts of £56-15s. Rovers won the replay at the same venue by three goals to nil, and the takings – up by a pound on the first game – established a record for the whole of Northamptonshire (ladies were admitted free).

In addition to their four cup ties, Kettering played 17 friendlies at home; winning 13, drawing two and losing two. Only five of the scheduled away games were completed; one won, two drawn and two lost.

At least 29 players wore the club's colours this season, with no fewer than six of them – A. Bellamy, Jack Hutchen, Fessor Lilley, Fred Palmer, J. Sumpter and C. Tebbutt – taking a turn between the posts, before Lilley (who continued to be involved with the rugby game at county-level) was given the job of goalkeeper.

William 'Ducky' Draper, 1889.

Part of a Kettering Revellers team group (many players turned out for two or more local sides), this photograph (possibly!) records Draper wearing Kettering FC's new chocolate and salmon jersey.

Seven

Professionalism

1890 - 1892

"The result of the match was made known in Kettering by various telegrams, and it is needless to say that there was considerable excitement in the town. The arrival of the last of the excursion trains was awaited by a numerous crowd, who filled the station yard, and who gave a hearty reception to the players when they emerged from the booking-hall. Pollard's pair-horse wagonette was in waiting to convey the team through the town, and a procession being formed with the drag in the centre, the whole concourse marched through the principal streets to the strains of the "Conquering Hero," played by the Rifle Band, while the Town Band, which had accompanied the players to Luton, brought up the rear."

Football had evolved as a sport played by amateurs purely for the love of the game. But the interest that the FA Cup and local knockout competitions generated changed all that. Results began to matter. Rumours of money left in players' boots after matches – 'shamateurism' – first emanated from Lancashire in the late 1870s, after an otherwise unexplained influx of good Scottish footballers. Before long, the rumours were substantiated and this inevitably led to protests by clubs who felt that their 'cheating' opponents held an unfair advantage.

At first the FA was divided. The old guard clung to the ideals of sportsmanship, whilst the more pragmatic saw professionalism as an inevitability and wanted to establish some degree of control over it. For a time the conservatives won the argument; in 1882 the governing body decreed that payments, other than expenses or compensation for lost wages, were prohibited and clubs found to have paid players were disqualified from the FA Cup. But the genie was out of the bottle and, on 20 July 1885, the Association bowed to the more powerful clubs and voted to legalise professionalism.

With professionalism came more competitive football. On 17 April 1888, at the Royal Hotel in Manchester, 12 clubs from the Midlands and the Northwest came together to form the Football League. The 'Invincibles' of Preston North End were its first champions, winning the League without losing a game (as well as carrying off the FA Cup without conceding a goal). The clubs that had embraced professionalism began to dominate the sport, and those from the south that remained staunchly amateur fell behind. For a while, at least.

Kettering's footballers played their second FA Cup tie on 4 October 1890, although there must have been those who wondered afterwards if it had been worth the trouble. Drawn away to Langley Green Victoria in the first qualifying round, the players gathered at the station on the Saturday morning, boarded the train at just gone half past ten and, after a short stop in Birmingham, reached the colliery village of Langley Green 15 minutes before the scheduled three o'clock start. Unfortunately, the whole team was suffering from a lack of practice, this being their first real test of the season, whilst their opponents had been very busy with matches and practice for some weeks prior to the fixture. On a lumpy pitch covered in rather long grass, Kettering were soundly beaten by five goals to nil. When it seemed that things could not get much worse, the travelling party failed to arrive home until late Sunday morning, having spent the night in a waiting room on Market Harborough station.

Whether or not the Langley Green debacle had any bearing on the deliberations is not recorded, but four months later the ground-breaking decision to pay the players had been taken. Kettering's last game as a truly amateur club was a 3-2 home defeat to Finedon Revellers in the second round of the Kettering Charity Cup, played on 2 February 1891. Just five days later, when the players took to the field for a friendly at home to Rushden (which resulted in a three-all draw), they were each being paid five shillings (25p) a week. The first football club in Northamptonshire to 'turn professional', Kettering was almost certainly the first club south of Birmingham to do so. Not that this impressed everyone – on 20 February the *Kettering Leader & Observer* commented: "It seems a pity that a club of the calibre of Kettering should have to resort to such means to keep their men up to mark. The love of the game must be at a very low ebb if the men won't put in an hour or two's practice once a week without wanting to be paid for it."

24 fixtures were completed during the season: resulting in seven wins, one draw and six defeats as amateurs (including a 16-1 loss to Aston Villa's reserve side on a snow-covered pitch) – and six wins, one draw and three defeats as professionals.

Two new cup competitions were entered: the Grantham Charity Cup and the Luton Charity Cup (both of which had been started with the help of the Kettering Charity Cup committee). In the former, Kettering knocked out Grantham Town but lost in the next round to Grantham Rovers, whilst in the latter, the highlight of the season was victory in the competition's first ever final, played at the Dellar Lane cricket ground in Luton before a crowd of about 3,500 – a record for that town. 38 years later, the *Football Telegraph* printed a grainy picture of the victorious Kettering team with the cup and told the tale of how it was won:

> A very interesting story is built round the winning of this trophy, and which no doubt will be read with much interest by present supporters of football locally. Kettering were drawn in the third round of the competition [having had a bye in the first round and dispatched Irthlingborough Revellers 10-0 in the second] to meet Rushden. The game was played at Kettering on the bitterly cold Monday afternoon of March 9th, before some 1,500 spectators. Kettering had a particularly strong team which included Benny Wood of Finedon, one of the most promising young full-backs in the county; Draper known as "Ducky," being included in the half-backs to enable Wood to play in his customary position... The Kettering team was W. ("Fessor") Lilley, Jack Langford, Benny Wood, W. ("Ducky") Draper, T. Newman, Geo. West, A.J. Bradley, C. ("Haporth") Dixon, A.B. ("Jummy") Panter, Harry Ball, and Harry Dixon.
>
> DISPUTED GOAL.
>
> Kettering won by 3 goals to nil. With regard to the first goal, Kettering claimed that the ball had been forced over the line. The Rushden players contended otherwise, but Referee F. Scott, of Luton, gave his verdict in favour of Kettering, whose other two goals were scored by Ball and Wood.

In the semi-final played at Luton on Saturday, March 28th, Kettering met Bedford and defeated that club by 6 goals to one, their goals being scored by "Jummy" Panter (4), "Harry" Dixon and "Nobby" Curtis. On that occasion about 1,000 supporters accompanied the Kettering team, a special excursion train being run. In that match "Nobby" Curtis appeared as centre-half for G. West.

THE FINAL.

The final was also played at Luton, the date being Saturday, April 18th, and Kettering's opponents were Windsor Phoenix, who had beaten Wolverton on the previous Saturday. Kettering won by 5-1, their goals being scored by "Haporth" Dixon (2), "Joe" Bradley (2), and Harry Dixon [contemporary sources credit Bradley with three goals and Charlie Dixon with two]. It was a great day for Kettering football "fans," 1,020 booked by the special train [actually, two trains were necessary due to the numbers travelling from the town; it was also said that the Windsor following amounted to just three – two pressmen and the baggage man, all of whom got in without paying – the rest of the crowd was made up of locals]. It was also a good day for Luton straw hat makers, for practically every Kettering person who made the journey donned a straw hat.

On that occasion "Jack" Langford was suffering from an injury, so "Ducky" Draper partnered Wood at back, C. ("Ching") Robinson came in as a half-back, but the forwards were the usual five. [Thus, the team for the final was Fessor Lilley, goal; William Draper and Benny Wood, backs; Harry Curtis, T. Newman and Charles Robinson, half-backs; Harry Dixon and Harry Ball, left wing; Jummy Panter (captain), centre; Charlie Dixon and Joe Bradley, right wing.]

FOOTBALL IN THE STREETS. – Owen Watson and George White, lads, pleaded guilty to playing football in the streets, on Nov. 28th, and were let off on paying 1s., and 5s. 9d. costs. The Chairman said future offenders would be more seriously dealt with. – Walter Loyd and John Starling, youths, of Kettering, pleaded guilty to a similar offence, and were dealt with in a like manner.

A small item that appeared in the Kettering Leader & Observer *some months after the Luton Charity Cup was won. With association football now firmly established in the town, were these boys emulating the players they had watched at Eldred's Field?*

Luton Football Charity Cup.

FINAL MATCH!

SATURDAY NEXT, APRIL 18.

KICK-OFF 4 P.M.

Admission 3d., Enclosure 6d., Pavilion 1s. *1891*

WINDSOR v. KETTERING.

POSITION:

Kettering 5

WINDSOR (Colour—White).

T Husted (goal)

H C Davenport, Capt. (left back)

A W Brown (right back)

C Thompson (left)

F Cashbourne (centre)

H Hill (right)

R Hyslop and H E Lewis (left)

F Nicol and J J Earle (right)

H B Phillips (centre)

A B Panter, Capt. (centre)

Windsor 1

KETTERING (Colours—Red and Blue).

Left

Whilley (goal)

W Draper (right)

A Wood (right back)

J Langford (left back)

Right

H Dixon and H Ball (right)

H Curtis (centre)

J Newman (left)

C Dixon and A Bradley (left)

Cups and Medals on view at Beecroft & Compy's, Bute Street.
Public Presentation at Town Hall, 6 o'clock.   Admission 3d.

BEECROFT COMPANY'S

SPECIAL VALUE.

TROUSERS TO ORDER, 13s.

TWO PAIRS, 25/6, Cash.

BUSINESS SUITS, 42s.

Made to Measure,

*Beecroft & Company's Lawn Tennis and
Athletic Rules ready shortly.*

DALTON, PRINTER, LUTON.

The 1891 Luton Charity Cup final programme. The oldest known programme for a match involving Kettering – and doubtless one of the very few that survive from any game of association football played anywhere in the world in the 1890s.

The man who led them, Avery 'Jummy' Panter, was quite a hero amongst Kettering folk. Before the semi-final against Bedford, an enterprising local photographer had mounted his picture on cards bearing the words: "Play up, Kettering". These, apparently, sold like wildfire and the majority of those who travelled down to Luton for the game wore one in their hat. Of course, the same happened again for the final, when two train loads of supporters left the town with the captain's image prominently displayed about their person.

At the conclusion of the game, the players and many of the spectators made their way to Luton Town Hall for the presentation of the cup. The *Kettering Guardian*'s correspondent takes up the story:

It is impossible to describe the feeling of intense delight that prevailed in Kettering on Saturday evening, when it became known that Kettering had succeeded in winning the Luton Cup, while at the straw-hat town the excitement amongst the Kettering noble 1,000 was a pleasure to see. "Three cheers for Kettering" was the incessant cry at night, and even many of the Lutonians entered into the excitement of the moment, and "all went merry as a marriage bell." No one could but admire the well-conducted hilarity of the Kettering contingent, who braved whatever the elements chose to dispense, in order to see their "pets" win the "mug." The Cup is truly a fine piece of work – a figure representing "Victory" surmounting the bowl, while on each side are figures of a lion and a greyhound, representing strength and fleetness, a representation that does adequate justice to Kettering's play on Saturday. A representation of a football field covers one side of the Cup, while on the other the name of the Competition appears. As the Cup stands, it is thought superior to that of the Kettering Committee, which is a matter of further congratulation to the winners. The medals bear the Luton borough coat of arms, and also the beehive and straw plait, representing the industry of the place. All the eloquence in the universe cannot describe the scene at the presentation – it was enthusiastic in the highest degree, and even the Chairman [Alderman P. Alexander, former Mayor of Luton] must have felt some of his Scotch blood rise at the thought of the sport which had awakened such keen interest amongst those assembled. Of course the speech of the evening, that was awaited for by the audience, was Captain A.B. Panter's maiden speech, and that worthy caused a deafening roar when he referred to the *article* they had won. Never mind "A.B.," it is a grand thing for you to have coached the team so successfully in the first year of your reign. May you long live to keep the team at such an excellent standpoint. All through the game on Saturday it was good to hear your voice steadily directing your team, not by yells and nigger dances, but by cool foresight and steadfast perseverance, which went a long way towards getting the five goals.

And the celebrations did not end in Luton:

WELCOME HOME OF THE VICTORS.

The result of the match was made known in Kettering by various telegrams, and it is needless to say that there was considerable excitement in the town. The arrival of the last of the excursion trains was awaited by a numerous crowd, who filled the station yard, and who gave a hearty reception to the players when they emerged from the booking-hall. Pollard's pair-horse wagonette was in waiting to convey the team through the town, and a procession being formed with the drag in the centre, the whole concourse marched through the principal streets to the strains of the "Conquering Hero," played by the Rifle Band, while the Town Band, which had accompanied the players to Luton, brought up the rear. The cup was displayed *en route* on the knee of the captain of the football team. On arrival at the Cross Keys Coffee Tavern cheers were given for the players and the committee, and the crowd gradually dispersed. The team afterwards adjourned to the house of Mr. N. Newman, where a social hour was spent. [*Kettering Leader & Observer*, 24 April 1891.]

Kettering FC, winners of the 1891 Luton Charity Cup.

Back row: George West, Jack Langford, Fessor Lilley, Benny Wood, Charles Robinson. Middle row: T. Newman, Harry Curtis, William Draper. Front row: Joe Bradley, Charlie Dixon, Jummy Panter (captain), Harry Ball, Harry Dixon.

Receipts:	£	s	d	Expenditure:	£	s	d
gate money.................	278	15	3½	half gate and guarantees	111	9	11½
174 members at 2s. 6d.........	21	15	0	travelling expenses and fares to			
37 hon. members.............	11	5	0	out matches..............	29	16	0
use of ground, staging, wire,				work on ground, staging, posts,			
compensation, &c..........	20	16	2	wire, tan, &c.............	33	0	11
refunded fares	10	8	10	payments to players..........	45	16	0
share on special to Luton.......	11	0	2	rent of ground	15	0	0
advertisements..............	1	17	6	shirts, &c., for team..........	6	1	3
sale of old goal posts..........	0	10	0	dressing and committee rooms,			
collected for Clarke's accident				&c...................	5	15	5½
fund....................	0	12	6	referees	2	15	6
insurance company	3	0	0	paid for accidents	6	10	0
	360	0	5½	footballs, bags, repairs, &c......	4	7	9
				printing	20	11	6
				insuring team...............	10	8	0
				subscription to English			
				Association and cup			
				competitions.............	2	0	6
				bill posting and distributing.....	9	6	9
				postage, telegrams, &c.........	6	7	6½
				gate keepers and ground man ...	10	14	6
				secretary's salary.............	5	0	0
				professional forms, &c.........	0	15	0
				crier......................	1	10	6
				miscellaneous items..........	4	3	3
				advertising.................	0	16	3
					332	6	7½
balance brought forward	22	5	0	balance in hand	49	18	10
	382	5	5½		382	5	5½

A representation of the club's 1890-91 balance sheet, gleaned from an article published in the Kettering Leader & Observer *on 29 May 1891, clearly showing, for the first time, 'payments to players'. Considering that payments were only introduced in February, £45 and 16 shillings represents the 'wage bill' clocked up in just under three months. Already a significant item of expenditure, and an indicator of things to come.*

This was to be Kettering's first full season as a professional club and subscriptions were raised to cover the cost of players' wages. The princely sum of 10s-6d entitled a member to a seat at every game at Eldred's Field, 7s-6d secured entry to the standing area on the reserved side, whilst for five shillings members could jostle for position amongst the Great Unwashed on the unreserved side. General admission prices varied according to the quality of the opposition, rising to as much as two shillings on occasion for the best seats in the new grandstand, which could accommodate 1,000 spectators. A packed Eldred's Field must have been quite a site.

For the first time, players from outside the locality were brought in. The honour of being the first professional footballer from another club to sign on went to Loughborough Town's Albert Peters. From Burnley came G. McBirnie – a prestigious signing and the first Scotsman to play for Kettering, he even had his photograph placed in Mr Harrison's shop window in Gold Street so that supporters would know what he looked like. Others to arrive were George Davies from Oswestry, W. Evans (Stockton-on-Tees), Levi Freeman and William Mablestone (both Grantham Rovers), Jackie Starr (Notts Jardines) and W.R. Cashmore of Wellingborough. It was agreed that the players' kit – boots, pants and jerseys – would be provided by the club and taken charge of by the groundsman after each match.

Not only would the Kettering faithful have to grow accustomed to strangers in the field, there was a radical new rule to take in as well, with the introduction of the penalty kick. This necessitated the marking of a line all the way across the pitch 12 yards from each goal-line. A penalty might be won for an infringement of the rules anywhere within this area, and the kick taken from anywhere along the 12-yard-line. (Not until early in the 20th century would the 'penalty area' be narrowed in width and the distance from the goal extended to 18 yards – and a penalty spot added.) The earliest known occasion of a penalty being awarded in a game involving the club (a reserve team friendly at Wellingborough, played on 26 September 1891) is recorded in the *Northampton Herald*: "Shortly after resuming, a foul close to the Kettering goal gave Wellingborough a clear free kick under the new rule, and all the players were set back with the exception of the goal-keeper. Mundin, however, failed to use this grand opportunity, shaving the outside of the upright."

As the club's standing in the footballing world rose, so did the quality of opposition that could be attracted to Eldred's Field and, on 24 October, Nottingham Forest arrived with a very strong side. Members of the Football Alliance, a league they had been instrumental in forming in 1889, Forest would go on this season to reach the semi-finals of the FA Cup as well as finishing top of the Alliance (which would then be disbanded and all but one of its 12 clubs voted into the Football

Kettering's First Professional Team.

SEASON 1891-2

A montage of players celebrating Kettering's professional team at the beginning of the 1891-92 season. The images are laid down in a classical 2-3-5 formation: Fessor Lilley, goalkeeper; George Davies and William Draper, backs; George West, Albert Peters and William Mablestone, half-backs; W. Evans, Jackie Starr, Jummy Panter, Harry Ball and Harry Dixon, forwards.

League). The *Kettering Leader & Observer*'s account of the match astutely picks up on the Nottingham team's 'scientific play', recognising that the age of running with the ball at feet until tackled, or simply kicking it long for everyone to chase, was coming to an end – the most accomplished footballers were now comfortable with controlling the 'leather' and distributing it accurately to team-mates:

NOTTS. FOREST v. KETTERING.

Lovers of the dribbling game in Kettering and district, experienced a fine treat last Saturday, from the visit of the renowned Notts Forest. The committee of the Kettering Club guaranteed that the Forest should bring their *bonâ fide* first eleven, and the many spectators who assembled in Eldred's field on Saturday, were able to certify that the promise had been faithfully kept, and the team from the lace town included no less than three "internationals." The most violent partisans of the Kettering club never expected that the home team would have a "look-in," and the only subjects for speculation before the match, were the amount of goals that Notts. would pile up against them, and the chances there were of Kettering being able to register a point at all against such a champion goal-keeper as Brown. As results turned out, Kettering were able to get off with a defeat of five goals to one, although there would not have been such a margin if Lilley had played in anything like his old form. However, a little must be granted the home team, who, from the outset, showed signs of nervousness at meeting such a formidable team. As luck would have it, Kettering was unable on this occasion to put its best team on the field. Davies was not sufficiently recovered from the kick he sustained the previous Saturday to play, and to make up for his absence, Peters played at full back. This let in Curtis amongst the halves, but it was generally admitted that "Nobby" was a poor substitute, and did not do half as well as he did at the latter end of the last season. Then a change had been made on the left wing, little Brigstock taking Ball's place, and this could not be regarded as any change for the better. Of the exhibition of the game by Notts. Forest, it is deserving of the highest praise. Their combination seemed almost perfect, their passing being a treat to watch, and the results attained was sufficient proof that the scientific play is the best in the long run.

The weather during the match was all that could be desired, but the ground was greasy from the effect of the recent heavy rainfalls, and from the cutting up it had received in an amateur match played upon it on the previous Thursday [there is a report of sawdust having to be scattered in the vicinity of the goals to negate the effects of the mud]; the air, however, was almost perfectly still, and the conditions were fairly even, though Notts had the sun in their eyes in the first half.

Higgins set the "leather" in motion a few minutes after three o'clock, and Notts. immediately began to invade, and Kettering halves and backs were soon given plenty to do, Draper saving remarkably well. The visitors early began to press, and three times in succession were shots tried at the goal, but Lilley managed on each occasion to keep them out. Kettering soon afterwards got near the Notts. goal line, but "Tich" Smith soon transferred the play into the Kettering territory by a good run on the wing, which was spoiled by Peters, who, throughout, played a sterling game amongst the backs. Following this, Kettering gave Brown a little work to do, and Dixon put the "leather" in Curtis's possession, but he finished up by shooting over the bar. Twice in succession did Dixon get the ball well in front of the goal, but the Notts defence proved too strong. The visitors followed this up by pressing the home team, and a quarter of an hour after the commencement of the game, "Tich" Smith, to whom the ball was passed out of a scrimmage close up to the home goal, sent it through, "Fessor" going so far as to touch it, and then allowing it to roll between the posts. Lindley then got very dangerously near, but Lilley was able to save well on this occasion. Five minutes later, Notts. were able, from a somewhat easy shot from Higgins, to register their second point, Lilley tantalising the spectators by letting the ball go through after he had touched it. Kettering then rallied a little, the forwards breaking away with the ball, the right wing especially, but Notts managed to foil their efforts. Eventually, however, from a pass from Evans to Dixon, the home captain was able to send in a shot which Brown could not stop, giving Kettering their one and only goal. The score did not remain at this for very long, and just before the interval, Higgins was able to elude Lilley, and give Notts their third goal. With the change of ends, the combinations of the visitors showed to even greater advantage than in the first half, and they were able not only to keep the Kettering backs busily engaged, but to pay such particular attention to the more prominent of the home forwards as to prevent them from making any effective break-away, and Brown's position during this half was almost a sinecure. Two additional goals were added to the visitors' score before the finish, and a lively struggle was progressing close up to the Kettering goal, when the signal was given for the cessation of hostilities, a thoroughly interesting game ending in favour of the Forest by five goals to one. Teams:–

Notts. Forest.– Brown, goal; Scott and Russell, backs; Thompson, M'Pherson, and A. Smith, half-backs; Pike and Shaw, left wing; Higgins, centre; Lindley and T.M. Smith, right wing.

Kettering.– Lilley, goal; Draper and Peters, backs; Mablestone, Curtis, and West, half-backs; Dixon and Brigstock, left wing; Panter, centre; Evans and Starr, right wing.

Referee, Mr. T.S. Ashmole, Leicester. Linesmen, Messrs. H.J. Williamson (Nottingham) and T. Maycock. [The 1891-92 season saw the introduction of a referee controlling the game *on* the pitch, assisted by linesmen on the touchlines; and the term 'umpire' was dropped from association football.]

Professionalism and the influx of players from outside the district naturally raised expectations of what the club might achieve, and there was no lack of criticism in the local press when victory upon victory did not materialise. On 6 November, writing under the pseudonym of 'Spectator', the *Kettering Leader & Observer*'s 'Sports and Pastimes' columnist made his feelings very clear:

After Kettering's miserable performance against Leicester [a 2-0 home defeat a week after the Forest game], I would suggest to all concerned, that they put up the shutters and chuck up the job. If this is a sample of our highly paid proficient professionals, then pray let us have a team of amateurs in the field again. Now Kettering have been searching the country through for men, and lavishing money on the acquisition of a team which was to take the world by surprise, we are treated to an exhibition about on par with the "fixture" which was played down our back street the other evening when a salmon tin, denude of its contents, did duty as the ball.

It is true to say that Kettering's well paid footballers did not 'take the world by surprise', but they did reach two cup finals and one semi-final, and of 36 friendly and knockout matches played, just over half were won. (One game was scratched: after being drawn away to Hereford in the first preliminary round of the FA Cup, it was decided there was little point in the team spending a day travelling there and a day travelling back when a poor gate was anticipated anyway.)

On Saturday, 12 March 1892, the club travelled to Luton to play Millwall Athletic in the semi-final of the Luton Charity Cup. A 1-0 defeat sent Kettering – the cup-holders – out of the competition, and to make matters worse the game was marred by an incident involving the referee, Mr R.E.A. Maynard, and William 'Smiler' Mablestone, leading to some unsavoury scenes at the end of the match. The following Friday, the *Northampton Herald* printed Mr Maynard's version of events:

Sir, with reference to the unseemly attack which was made on me by several hundred of the riff-raff of Kettering at the conclusion of the game. Briefly, the wrath of these people was aroused by the fact of my acting in accordance with the rules of the game, i.e.; after having twice cautioned one of the Kettering players [Mablestone] for foul language and foul play, he committed a like offence a third time, whereupon I asked him to leave the field. This he refused to do. I then appealed to his captain to ask him to leave, but this he would not do till I threatened to report his conduct to the F.A., and to suspend play. This action of mine so incensed the several hundred roughs of Kettering that it was with the greatest difficulty they were prevented from taking to the field there and then. The Luton Charity Cup Committee at once whipped up a strong body-guard, at whose head was the superintendent of the local police. He was supported by several constables, the Committee of the Luton F.C.; a number of independent gentlemen, and the members of the Millwall Athletic Club; but even then I was rather severely handled at the finish of the game, as a number of bruises on my body go to testify. Once in the pavilion, there I had to remain for a considerable time till the Kettering roughs thought fit to leave the ground. As I am fully reporting the circumstances to the F.A., I will forbear making any further comment.

Dear Spectator, – I venture to think it would have delighted your sporting mind to have been at Leicester Station last Saturday midnight, to have seen the "splendid combination" of the Town Football Club and the Town Band when they met and mutually congratulated each other upon their successes at Grantham and Derby respectively. Such cheering, and such a display, I venture to think, is seldom seen at Leicester. After the united cheers had somewhat subsided, out came the bandsmen with their instruments. Off goes the word of command, "Single file," and then, to the strains of "Palmer House" – or, as a certain bandsman will have it, "Huntly and Palmer House" – they marched up and down the platform, in and out of the arches, delighting a group of passengers and officials, the latter pausing to admire regardless of duty. The "Little Welshman and Scotchman" joined in the parade with a jolly polka, whilst Evans, putting on his best style, paid special attention to the goalkeeper – one of the feminine persuasion. Then the enthusiastic spectators who had accompanied the team to Grantham could not resist, and so joined in the procession, feeling no little pride they were indeed "natives of Kettering." Just fancy this sort of thing going on, full swing, for nearly half an hour, and in the meantime the "red scarf" was espied doing duty. Then up came some straggling footballers, who turned out to be members of poor Wellingborough F.C., when they were sympathetically (?) asked how they had got on, "Just managed to lose again," said Joe Hacksley, "and I am nearly killed." Just as the Kettering linesman, from behind a big cigar, was having a farewell shake of hands with a very particular friend, a bandsman was heard to exclaim, with pride, "Well, if we can't beat Derby at football we can at band-playing." During the homeward journey, the time was pleasantly enlivened with strains from "Edwinstone," and songs and Irish melodies from the company. Then two were enquiring where a certain member of the F.C. had been to, as he was not seen at Grantham, and certainly not at the contest at Derby, so they concluded he had been somewhere else, but echo answers where? All those who knew anything of the experience at Harborough "all night" thought it almost equal to it, but a 2s. breakfast. At least, Jummy thought so.   ONE WHO WAS THERE.

A letter that appeared in the Kettering Leader & Observer *on 27 November 1891. It relates to the journey home after the club's 0-0 draw with Grantham Rovers the previous Saturday, and the meeting on Leicester Railway Station with the Kettering Town Band and Wellingborough Town FC, both of whom had been involved in contests in Derby that day.*

The Millwall incident was not the first episode of trouble involving Kettering's followers this season. The previous December, en route to the final of the Grantham Charity Cup (which Kettering lost 1-0 to Derby County Wanderers), the visit of Grantham Rovers to Eldred's Field ended in a chase through the streets of the town. There was already some ill-feeling between the two clubs after Freeman and Mablestone ('poached' from Rovers during the summer) had been given a hard time by the locals during Kettering's game at Grantham's Harlaxton Road ground a few weeks earlier, so when the Grantham secretary Mr A. Martin – better known to most as 'Tatler', editor of the *Football Chronicle* and regular critic of all things Kettering – appeared in the field to act as a linesman, it seems almost inevitable that things would get out of hand at some point...

> As soon as the game was over there was a general rush into the middle of the field, where the Grantham linesman was. From his first appearance in the field it was evident that he was by no means popular with the spectators, as many were of the opinion that this was the writer of some caustic remarks anent the Kettering club in a certain football paper. Throughout the match he had to undergo pretty strong verbal castigation from both sides of the field, but when the game was over the crowd surrounded him so that the secretary and the vice-captain of the Kettering club thought it advisable to escort him to the dressing-tent. After some difficulty, the crowd were induced to leave the ground, but they did not go farther than the bottom of Green-lane, where they hoped to see the offending journalist. The omnibus coming up for the Grantham team caused many to think that he would ride down with them, and whilst the crowd were surging round the vehicle the person whom they were in quest slipped out of the entrance on the London-road, and, taking advantage of the narrow lane which runs parallel with the church, he was able to give his pursuers the slip for a time. However, they soon got on his scent, and both pursuers and pursued went at the double towards the Midland Station. Arriving near to the entrance, a few of the crowd picked up some handfuls of gravel and threw it at the fleeting scribe. Eventually, by the aid of Mr. Favell, he got safely on the platform, and was able to return in safety with the Grantham team. [*Kettering Leader & Observer*, 11 December 1891.]

Northamptonshire-Lincolnshire rivalries would be renewed a few months later when, for the first time, Kettering reached the final of their own charity cup competition, and once again found themselves face-to-face with Rovers – but not before there was yet more off-the-pitch drama. Having dispatched Leicester Fosse 5-0 and Kettering Anchor 12-0, the club should have faced Finedon Revellers in the semi-finals, a game that would have been keenly anticipated. But it was a game that was never played.

On Friday, 19 February 1892, the day before the semi-final was scheduled to take place, Finedon's half-back Tom Rowe (aged 25) died in Northampton Infirmary from the effects of an accident sustained at work the previous Wednesday. Revellers refused to play any football until after Rowe's funeral and asked for the tie to be postponed. However, under the rules of the competition, a club was required to give 14 days' notice to alter the date of a fixture, so the match was awarded to Kettering. A bitter row ensued – resulting in the two clubs refusing to play one another for a year – when it was alleged that it had actually been a ploy by Finedon to have the game postponed because A.G. Henfrey, their famous England international, could not turn out on the 20th. And, in Kettering's defence, it should be noted that five weeks later, Finedon were content to beat Wellingborough 3-1 in the final of the Senior Cup, only hours after their full-back Benny Wood (formerly of Kettering) had passed away.

On the same day that Finedon and Wellingborough were battling it out for county honours – 26 March – the Kettering Charity Cup final was played before a record crowd at Eldred's Field. It was the third year on the trot that Grantham Rovers had reached the final and the fourth successive season that a club from the 'gingerbread town' would contest it. Fortunately, on this occasion the linesmen were neutral and the *Kettering Leader & Observer* had only a game of football to report on:

THE FINAL.

GRANTHAM ROVERS v. KETTERING.

One of the largest crowds that have ever been drawn together to see a football match in Northamptonshire was that of Saturday last, when between five and six thousand lined the ropes of the Town Ground to see what was expected to be the final encounter; but strange to say, and luckily for the charity funds, at the call of time scores were equal, so that the teams have yet to meet again. In passing, it is worthy of note that the gate realised

£124.

The day was beautifully fine, and it is doubtful whether a better day could have been chosen, there being no wind or sun to contend against. Each team, as it emerged from the dressing-tent, was warmly welcomed by their respective admirers, the Rovers having brought a fair contingent with them by a cheap trip from Grantham. Peters, having named the coin, decided to kick down towards the London-road. Within a minute or so of the advertised time Flinders moved the ball off the centre, but he had hardly got over the line when the Kettering right wing got possession, and, amidst cheers, invaded, but Tucker came to the rescue and relieved. Southwell, in a dexterous manner, then carried the leather well into the Kettering quarters, and Lilley had to thump out twice in succession, which he did in his old style. Gradually, the scene of action was shifted, and the home team had just got over the line of demarcation when Hollingsworth "fouled." Following up the free kick awarded, Dixon and Freemen very gamely brought the leather along the outside, and then crossed over very nicely in front of the Grantham goal, but

MABBOTT MISSED THE OPENING.

Panter shortly afterwards tried the Grantham defence with a good shot, but it was well sent back. Peters returned it, but his shooting was wide of the mark. Continuing to press, Kettering still kept well in the Rovers' quarters, and safety was only found in putting by. Dixon took the corner, but nothing came of it, as Peters shot by. From a free kick against Kettering the Rovers were able to get away, and some vigorous play followed, in which

PETERS WAS STUNNED

after heading back a hot shot. After a short interval play was again resumed, and from some good passing on the part of the Rovers' right wing Kettering had to concede a corner, but it proved of no value, as it went behind. Pulling themselves together better, the Rovers still continued to act on the aggressive, but Panter relieved in splendid style. A few minutes later the Kettering forwards were able to break away, and gave Hollingsworth an opportunity of relieving very gamely. Whilst near the Grantham citadel hands were given against the visitors. Peters was entrusted with the kick, and dropped the ball well in front to Mabbott, who helped it on, but Brittain headed it back very cleverly. Shortly after this Draper was "winded," but a few seconds' rest put him right, and, getting scent of the leather again, made an incursion into the "Gingerbread" quarters, and Tucker was forced to yield a corner. Panter dropped the leather nicely in front of the sticks, but it was well headed away. The Rovers then renewed the attack, and after the match had been in progress twenty-five minutes, Southwell followed up a splendid run on the right wing by planting the leather well near the mouth of the goal, where Mulvey was in waiting, and, taking his aim, sent the ball through just out of Lilley's reach, thus giving

GRANTHAM THE LEAD.

It is needless to say that the result was hailed with tremendous cheering from the Rovers' supporters. This had the effect of putting increased vigour into the match, the Rovers for a time having the best of it, Mulvey shooting over the bar twice, and Pulling once. At this point Draper and Mabbott changed places, and then Kettering showed up better, and were able to renew the attack. A good opening presented itself, but Starr relied on a kick over his head with non-effect. This was followed by a splendid effort by the Kettering left wing, but Starr again spoilt it by shooting too high. The interval then arrived, the position of affairs being–

Grantham 1

Kettering 0

FOOTBALL.

KETTERING CHARITY CUP FINAL,
GRANTHAM ROVERS
(CUP HOLDERS) *V.*
KETTERING F. C.,
Will be Played
ON THE TOWN GROUND, KETTERING,
ON SATURDAY, MARCH 26TH, 1892.
KICK-OFF 3.15 P.M.

THE Splendid BAND OF THE KETTERING RIFLES will Parade the Town before, and play selections during the game.

Weather permitting, the Cup and Medals will be presented to the players from the stand in the field, immediately after the match.

Admission—1s., and 6d.; stand, 3d. extra.
For Special Trains see bills.

FOOTBALL.

GRAND MATCH AT KETTERING.
WEDNESDAY MARCH 30TH.

EVERTON
(BONA-FIDE LEAGUE TEAM) *V.*

KETTERING.
KICK-OFF, FOUR O'CLOCK.   Admission, 1s, and 6d.

Everton Team :—Jardine, goal ; McLean and Howarth, backs ; Kelso, Holt, and Robertson, half-backs ; Latta, Geary, Maxwell, Chadwick, and Milward, forwards.

The Midland Railway Company will issue cheap return tickets from Irchester, Wellingborough, and Desborough.

NORTHANTS FOOTBALL ASSOCIATION
CHALLENGE CUP COMPETITION.

THE FINAL WILL BE PLAYED BETWEEN

FINEDON AND

WELLINGBOROUGH TOWN,
ON SATURDAY, MARCH 26TH 1892.
KICK-OFF AT THREE O'CLOCK PROMPT.

Admission :—
Pavilion, 1s; reserved, 6d; unreserved, 3d.

The Kettering Rifle Band than gave us a little inspiriting music whilst the players refreshed. The second half, perhaps, was the most exciting. Grantham commenced with an incursion towards the Kettering citadel, where Pulling tried a shot which went over the cross-bar. Closely following this, Archer shot wide, and a minute or two later Davies had to concede a corner, but this was shot behind. After this pressure

KETTERING RALLIED

beautifully, and during the rest of the match showed up in much better form than the Lincolnshire eleven, Broadbent and his two backs having a lot to do. Archer's hands having come in contact with the ball, Peters was able to drop the leather in quarters rather dangerous for Grantham, and Freeman tried to head through, but Broadbent was well at home. At last, fifteen minutes from the interval, Kettering were rewarded. From a throw-in Peters obtained possession, and, with a well-judged shot, landed the leather between the posts, well out of the reach of the Rovers' custodian. This made the

SCORE EQUAL,

a result which was hailed with unbounded enthusiasm, hats being waved, and a few excited ones even turning somersaults. The excitement amongst the spectators was intense, and the cheering and chevying, as one team after the other temporarily gained the upper hand during the next ten minutes, were tremendous. For a time the struggle was maintained in the centre of the ground, and then the Rovers, having forced their way into the Kettering quarters, obtained hands just beyond the 18yds line, but the shot from this point was sent back by McBirnie, and carried right into the Rovers' territory, where another exciting scrimmage occurred. Following on hands on the left front of the Grantham goal, a close shot was sent in by Draper, and then again the leather was transferred to the Kettering end, where it was met by Lilley, about twenty yards in front of his post, and sent back to the other side of the centre line; but it was almost immediately brought back by Pulling, who was about to shoot for goal when Davies fairly leaped on to the ball, which collapsed

LIKE AN OLD SILK HAT.

A new ball was instantly thrown in, and, on re-starting, Dixon centred to Draper, who shot obliquely across close to the ground, from left to right of the Grantham goal, and Broadbent only saved by throwing himself on the turf, and, touching the ball with his

Opposite: Advertisments in the Kettering Guardian, *Friday, 25 March 1892. A number of big-name clubs visited Eldred's Field during Kettering's first full season as professionals, including Nottingham Forest, West Bromwich Albion (FA Cup winners this season) and 1891 Football League Champions Everton. Interestingly, the Kettering Charity Cup final was played on the same day as that of the Northants FA's Challenge Cup (Senior Cup) – an organisation and competition that Kettering continued to have nothing to do with. In the event, the Association's competition realised a paltry £15-18s in gate receipts compared with Kettering's £124.*

extended fingers, giving it just enough spin to send over the line on the outer side of the goal-post. The Kettering men were just now doing all the pressing, and the ball was once more sent through by Dixon from the left, but on appeal was adjudged off-side, the home team, who thought the trick was done, was brought to an end. Up to within five minutes of the end the

HOME TEAM HAD THE BEST OF THE GAME,

and several very close shots were sent in by Panter, Mablestone, and Peters, but nothing could be scored, and a grand game, therefore, ended in a draw. Teams:–

Kettering.– Lilley, goal; Davies and McBirnie, backs; Peters, Panter, and Mablestone, half-backs; Dixon and Freeman, left wing; Mabbott, centre; Draper and Starr, right wing.

Grantham Rovers.– Broadbent, goal; Tucker and Brittain, backs; Hollingsworth, Archer, and Fisher, half-backs; Cockman and Mulvey, left wing; Flinders, centre; Southwell and Pulling, right wing.

Linesmen, Mr. M.A. Barber (Bedford) and Mr. Marshall (Leicester); referee, Mr. T. Ashmole (Leicestershire Association).

The replay was set for 23 April when, in front of another large crowd (receipts of £120-10s were recorded), Rovers won by a goal to nil – and Kettering's bitter rivals were allowed to keep the trophy they had now secured on three successive occasions. This time, it seems, it was Tatler who had the last laugh.

The club's first full professional season had ended without silverware, and the *Kettering Guardian*'s 'Don' had his own theory as to why: "What has been the cause of the falling off in form? Not over-training, I am sure. Perhaps a little more outdoor exercise during the evenings that precede the matches on Saturdays would be more beneficial than the heated smoking-rooms of the places a good many of the team at present frequent."

A cartoon of William Mablestone that appeared in a Football Telegraph *article in 1925. The reference to throwing the ball 'further than some people could kick it' alludes to a time when the rules were less strict about run-ups and jumps before delivering a two-handed throw-in. (Throw-ins had been one-handed prior to 1882.)*

Kettering FC, 1891-92.

Back row: Charlie Dixon (trainer), Jummy Panter, Fessor Lilley, A. Dixon (assistant trainer), G. McBirnie, William Hart (linesman). Middle row: Jackie Starr, Albert Peters (captain), William Mablestone, William Draper. Front Row: George Davies, W. Evans, Levi Freeman, Harry Dixon.

After defeating Lincoln City Swifts 3-1 in the semi-final of the Grantham Charity Cup, and prior to the final, which Kettering would lose 1-0 to Derby County's reserve side, a short verse was written (author unknown) that incorporated the names of the 11 players in the photograph above:

> *"McBirnie" saw a "Starr" in the "h-Evans,"*
> *Standing by the side of good old "Jum,"*
> *There stood "Mabe" sweetly smiling in the sun,*
> *"Dixie" flapped his wings with joy,*
> *"Davies" thought the picture fair,*
> *"Levi" smiled when "Peters" told him*
> *That old "Fess" would not get there,*
> *"Ducky" saw with extreme pleasure*
> *Lincoln City bottled up,*
> *Kettering people begin to wonder*
> *If they will win the Grantham Cup.*

KETTERING v. EVERTON.

By the enterprise of the committee of the Kettering Football Club, lovers of the dribbling game had an opportunity last Wednesday of seeing one of the crack League teams, viz., Everton. Owing to North-ampton Races, and one or two other causes, the "gate" was not quite so large as might have been expected, but nevertheless, there was a good company present, including football enthusiasts from all parts of the county. The day was a glorious one, the only drawback, if it could be so termed, being that the sun was a trifle too warm for the players. Everton won the toss, and wisely chose to play against the wind, with the sun at their backs, whilst Kettering had to face a dazzling light. The visitors were the first to invade, being favoured with a free kick in the home territory. Davies headed away, and the ball afterwards went by. The Kettering forwards then travelled into the Everton ground, and Dixon placed the leather well in the centre, but McLean relieved. The visitors again obtained a free kick in the home quarters, but Waley shot too high, and Maxwell, who had a fair opening, put too much screw on, and the leather just passed outside the uprights. The League men continued the attack, but could not get through, and from a long kick by Panter, Dixon made another run on the left, but his centre was not followed up quickly enough. The game returned to the Kettering end, but Waley again kicked by, followed by Panter doing a similar action at the opposite citadel. Peters put in a shot, but the sphere rolled by off Freeman, who tried hard to head through. After a fruitless attempt on the home fortress by Maxwell, Draper and Starr brought the game into the enemy's land. The first-named kicked over the bar, but when Freeman tried his foot Jardine was compelled to handle. He dropped the ball, however, and only saved by kicking away, the home forwards again being late in coming up. A free kick was allowed in the left corner, but the custodian again fisted out a good shot. The first corner fell to the homesters, but McLean headed away, and directly afterwards Dixon shot just by the uprights. The ball was quickly transferred, and a struggle took place in the Kettering goal. Latta struck the uprights, and Geary kicked by, the attack ending by Milward kicking over. Dixon next travelled into the visitors' quarters, but before getting dangerous he was stopped by Collins. Draper put in a good bit of play, and Freeman compelled the custodian to use his hands. Kettering now had hard luck in not scoring. Panter sent in a long shot, which Jardine nearly missed, being only able to touch it over the bar. The corner was of no avail, and the Everton players rushed the leather into the Kettering ground, but Geary shot over. The visitors kept up the attack, but were unable to obtain a point, Davies showing good defensive work, and the interval came with the score unopened.

After the interval the visitors were the first to become dangerous, but Geary again kicked too high. Kettering had an opportunity by a free kick near the Everton goal, but nothing came of it. Some good passing on the part of Dixon and Freeman enabled the home forwards to make a rush. Starr and Draper slipped by the visitors' backs and passed across, but Starr headed by. Dixon also centred beautifully, but McLean used his head, and, Panter returning quickly, Dixon headed over the cross-bar. The home men led the attack for a time, some plucky play being put in by Starr, who made frequent en-deavours to evade the visitors' backs. About half-an-hour from the re-commencement the Everton right wing brought the leather into the home ground, and Latta having passed straight across the goal, Maxwell put through, being close in, thus scoring the only point during the encounter. The visitors continued the attack, but Peters relieved; and excellent defensive tactics were shown by Panter. Starr was the means of bringing the leather into the visitors' quarters, and a scrimmage occurred in the mouth of the Everton goal, and Kettering appeared likely to score. Dixon headed just by, and Draper compelled the custodian to handle. Soon afterwards the whistle was blown for time, the visitors winning by one goal to *nil*. Teams:–

Kettering.– Lilley, goal; Davies and McBirnie, backs; Panter, Peters, and Mablestone, half-backs; Freeman and Dixon, left wing; Evans, centre; Draper and Starr, right wing.

Everton.– Jardine, goal; McLean and Collins, backs; Kelso, Jones, and Robertson, half-backs; Milward and Waley, left wing; Maxwell, centre; Latta and Geary, right wing.

Linesmen, Mr. J. Hutchen and Mr. A. Chadwick; referee, Mr. T. Ashmole, Leicester.

The Kettering Leader & Observer*'s match report of Kettering's 1-0 defeat at the hands of Everton, one of the top clubs in the country and reigning champions of the Football League. The game was a friendly fixture, played at Eldred's Field on 30 March 1892.*

Eight

Debt, the Midland League and North Park

1892 - 1895

"Sir, – Through the medium of your columns, the committee of the Kettering Football Club wish to place before the public the present position of the affairs of the club, what has been, and what is being done for the improvement both of the team and of the financial position of the club. When the present committee – which is composed solely of working men – assumed the management, they were confronted with an empty exchequer, a heavy debt, and a team weakened by the loss of some of the best men of last season. The tide of affairs seemed to be at the very lowest ebb – without money, or players, or available funds – and it was only their confidence in the football-loving public that decided them to do their best to keep the old club going."

On 14 May 1892, at the Annual Meeting of the Midland League held at the home of the reigning champions, Rotherham Town, Kettering's application to become a member was accepted. Formed in 1889, an indication of the league's standing in those days was that its champions were usually elected into the Football League.

For the first time in the club's history there would be more competitive matches than friendlies. Supporters could look forward to league fixtures against Burton Wanderers, Derby Junction, Doncaster Rovers, Gainsborough Trinity, Grantham Rovers, Leicester Fosse, Long Eaton Rangers, Loughborough Town, Mansfield Town, Newark, Rotherham Town and Wednesbury Old Athletic. But joining this select group came at a price: being the most southerly town, Kettering's membership carried the condition that the club would pay one third of every visiting team's railway expenses – and costs were already starting to spiral out of control.

The 1891-92 balance sheet had revealed a huge deficiency of just over £245. Professional football was proving difficult to administer. Members were told that the secretary had been obliged to let the players have money whenever they came for it – because if it was not granted them they might refuse to play! Funds were in such an unsatisfactory state that it was evident things would come to a crisis one way or another. As a result, it was decided that the best solution was to form a limited liability company and, on 26 August 1892, the Kettering Football Club Company Limited was registered by Messrs Iliffe, Henly & Sweet of 2 Bedford Row, London:

Memorandum of Association

OF

THE KETTERING FOOTBALL CLUB COMPANY, LIMITED.

1. The name for the Company is "THE KETTERING FOOTBALL CLUB COMPANY, LIMITED."

2. The registered office of the Company is situate in England [the address given is 11 Gold Street, Kettering].

3. The objects for which the Company is established are:–

(*a.*) To acquire and hold the Furniture, Fixtures, Football and other implements and effects of an unregistered Association or Club, now known as the "Kettering Football Club," subject to all the existing engagements, debts and liabilities of the said Club, and to take over such engagements, debts and liabilities, or any of them, upon such terms and conditions as may be determined.

(*b*.) To promote the game of Football in the Town of Kettering and the County of Northampton, by the holding of Matches there or elsewhere, in Great Britain, and for that purpose to engage, establish, and maintain teams of Football players whether composed of amateur or professional players or partly of amateurs and partly of professionals.

(*c*.) To hold and promote Athletic or other Sports in or near to the said Town of Kettering and for that purpose to give at such Sports prizes in kind or in money.

(*d*.) Subject to the provisions of the 21st section of the Companies' Act of 1862 to purchase, take on Lease, or in exchange, or to hire, or otherwise acquire, a ground or grounds, or any other real or personal estate necessary or convenient for the objects of the Company.

(*e*.) To construct, fit up and maintain any Buildings, Pavilions or Stands upon such Ground or Grounds: To fix and enforce a scale of charges for admission to the ground, or any buildings Pavilions or Stands thereon, and generally to set out and manage the same as may be required for the objects of the Company.

(*f*.) To acquire money by gift or subscription and to distribute the same in or about the furtherance of all or any of the objects of the Company. And to raise or grant sums of money to be awarded in prizes or otherwise in connection with any such matters as aforesaid on such terms as may be prescribed.

(*g*.) To join in and promote the competition for Challenge Cups or other similar Competitions for the purposes of the Company or for the benefit of Charities or other like objects.

(*h*.) To become a Member of, and subscribe to the Football Association, the Football Alliance, or any other Alliance League or Association having objects altogether or in part similar to those of this Company.

(*i*.) To permit and allow any person or persons, Club, or Society, to use and enjoy any Ground or Lands of the Company for such purposes and upon such terms and conditions as shall be fixed and determined.
[There was no *j*.]
(*k*.) To insure the players of the Company against accident for their own benefit.

(*l*.) To invest the monies of the Company not immediately required upon such securities as may from time to time be determined.

(*m.*) To borrow monies required for the objects of the Company upon such securities as may be determined.

(*n.*) To sell, improve, manage, develop, lease, mortgage, dispose of, or otherwise deal with, all or any part of the property of the Company.

(*o.*) To do all such other lawful things as are incidental or conducive to the attainment of the above objects or any of them.

4. The liability of the Members is Limited.

5. The Capital of the Company is £1,500 divided into 1,500 Shares of £1 each.

Directors were required to hold five shares, and seven gentlemen signed to state they were willing to do this: John Winter Dryland, Charles William Lane, William Thurnall, George Cleaver, Nathaniel Newman, Frank Mobbs and W.H. Wall. (National Archives document.) Three days after the company was registered, a meeting was held at the Dalkieth Coffee Tavern to explain to one and all what had been done and to promote shares in the new company. J.W. Dryland took the chair and solemnly told those present that the days of the 'old' club were no more.

Irrespective of the financial situation, preparations for the new season continued apace and players were brought in to replace those who had left: Bob Hopewell, C. McUrich, Evan Roberts and Jimmy Stott all travelled some distance to sign. But it was a lad from closer to home that would one day outshine them all – Benjamin Walter Garfield, better known as 'Benny'. Born in August 1872 at Raunds Lodge, Garfield lived as a young boy in Higham Ferrers, playing football for Higham and Finedon before joining Kettering. Of slight build but described as hardy, tricky, fast and someone who could centre well, Garfield would score nine goals for the club in 18 competitive games this season. Destined to play in the Football League for Burton Wanderers and West Bromwich Albion, the highlight of his career would come on 5 March 1898, as an England international at inside-left in their 3-2 victory over Ireland at the Solitude Ground in Belfast.

Opposite: The club having already, in its short history, been involved in games of rugby union, Uppingham rules and association football, the 1892 close season saw Kettering's players form a cricket team. A report of their first game, versus the Working Men's Cricket Club on 14 May (the same day as the Midland League Annual Meeting in Rotherham), was carried in the Kettering Leader & Observer *the following Friday.*

CRICKET.

KETTERING FOOTBALL CLUB
V. WORKING MEN'S CRICKET CLUB.

These teams met on the North Park Ground on Saturday afternoon, in fine weather. As usual, there was a large concourse of persons, numbering about 200, assembled, to see what the football team could perform in the way of cricket. Albert Peters winning the toss, selected to bat, and sent in Tunnicliffe and Starr. The former man had but a short stay, being clean bowled with the first ball, and not much of a stand was made until Peters and Stott were partnered, and who made the score-sheet show an altogether changed aspect, knocking up fifty between them, but unluckily were both run out after scoring 28 and 22 respectively. Nothing of note afterwards took place, except that Davies caused some amusement by his "knowledge" of the willow, and the innings closed with a creditable 76 runs. F. Page and A. Taffs trundled best, the former taking four wickets for 21 runs, and the latter three for twelve. Going in to bat, the Working Men's Club scored freely from the bowling of Stott and Peters, although a large number of runs were gained by the bad fielding of their opponents. Numerous catches were also offered but lost, and the innings closed at six o'clock with nine runs and a wicket in favour of the Working Men's Club. For the losers G. West performed best in the bowling department, taking three wickets for twelve runs. The following were the full score:–

FOOTBALL TEAM.		WORKING MEN'S CLUB.	
J. Starr, c and b Taffs ...	4	H. Toseland, c West, b	
E. Tunnicliffe, b Page ...	0	Starr	11
Harry Dixon, b Taffs ...	6	A. Wilford, c and b West	13
G. West, b Taffs	5	G. Wilson, b Stott	10
A. Peters, run out	28	W. Joyce, c Tunnicliffe, b	
J. Stott, run out	22	Starr	4
H. Payne, st Abraham, b		A. Taffs, run out	7
Page	6	A. Watts, b West	15
Horace Dixon, b Page ...	2	T. Dunkley, c Peters, b	
C. Dixon, c Toseland, b		Stott	3
Page	0	H. Percival, run out ...	8
G. Davies, st Abrahams,		R. Abrahams, c & b West	0
b Taffs	0	F. Loasby, not out	2
Henry Dixon, not out ...	0	F. Page, not out	1
Extras	3	Extras	11
	—		—
Total	76	Total	85

The club's first league fixture was played at Eldred's Field on Saturday, 17 September 1892, when Derby Junction were the visitors. The match finished 2-2. Kettering's team that afternoon was Evan Roberts, William Draper, George Davies, William Mablestone, Albert Peters (captain), Jummy Panter, C. McUrich, Jackie Starr, Jimmy Stott, Harry Dixon and Benny Garfield. It was the first time anywhere in Northamptonshire that nets (an invention of Liverpool engineer John Alexander Brodie) had been attached to the goals, which were by now solid affairs with fixed wooden crossbars. Life in the Midland League proved tough and defeats in the next three games left Kettering hovering close to the bottom of the table.

But it was not all doom and gloom; the club finally won an FA Cup tie (four years after playing its first), beating Langley Mill Rangers at Eldred's Field by three goals to one in the first qualifying round. The *Kettering Leader & Observer* described a welcome victory:

THE ENGLISH CUP.
KETTERING V. LANGLEY MILL RANGERS.

Among the many contests that took place last Saturday [15 October] in connection with the national trophy, not the least interesting was that which took place at Kettering, when the home team tried conclusions with Langley Mill Rangers, and finally succeeded in ousting them. The game took place on the ground in Green-lane, and was watched by a fair number of spectators, but for some reason or other the attendance showed a falling off. Footballers in Kettering were more fortunate with the weather than they were in some other places, the day being all that could be desired, and scarcely any wind. On the tick of three the ball was moved from the centre, and Kettering early showed that they were on aggressive tactics, but they did not have it all their own way, and the Langley centre forward got near enough in the home quarters to shoot over the cross-bar. Hopewell missing the ball let Langley again get in close quarters, and Mablestone could do nothing but concede a corner. Peters early showed that he was in his best form, and was not long before he tried to effect an opening with a low clean shot, but Carlin was able to return it. When the game had been in progress about ten minutes, Panter, who on this occasion was playing centre forward, got the "leather," and with a smart bit of play

LOWERED THE LANGLEY CITADEL.

The result was hailed with tremendous cheering and cries of "Good old Jum." With the score against them, Langley made a gallant effort by an attack, but found the home halves tough nuts to crack. Once things looked a bit dangerous for Kettering when "hands" were obtained against them within a short range of the goal-posts, but the venue was quickly changed, and the home team spent a little time in close quarters to the Langley goal, until McUrich offended the off-side rule, and this gave Langley a welcome relief. For a few minutes Kettering seemed a bit disorganised, and two or three rushes by the visiting forwards were only stopped by kicking out, a style of play which is never popular with the spectators. At length Langley were able to send in a soft one to Roberts which he quickly returned, but Draper "mulling" the "leather," the home custodian had a more difficult shot to deal with. The Kettering left wing then raced away and put the "leather" well across the Langley goal, but could not keep it long in this desirable quarter, the visiting forwards being on the alert. Hopewell exhibited some very sound defensive work, and the home custodian again had to save, and Kettering were soon back in the territory of the Rangers. Here Dixon tried a shot, but the "leather" dropped on the outside of the strings [net]. From the goal kick Langley got into the home quarters, when Phillips saved well. Then Panter again got possession and led an attack on the Langley citadel, Dixon passing the "leather" well across the mouth of the goal, Stott finally heading it through, thus making

KETTERING TWO GOALS AHEAD.

"Nothing succeeds like success" was proved in this contest, for with the score still further improved Kettering were incited on to add still further to it. The Kettering left wing again became conspicuous, and then the right wing put in some smart work, and Stott, seven minutes from the last goal, scored

KETTERING'S THIRD POINT.

Before half-time arrived the home goal was once again closely invaded as the consequence of a miss by Phillips. A very hot shot from his left front was cleverly met by Roberts, who sent it back with both hands, but on the return it was met by the Langley captain, who butted it into the net and

SCORED FOR THE VISITORS,

to the intense delight of their friends outside the ropes. A fourth goal by Panter for Kettering was disallowed on the appeal of off-side. At half-time the score was–

Kettering 3

Langley Mills 1

The second half was not so interesting as the first. However, it opened very well, McUrich putting in some brilliant work, but could not effect any opening. Langley seemed to put additional zeal into the contest, and Kettering had to act a bit on the defensive. Again Langley failed to get any advantage from "hands" in front of their opponents' goal, and this was followed a minute or two later by Mablestone (who up to now had been a bit off) dropping in a beauty just under the cross-bar, which the Langley custodian could only save with difficulty. Dixon and Stott made it rather warm for Carlin for a time, and then Roberts found things equally as exhilarating in his quarter, bad play on the part of the home team accounting for a good deal of this. Getting away at last, Panter sent in a skier with some pace behind it, and Carlin did the only thing he could and saved by putting it over. McUrich took the corner and dropped the ball on the nets. A few minutes later another cheer went up as many

THOUGHT KETTERING HAD SCORED.

Some splendid passing had taken place amongst the Kettering forwards, and Starr at length tried to head it through when the ball was caught in the net just outside the post, and of course no point was obtained. In the last few minutes Kettering seemed to gain the upper hand again, and when the referee's whistle blew they were in dangerous proximity to the goal, the game thus being the same as it was at half-time. Players:–

Kettering.– E. Roberts, goal; Draper and Phillips, backs; Mablestone, Peters, and Hopewell, half-backs; McUrich and Stott, right wing; Panter, centre; Dixon and Starr, left wing.

Langley Mill Rangers.– R. Carlin, goal; J. Clarke and J. Farnsworth, backs; W. Booth, J. Brown, and W. Gellatly, half-backs; T. Chambers and G. Bestwick, right wing; T. Rose, centre; G. Pinegar and F. Eyre, left wing.

Linesmen, Messrs. J. Chester and B. Garfield [did Benny Garfield recall his stint "waving the flag" – as the *Kettering Leader & Observer*'s correspondent put it – when he represented his country in Belfast a few years later?]; referee, Mr. J.H. Strawson (Lincoln).

Beeston were dispatched 6-1 in the second qualifying round, but the run eventually came to an end with a 2-1 defeat at home to Loughborough. (The first team entered no other cup competitions this season.) The win against Langley Mill must have had a positive effect because Kettering secured their first Midland League victory (by three goals to nil) at home to Newark the following week.

The campaign was well underway before the committee finally decided on what the distinctive colours of the club should be in the league. Red jerseys were favoured, but it was thought likely that something different would have to be used because many other clubs played in red – a popular colour of the period. However, it was other clubs that changed and Kettering took to wearing an all red strip. Often referred to in the local press up to now as the 'Holy City Boys' or 'Holy Citizens', the team gradually acquired two new nicknames – the 'Ketts' and the 'Reds'. ('Poppies', which has now endured for more than a century, would not appear until 1907.)

November was a bad month for refereeing Kettering games: Grantham Rovers were due to play a Midland League fixture at Eldred's Field on the 12th, and Kettering submitted the names of three men – any one of which might have acted as referee – but for some reason none of the names met with Grantham's approval (there remained quite a rivalry between the two clubs, to say the least). It was therefore left to the secretary of the league to select an official and Mr J. Jeffries of Derby was duly appointed. On the day of the game Jeffries, who worked for the railway company, caught a south-bound express that did not stop at Kettering. He continued to Bedford where he alighted, still with the intention of refereeing the game, and went to board a north-bound goods train; only to slip, fall on to the track and fracture a leg. The game eventually went ahead without him but had to be regarded as a friendly (Kettering won 3-1). A fortnight later, the team arrived at Newark after a period of heavy rain, only to find the referee had declared the pitch unfit for a league fixture, but good enough to play a friendly on. The state of the playing surface after the match can only be guessed at but the result is recorded as 0-0. The club received just £1-6s as their half-share of the gate, which was less than the cost of travelling there.

On 29 April 1893, Kettering played their last match at Eldred's Field, defeating Doncaster Rovers by three goals to nil in front of about 1,000 spectators. The question of how long the club would be able to use the ground had been raised at the beginning of the season. As long as Mr Eldred's tenancy lasted the club was secure, however, this was coming to an end and it was an open secret that the land would eventually be sold. There was a general wish expressed in the town that the football club might be kept on as tenants until that time, but the new rector of the parish had a desire to foster athletics and gave the Church Institute first refusal; an offer which they accepted. All of which proved irrelevant because, within weeks, the field, along with other land in Green Lane, had been sold for £11,000 to Messrs Hanger and Payne who were about to build houses.

The club finished its first league campaign in a reasonable seventh position. Champions for the second successive season were Rotherham Town and they were duly voted into the Second Division of the Football League. Kettering's 4-0 win at Eldred's Field being one of only two defeats suffered by the northerners in 24 league matches.

So that supporters could be informed of the club's finances, a meeting was held in the Iron Room on Workhouse Lane (now Dryland Street) on 29 May. It was revealed that the bank was owed £153, and that the Kettering Football Club Company Limited, registered back in August, had not been the answer to everyone's prayers. It had in fact been wound up just before Christmas after only around 130 shares had been applied for. The club's affairs remained in something of a mess.

Overleaf: The Kettering Leader & Observer's *report of Kettering's last match at Eldred's Field – a 3-0 victory over Doncaster Rovers, and the* Kettering Guardian's *take on their first game at North Park – a 2-1 win against Notts St John's. Although the club's stay at its new home would be short (just four years), North Park would see more than its fair share of triumph and tragedy.*

FOOTBALL.

KETTERING v. DONCASTER ROVERS.

There were about a thousand spectators on the ground of the Kettering club last Saturday, to witness a match between the above in the Midland League. Some interest was caused in the fixture, as it was the last of the home team in the League, and it was also the concluding match of the season. The band of the Kettering Rifles on this occasion played to the field, and at the interval played a selection. The play was not of a very exciting character, but at times a certain element of roughness was introduced, mostly by the visitors, and this led to some strong comments from the spectators. For some time after the commencement the honours were about equally divided, but, at the end of twelve minutes' play, the visitors forced their way into the home quarters, and a low swift shot from the right very nearly went through. The ball, however, struck the post, and, with the screw, sailed right across to the other post, where it was bustled out by Roberts, and soon carried back up the ground. After this Kettering did most of the attacking, and, with the wind in their favour, they made it warm for Massey and the Doncaster backs, but it was not until thirty-five minutes had passed without result that a centre by McUrich enabled Starr to head through, and score the first goal for Kettering. Nothing more was done up to half-time, but about a quarter-of-an-hour after the second start Starr again did the needful. Playing with the wind, the visitors did most of the attacking this half, but the Kettering defence was well maintained, and about five minutes before the finish they managed again to break through and score goal number three, the leather being neatly dropped in by Garfield over the head of the Doncaster custodian, who had rushed out in the attempt to clear. For nearly twenty minutes the visitors played only ten men, in consequence of the retirement of Bridgewater, who appeared to be suffering from a weak knee, which bothered him several times during the earlier portion of the game. Teams:–

Kettering.– Roberts, goal; Draper and Wallis, backs; Hopewell, Peters, and Mablestone, half-backs; McUrich and Goode, right wing; Garfield, centre; Dixon and Starr, left wing.

Doncaster.– J. Massey, goal; Parr and Attice, backs; Waddington, Morris, and Gill, half-backs; Hill and Smith, right wing; Lee, centre; Lester and Bridgewater, left wing.

Linesmen, Messrs. Taylor and Maycock; referee, Mr. T. Ashmole.

THE BALL SET ROLLING AT KETTERING.

NOTTS. ST. JOHN'S V. KETTERING.

The ground used by the Town Club last year, known as Mr Eldred's field, not being available this year, the North Park is to be used for the purpose. Notwithstanding the distance to the North Park, and the disappointment at the license not being granted for the supply of refreshments on the ground last Saturday, there was a good gate, and much interest was manifested in the first match of the season, the competing teams being the Kettering Town and Notts. St. John's.

Considerable changes have been made in the personnel of the home team since the end of last season, and it may be difficult to gauge the merits of each individual member; but to judge from Saturday's display, there is good reason for being satisfied with Mablestone, Peters, Starr, and McUrich, the old players; and also with the form shown by Brookes (Burton Swifts) and Armstrong (Newark), two of the new-comers. S Wallis and A Toseland, who have previously played for the club, did fairly good work at back, although the last-named was slow at tackling; and H E Dixon (Kettering Crusaders) did well in goal. Atkinson (Stafford), another new comer, who created a good impression in practice games, was overmatched by Notts. right half, and made a very indifferent show all through the game; as a successor to H Dixon, who has been captured by Notts County, he certainly is a great disappointment.

Play commenced at 3.40, and the Kettering men, having to contend against a strong breeze from the right front, were penned in for a considerable portion of the time, and Dixon had several times to hit or throw out. The proceedings were diversified with occasional excursions into the Notts. territory, and there were numerous spells of lively play, but neither side was able to score, and when the whistle blew for the half-time interval the score was *nil*. On re-starting, the home players made a vigorous attack, and although some exceedingly close shaves were experienced, bar and posts being struck in turn, no point was made until nearly 20 minutes had passed, when another attack developed an opportunity, from which Brookes scored with a brilliant shot. Kettering continued for a time to press very closely, and made several close attempts to score, but the Notts. forwards, among whom Shaw was very active, got possession two or three times, and made it necessary for Dixon to bestir himself. About half-an-hour from the re-start, Kettering again invaded, and McUrich cleverly headed in from a pass by Peters, making the second goal for Kettering; but shortly afterwards Notts. gained the upper hand, and scored from a shot by Petchell. After this nothing further was added, although Kettering pressed closely for most of the time, and at the close the score was – Kettering, two goals; Notts. St. John's one goal.

The teams on Saturday were constituted as follows:

Notts. St. John's:– Goal, G Sykes; backs, R Smith and C Sturbitant; half-backs, H Brothwell, W Maltby, and J McGinns; right wing, W Petchell and F Dean; centre, W Shaw; left wing, R Barker and J Knowles.

Kettering:– H E Dixon, goal; backs, S Wallis and A Toseland; half-backs, T Newman, Albert Peters, and Mablestone; right wing, Armstrong and Brookes; centre, McUrich; left wing, Starr and Atkinson.

Linesmen, Messrs H Sands and J Smith. Referee, Mr C Dixon.

Two Kettering stalwarts moved on in the close season; fortunately neither would stay away for too long. Harry Dixon's talents had come to the attention of Notts County, for whom he signed. But he missed the town too much and, after just five appearances for the Nottingham club, Dixon would return to once again don a red jersey. William Draper disappeared for slightly longer after accepting a place in the Burton Wanderers side that was destined to win the Midland League and be elected into the Second Division. Draper would, however, make his way back to Kettering after a year in the Football League.

Of the club's new signings, none really stand out as being a great success, although Ike Hitchcock from Notts Jardines would at least play a part in the majority of games this campaign and stay with the club until the middle of the decade.

At 3.40 pm on Saturday, 2 September 1893, Kettering kicked-off their first match (beating Notts St John's 2-1 in a friendly) at the club's new home – North Park. Situated, as the name suggests, at the north end of town, North Park was bordered by Bath Road along its western flank and open fields to the north and east. It must have been quite a sporting venue at the time, hosting athletics, cycling and cricket as well as football.

Judging by the prices advertised in the *Kettering Leader & Observer* on the eve of the first home league fixture of the season, the cost of spectating may well have been less than it was at Eldred's Field, possibly reflecting the fact that the new ground was further out of town: "The match for Saturday, Sept. 30th. Kettering v. Doncaster Rovers. Kick-off 3. Admission: Stand and whole of west side, 8d.; unreserved, 4d.; ladies half-price to reserved side."

The match against Rovers finished 0-0, which was probably something of a relief considering the opening league fixture had been a 6-1 mauling at Newark. But the omens were not good. The day before the Doncaster game, as well as advertising admission prices, the *Kettering Leader & Observer* had printed an open letter from Kettering's secretary Charles Bullock and committee chairman Frank Abraham, appealing for the public's support in overcoming the club's monetary woes:

THE KETTERING FOOTBALL CLUB.

Sir, – Through the medium of your columns, the committee of the Kettering Football Club wish to place before the public the present position of the affairs of the club, what has been, and what is being done for the improvement both of the team and of the financial position of the club.

When the present committee – which is composed solely of working men – assumed the management, they were confronted with an empty exchequer, a heavy debt, and a team weakened by the loss of some of the best men of last season. The tide of affairs seemed to be at the very lowest ebb – without money, or players, or available funds – and it was only their confidence in the football-loving public that decided them to do their best to keep the old club going.

They have, after many attempts and much expense, succeeded in securing several good men, and they hope quickly to further materially strengthen the team. To do this, however, it is absolutely necessary that the public should give their support, by putting in an appearance at the matches or purchasing season tickets. The committee have decided to hold an archery tournament, and will be glad of any help in this direction, either by gift of prizes or purchase of tickets. They know that there are sufficient lovers of the game in Kettering to support a really first-class team, and this is the end at which they aim.

At the start of the season the Midland League had rescinded the rule requiring the club to pay one third of a visiting team's railway expenses. Nevertheless, finances remained in a parlous state and results on the pitch were proving no tonic. Interest in the FA Cup ended at first qualifying stage with a 4-1 reverse at Loughborough. Supporters who travelled to the last match of 1893 – the Kettering Charity Cup semi-final – had a miserable journey home after seeing Leicester Fosse score eight without reply. And things did not improve at the beginning of 1894; a 5-1 (friendly) defeat at home to Notts County on New Year's Day was followed five days later by a 12-1 (Midland League) humiliation at the hands of Long Eaton Rangers.

On a day when nothing went right, goalkeeper George Pack and full-back W. Boddington both missed the train to Long Eaton (another full-back, Tommy McLean, had broken his arm the previous week), half-backs Albert Peters and William Mablestone were both unable to play and forward Jummy Panter was suspended. In the end, just eight players arrived at the ground, which was heavily covered in snow. Long Eaton offered two further men, allowing Kettering to take to the field with a 'team' of ten, made up of six regulars – including full-back Sammy Wallis in goal – two reserves and two opposition players!

After an absence of five years, the club again entered the Northants Senior Cup. But after winning 4-1 at Wellingborough, the semi-final against Rushden on 24 February was forfeited because Kettering were due to play a league fixture at Leicester. The club declined to fix an alternative date and not surprisingly the county FA took a dim view of the situation, not least because of lost revenue. The day before the game should have been played, the *Kettering Guardian*'s correspondent pulled no punches in his appraisal of the situation:

I regret to hear that Kettering Town cannot see their way clear to set apart a date on which to play a match for the benefit of the Northants. Football Association; Rushden having consented to meet Kettering on some date convenient to both teams. It cannot be that Kettering misunderstood the application made to them, and yet they consent to play if the 'gate' is divided between the competing teams! Nothing will so quickly ruin the reputation of any club as selfishness and greed, and I regret to find any club permeated by a love of money to the utter obliteration of a pure love of sport. The Northants Football Association seeks to exercise a maternal care over the destinies of football, and yet in an endeavour to raise funds, the parent association is spurned by her children! How much better, in the eyes of the world, would it be to join hands, and once more sing 'Auld Lang Syne?'

It was a miserable season all round, with no less than 35 players (including the two loaned by Long Eaton) used in just 24 competitive games – the last of which, a Midland League fixture, saw Kettering visit William Draper's Burton Wanderers, who had already chalked up 16 wins in the competition (four times as many as the Reds). Result: Kettering lost by eight goals to nil, finished two places above bottom club Mansfield Town and had to (successfully) seek re-election, whilst the champions from Burton-on-Trent and runners-up Leicester Fosse were both welcomed into the Football League.

At a meeting of the members in June 1894, it was suggested that the financial position of the club might be improved if a ground could be obtained in a more central location, with the Gas Company's land in Gas Street (Meadow Road) being specifically mentioned. However, the majority of those present did not favour the suggestion and Kettering would continue to play their home games at North Park.

Incredibly, despite the ongoing concerns over the lack of money, eight new players were signed: Alf Ball from Preston North End, John Barker (Bailliston), J. Palmer and Jackie Whitehouse (Brierly Hill), William Pell (Stoke), Charles Robinson (Burslem Port Vale), Charles Rose (Derby County) and Jack Thorpe (Heanor). Although two of the eight would not last until Christmas – Barker was suspended after playing seven games when it was discovered that he was still registered with his previous club, whilst Rose, who had been engaged on 25 shillings a week, had his services dispensed with on 12 December after he declined the club's request to move to the town from Derby to cut down on travel expenses – a few of the new signings would stay long enough to have quite an impact on the club's fortunes over the next few years.

Making the most immediate impact was the one-handed Jack Thorpe, whose disability affected neither the player – he would appear in more competitive games (27) and score more goals (13) than anyone else this season – or the officials – on more than one occasion the ball striking his stump would be declared 'hands'!

Although a better campaign overall, there were still a few disasters in this one that mirrored the last. Drawn away to Loughborough in the first qualifying round of the FA Cup, the Reds went down by four goals to nil – the third year on the trot they had been dumped out of the competition by the same team. Another trip to Leicester in the Kettering Charity Cup resulted in another heavy defeat, 6-1 being only a marginal improvement on the previous season's eight goal thrashing. And there was again controversy involving a Senior Cup game with Rushden – only this time it was the final that the club chose to snub.

Opposite: Kettering FC, 1893-94.

Back row: Charles Robinson (chairman of the committee), Sammy Wallis, George Pack, Albert Toseland, Charlie Dixon (trainer). Middle Row: Ike Hitchcock, Jummy Panter, Albert Peters (captain), William Mablestone, Harry Dixon. Front row: Jimmy Meecham, Jackie Starr, Jack McDermott. The photograph was apparently taken at the back of the Victoria Hall (later the Odeon) prior to the team travelling to London to play a friendly at Millwall. (By now, most clubs had adopted white shirts as a second strip.)

The climax of the competition was due to be played at Wellingborough on 23 March 1895, but Kettering had a Midland League fixture at Ilkeston that day and the reserves were otherwise engaged in the newly formed Leicestershire & Northamptonshire League. So a scratch team was raised, mostly from other clubs across town. Kettering played the final with nine unregistered men – and lost 4-1. Afterwards, it was suggested by the county FA that the match should be replayed (no doubt to their financial reward!) but this was overruled by the game's lawmakers in London, who judged that to be unfair on Rushden and the result stood. The side that represented Kettering was Perkins, Coles, Cox, Clough, Curtis, Newman, Taffs, Glover, Shrives (the goal scorer), Newberry and Loake. Only the club's two registered players were awarded runners-up medals, but it cannot be stated with any certainty which two they were.

Five wins out of their last six Midland League games – sparked by a 7-0 trouncing of Matlock – saw Kettering achieve a respectable fifth place finish. Just one visiting team left North Park with both points (it was two points for a win in those days) and that was Loughborough, heading towards the title and a place in the Football League.

On 16 April, a day after their final league fixture, Kettering travelled south to play Millwall Athletic (and beat them 3-2) in a friendly. Millwall's secretary, William Henson, had been instrumental in founding the Southern League this season, a competition which his team (one of only two professional clubs in London – the other being Woolwich Arsenal) won without losing any of their 16 matches. Invited to join the Football League, Millwall declined because of the travelling involved, which was probably the sensible approach to take at the time because Kettering was not the only club finding it hard to come to terms with the costs of professionalism.

The situation is best illustrated by the plight of Accrington (not to be confused with Accrington Stanley), who had visited North Park earlier in the season to play a friendly. The movement to pay players for their services can be traced to the Lancashire mill towns, and Accrington were temporarily expelled from the FA in 1883 for doing just that. But they, along with others, succeeded in changing the course of the game. By the time the club became founder-members of the Football League, payments were the norm and all the top sides did it. But it was to prove Accrington's undoing. The town was simply not big enough to sustain football at the highest level. In 1893 the club was forced to resign from the League, unable to pay its debts. Just over 12 months after sending a team to Kettering (and being beaten 4-2), Accrington would fold. The warning signs were there for all to see.

Nine

Famous Opponents

1895 - 1897

"Together we proceeded in the direction of the station, and from the deserted appearance of the streets, it seemed likely that we should be the only supporters enthusiastic enough to follow the fortunes of our players on such a day. However, I was pleased to see a nice little company waiting at the station, eagerly discussing the probabilities of the weather. The special was only a few minutes late, and eventually ran into the Central Station at Manchester at 12.45, only half an hour behind time. If the weather in the Midlands was rough, it threatened to be still worse at Cottonopolis. The air was exceedingly heavy and very raw, and a fine rain made everything damp and miserable as we emerged into Manchester's dirty streets."

Today, the dream of all non-League clubs must surely be to draw Manchester United away in the FA Cup. It actually happened to Kettering twice in successive seasons during the 1890s, although it would be fair to say that the Manchester club was certainly not as well known in those days as it is now. Formed in 1878 as the Newton Heath Lancashire & Yorkshire Railway Cricket & Football Club, the 'Heathens' joined the Football League in 1892 and moved to their Bank Lane ground in Clayton – which is where both the Kettering games were played – a year later. The name change to Manchester United would not occur until April 1902, when the club, in debt to the tune of more than £2,500, was saved from extinction by a group of businessmen.

After slowly coming to grips with professionalism, Kettering's journeys to the industrial Northwest formed part of a very progressive period for the Reds; as well as creditable FA Cup runs there was to be a championship, local cup successes and a new league that would see teams from the likes of Tottenham Hotspur and Woolwich Arsenal visiting North Park.

At the start of the 1895-96 campaign, the centre-forward position rendered vacant by the departure of Charles Robinson was filled initially by Babes (formerly of Clyde and Celtic) – only for Babes to be replaced after just three games (and one goal) by Joe McMain from Preston, who would prove to be one of Kettering's most influential captures. Leicester Fosse's William Miller, whose services were secured for a fee of £15, took one-handed Jack Thorpe's place at inside-left after Thorpe joined Sheffield United, whilst Manchester City's Alf Heskin arrived to shore up the half-back line. And there was a prominent local signing, too – Burton Latimer's William Perkins. An outstanding goalkeeper, Perkins would later become an integral part of Liverpool's 1900-01 First Division Championship-winning side.

The season opened at North Park on 2 September 1895 with a 2-1 friendly victory over Glossop North End. This proved to be the beginning of an unbeaten run of 13 Midland League, six cup and six friendly games; a run which finally came to an end at Gainsborough Trinity with a 2-0 league defeat on 25 January 1896. The 25 matches yielded 20 wins and 79 goals (with just 18 conceded). Even the reserves got in on the act when, on 16 November, they trounced Bedford Town 19-1 – a result that was a mere two goals better than the previous season!

Kettering reached the first round proper of the FA Cup for the first time in their history after knocking out Gedling Grove, Coalville Town and Football League Division Two clubs Loughborough Town and Leicester Fosse. The first round was then the equivalent of today's fourth, with 32 teams in the draw, which this season comprised all 16 First Division clubs, ten from the Second Division and Blackpool, Chesterfield, Kettering, Millwall Athletic, Tottenham Hotspur and Southampton St Mary's from outside the Football League. Kettering were drawn away to Newton Heath, a relatively anonymous Second Division team from the Manchester suburbs with a large chemical works adjacent the ground.

The tie was played on Saturday, 1 February 1896 (a week after the club's 25-game unbeaten run had come to an end), and the *Manchester Evening News* covered the match in some detail:

It need hardly be said that the supporters of the Heathens had very grave doubts as to the performance of the team against the Midland club. This is the first appearance of Kettering in Manchester, and beyond the fact that they are practically at the head of the Midland League, nothing is known of them in this district. The ground at Bank Lane looked in excellent condition. It will be remembered that in the first round of the English Cup last season Stoke beat the Heathens on this ground. During the week the Manchester eleven have been training under the control of Mr. Albut. The teams lined up as follows [with corrections to the Kettering side]:–

Newton Heath: Ridgeway; Dow and Collinson; Fitzsimmons (D), Perrins and Cartwright; Kennedy, Donaldson, Cassidy, Smith and Peters.

Kettering: Perkins; Wallis and Draper; Pell, Heskin [who would suffer a broken leg at the end of the month] and Mablestone; Whitehouse, Panter, McMain, Miller and Dixon.

The Heathens were of course, minus Douglas, who has been suspended. Ridgeway taking his place. Errentz was unable to turn out, but Cassidy reappeared. However, Clarkin and M'Naught were unfit, and this about filled the Heathens' cup of bitterness. The team was thus a very weak one, whilst Kettering were without Ball and Ashworth.

There was a good attendance when, Mr. Byr, of Sheffield, referee, appeared. Cassidy won the spin of the coin, and M'Main started. The Reds [Kettering would have been playing all in red, Newton Heath were probably in green shirts and white shorts] went down, and Perrins almost let them in. The attack was repulsed, but the visitors were soon back again, and Collinson gave a corner. From this the home left got away, and several shots were directed at the Kettering goal, but all to no purpose. Kennedy went away on the left, and the ball travelling across the Kettering goal had a narrow escape. The ball came up again and Perkins had to save. This was followed by a corner. Pell sent the leather nicely forward, and Whitehouse darted off, but ran the leather out. Kennedy on the other hand beat several opponents, but was forced into touch. The Heathens were displaying more dash than they have done of late, and Draper had to punt out again. Whitehouse got down and from a bully M'Main missed a capital chance. Still the visitors kept the play in the home quarters and Ridgeway had to clear from Whitehouse. Play was transferred to the opposite end and Kennedy passed to Donaldson, who scored the first point for the Heathens. Cassidy was limping very badly, and on receiving the ball he quickly sent it on to the left. The Reds were playing a capital passing game, and again invaded the home quarters. Ridgeway bringing off a brilliant save. The Reds were not done with and for several minutes the home defence was tried, and Ridgeway, who was paid close attention, again cleared finely. Cartwright put the ball up, and Cassidy practically playing with one leg just missed the mark. Perrins sent the ball up, but Wallis returned, and then the visitors were penalised for fouling Collinson. The visitors continued to show dashing form, and looked like scoring, but the home defence prevailed. Cassidy had to leave the field, but the four forwards forged ahead, and Smith just missed the posts. Heskin was the means of transferring play into the home quarters, and a capital shot from Miller hit the post. Collinson was next called upon, and he did his work well. There was no doubt about the visitors' ability, and after some smart passing they forced a corner. Dow cleared another attack, and then the ball was run out at the Kettering end. Perrins again let the Reds in, but Panter sent the ball out. Peters tried, and then after a sharp run Perkins had to run out to clear. At half time the Heathens were leading by one goal to nil.

The Heathens started the second half with only ten men, and by a pretty movement they carried play into the visitors' half, a couple of corners having to be conceded, but nothing accrued from them. From a goalkick Kettering broke away, but Fitzsimmons stopped them. It was only for a moment, however, as M'Main pounced upon the leather. He was quickly robbed by Collinson. Twice in succession the visitors were penalised for tripping, but the halves were fairly strong and held a big advantage, having only four backs to contend with. Perrins was not a success at centre half, and M'Naught would have made a great difference. Cartwright came in for a round of applause, he taking the ball from the toes of his opponents. The game continued to be very fast, both sets of players going for all they were worth. Collinson took another free kick, but Wallis headed out of danger. The visitors were doing their utmost, but Cartwright repeatedly checked the Reds. Dixon sent in one which Ridgeway threw away, and then Dow had to give a corner. The ball was well placed, and a warm bully was made on the home goal, the ball going through, but the point was disallowed on account of Ridgeway being obstructed. The game being transferred to the other end Peters let go. Perkins first clearing, and Donaldson had hard lines with a good shot. A free kick to the visitors caused the home partisans to hold their breath, but the leather went through untouched by a second player. Offside spoiled a visit by the Heathens, and then Dow allowed Dixon to beat him, but his final was well met by Collinson. Cartwright, who was playing a splendid game, was again instrumental in sending the Reds back, but a couple of free kicks again put the home team on the defensive. Smith worked the ball away, and Kennedy got down. A corner came, and with this Smith landed a second point. On resuming the Heathens were again found in the visitors' quarters, but another free kick was given against Perrins, and Pell scored for the visitors. The visitors made a desperate effort. Dixon put in a capital shot, but Ridgeway, who had played a capital game, saved, although he was hurt in doing so. The whistle shortly afterwards sounded, with Newton Heath winners of a good game, and ready for round two.

COMMENTS.

Considering that the Heathens had only ten men for nearly the whole of the game, they did very well. The game was the best seen at Clayton for a long time; it was fast, exciting, for the whole ninety minutes. Ridgeway played a capital game throughout, and some of his saves were very good. Dow, Collinson and Fitzsimmons all did very well, but Cartwright was without doubt the best man on the field. Perrins was a failure, and it was only through his foolishness that Kettering scored their only goal. The four forwards did exceedingly well, Kennedy being the best, but the whole team played for all they were worth. The defeat of Loughborough and Leicester at the hands of Kettering in the qualifying stages is not to be wondered at. They play a good game, and have plenty of dash. The only fault is that they use their weight rather too freely.

The following week, the *Kettering Leader & Observer* carried a version of events as seen through local eyes:

Kettering were "dished" out of it. That was a common expression amongst the football fraternity from this district after the match at Manchester against Newton Heath. The onlookers from this locality were not at all satisfied with the decisions of the referee – especially in one instance when the ball was put into the net off Wallis. What a great deal depended on that decision? If the referee had allowed a goal the match would have resulted in a draw, and that would have meant a big "gate" at Kettering. In addition to this, the Kettering Committee were very dissatisfied with the gate at Manchester. There were about 6,000 spectators, much below the estimate, and the total amount to be drawn by the Kettering Club will not be anything like what was expected. But it is of no use crying over spilt milk. It is gratifying to know that Kettering have done much more than was anticipated at the commencement of the season, and that the encounters at Leicester and Manchester have brought the much needed shekels to the club [Kettering began the season £450 in debt].

Between three and four hundred people journeyed from this district by the special train. After Newton Heath had been taken down by Fairfield, and the exhibition of Kettering in the qualifying rounds, which were escaped by Newton Heath, the travellers were in hopes of returning with the news of victory. But though defeated, Kettering were not disgraced. From first to last, they made a splendid fight of it. The result, a victory for Newton Heath, by two to one, was by no means a true indication of the nature of the game, for three quarters of the time the visitors were around the home citadel. Though Kettering were unlucky in losing, they will doubtless derive some consolation from the good opinions formed of them. Everyone was praising the play of the visitors; the forwards, who were very smart on the ball, played with commendable dash and combination, and the backs and halves showed a sound defence. They were distinctly ahead of the "Heathens" in point of play, the Second Leaguers owing their victory to a very great extent to a marvellous exhibition in goal of Ridgeway.

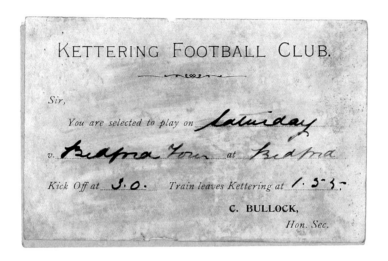

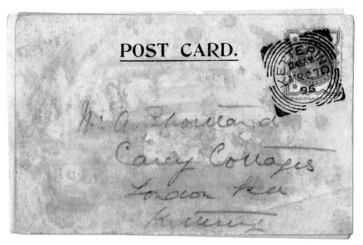

A Kettering FC selection card, postmarked 27 March 1896.

The card informs Mr A. Shortland – of Carey Cottages, London Road, Kettering – that he is selected to play (for the reserves) at Bedford Town the following Saturday. (There is no record of the gentleman ever having made the senior team in a competitive match.)

In all, 17 cup ties were played this season, of which only three were lost. Putting aside the disappointment of defeat in Manchester – and a 2-0 loss to Walsall in the semi-final of the Wellingborough Charity Cup – the club actually reached the final of three other knockout competitions and went on to win two of them. Although the climax of the Luton Charity Cup ended in a 3-0 defeat at the hands of Luton Town, Kettering lifted the Senior Cup on 23 April, beating Rushden 3-0 at Wellingborough; and, six days later, having dispatched First Division Nottingham Forest by a goal to nil in the semi-final, Second Division Burton Wanderers were beaten 2-0 at North Park in the (replayed) final of the Kettering Charity Cup.

But it was the Reds' performances in the league that must have drawn admiration from a wider circle of the game's observers. Going into the last month of the season the club was vying for top spot with Gainsborough Trinity, Walsall and Long Eaton Rangers.

Kettering were clearly favourites to win the title because on 3 April they drew the Midland League Championship Match 2-2 against The Rest Of The League – some time before the actual winners had been decided! This was one of 13 games played in 28 days, including the last six league fixtures, a benefit for Jummy Panter (versus the Grenadier Guards, which Kettering won 4-2) and, bizarrely, a long journey to Southampton St Mary's for a 1-0 friendly defeat. However, despite cramming in the football and spending hours travelling – severely testing everyone's fitness and endurance to the limit – come the end of the month, the Reds were top of the Midland League. Champions! Five points clear of runners-up Gainsborough, having won 20 and lost only three of their 28 league matches. (At the other end of the table were Matlock, who lost every single one of their games and conceded no less than 130 goals!)

41 years later, writing in the *Kettering Leader*, Albert Toseland, a member of the title-winning side, recalled the celebrations:

We had a drive round several villages by brake (there were no 'buses then), via Geddington, Stanion, Brigstock, etc., to Benefield, where we had a splendid tea provided for us. After we had had a walk round we started our journey home, and arriving at the Conservative Club again we were given a complimentary dinner to celebrate the winning of the Midland League. What a day we had (and night!) The two cups in front of the group [he is referring here to the team photograph overleaf] are the handsome Kettering Charity Cup and the Northants Senior Cup, both of which we won that season. We were also finalists in the Luton Charity Cup. After the dinner the cups were filled, and were handed round a few times. Mr. Charles Robinson, chairman of the committee [and newly-elected president of the Midland League], presented the championship medals to each one of the players, and I am pleased to say that I have still got mine, and proud of it, too.

1895-96 remains one of the best seasons in the club's history. Two major factors in Kettering's success were Joe McMain, who scored at least 28 goals in 42 competitive games (14 goals are still unaccounted for) and their home form – unbeaten in the town in 27 league, cup and friendly fixtures. Even so, looking back now, one fact stands out: Kettering were the first winners of the Midland League never to have (to date) tasted life in the Football League.

Kettering FC, 1895-96.

Back Row: Charles Robinson (chairman of the committee), Sammy Wallis, Alf Heskin, William Perkins, William Draper (captain), Jummy Panter, Alf Ball, Albert Toseland, George Campbell (trainer), Charles Bullock (club secretary). Middle row: William Pell, Teddy Panter, Jack Ashworth, Joe McMain, William Miller, William Mablestone. Front row: Jackie Whitehouse, Harry Dixon.

The photograph was taken at the conclusion of the season on the lawn of the Conservative Club, before the celebratory tour of the surrounding villages described on the previous page. The larger of the silverware on display is the Kettering Charity Cup, whilst on the ground sits the Northants Senior Cup.

The trainer, George Campbell, had taken over from Charlie Dixon the previous season and would continue to act in this capacity well into the 1900s. Albert Toseland later described him as "a very good trainer ... very strict, but he knew his job and did it well."

The only arrivals from outside the district this season were West Bromwich Albion's Thomas Green, and James Atherton from Leicester Fosse, the latter as a replacement for the popular William Mablesone, who departed for Reading before a ball was kicked. One man it proved impossible to replace was prolific goal scorer Joe McMain, whose last game for Kettering was to be at Woolwich Arsenal on 2 November 1896, before he signed for First Division Wolverhampton Wanderers for a fee of £50. Seven different players would be tried in McMain's centre-forward position, none of them with any real success.

Mr A. de Sales Turland of Isham accepted the club presidency after the position was rendered vacant by the untimely death of Harry Hanger, aged 40, on 2 October. Named Henry at birth, but generally referred to as Harry, he was a shoe manufacturer (of Montagu Works) who played for Kettering between 1872 and 1878 – taking part in the first game against Uppingham School when he was just 16 years old. His brothers Charlie and Fred also played for the club.

On 7 December, West Bromwich Albion sent a team to play a benefit match for William Draper. 'Ducky', as he was known, had had a successful trial for Kettering during the 1889-90 campaign, and in his third year with the club had played in every position on the field. In 1893 he joined Burton Wanderers but returned to Kettering at the end of the following season. Thereafter he became a regular in the side until 1904 when, following a brief spell at Wellingborough, he would take up a position as trainer with Queens Park Rangers. During his time at Kettering and Burton, Draper won five winners and five runners-up medals in assorted competitions. Married, he worked as a clicker at the same Montagu Works with which Harry Hanger was associated. His benefit match finished a goal apiece.

1896 saw the advent of the United League; a relatively short-lived, mid-week competition made-up mostly of East Midlands, Home Counties and London clubs that wished to add more competitive games to their fixture lists. The founder members were Kettering (Midland League), Loughborough Town (Football League Second Division), Luton Town (no other league commitments), Millwall Athletic (Southern League), Rushden Town (Midland League), Tottenham Hotspur (Southern League), Wellingborough Town (Midland League) and Woolwich Arsenal (Football League Second Division). As a consequence of Kettering effectively playing the first team in both the United and Midland leagues, only three cup competitions were entered and just six friendlies arranged.

Despite the Reds falling at the first hurdle in the Kettering Charity and Senior Cups, history repeated itself in the FA Cup when, after beating Rushden and Mansfield, they once more accounted for Leicester Fosse, this time by two goals to one in front of 5,000 excited spectators at North Park – and were again drawn away to Newton Heath in the first round. The *Northampton Mercury*'s Kettering correspondent made the trip up to Manchester to be amongst the crowd of 4,000 to record the day:

WITH THE REDS AT NEWTON HEATH

When I left home at eight o'clock on Saturday morning the prospects of a trip to Manchester were not at all inviting. The streets were covered in slush, sleet was falling, and, from appearances overhead, threatened to continue falling throughout the day. Half-way up the street I overtook another supporter, who voluntarily confessed himself to be a confounded fool for turning out a morning like that to see a football match, and almost repenting that he had left his comfortable bed so early. Together we proceeded in the direction of the station, and from the deserted appearance of the streets, it seemed likely that we should be the only supporters enthusiastic enough to follow the fortunes of our players on such a day. However, I was pleased to see a nice little company waiting at the station, eagerly discussing the probabilities of the weather. The special was only a few minutes late, and eventually ran into the Central Station at Manchester at 12.45, only half an hour behind time. If the weather in the Midlands was rough, it threatened to be still worse at Cottonopolis. The air was exceedingly heavy and very raw, and a fine rain made everything damp and miserable as we emerged into

MANCHESTER'S DIRTY STREETS.

After a good dinner, I set out for Bank-lane, Clayton, the home of the "Heathens." Now Newton Heath is not regarded as the Belgravia of Manchester; in fact, some parts of the East End of London would compare most favourably with this uninviting district, and although I am not very well versed in nationalities I should say that every nation upon earth has its representatives in the Newton Heath district. Lancashire clogs are in evidence on every hand, whilst hats or bonnets appear to be an unknown habiliment amongst the fair sex of the locality; and so far as one could judge, Luton does not make its fortune by Newton Heath. As the "Heathens'" ground is nearly four miles from the city, one has to look pretty smart in securing a seat upon one of the trams which stop close to the grounds. I reached the ground half an hour before the kick off, and found it almost as bleak as the North Park. No alterations had been carried out since Kettering were there last season, and the ground certainly looked worse than ever. The snow had been carted off, and the turf, or rather the place where the turf should be, covered with what appeared to be

A MIXTURE OF SAND AND CINDERS.

There were numerous pools of water about, a fact which the players quickly became aware of when they commenced running. Towards three o'clock the spectators arrived in crowds, and there was a very respectable gate when Captain Draper led his men on to the field amidst a storm of cheering. In the preliminary canter some of the players quickly came to grief. Heskin, Draper, and others suddenly finding an attachment for mother earth. Whilst this little exhibition was causing amusement to the spectators, Cesar Jenkyns led on the "Heathens" amidst a tremendous outbreak of applause from the home supporters. No time was lost, and Jenkyns having beaten Draper with the coin, chose to kick with the wind in his favour. The commencement was sensational in the extreme. Ball, Miller, and Graham got close to Barrett's charge before Errentz cleared. Wallis splendidly returned, and Heskin helping the ball across the Newton goal, Dixon dashed in and shot into the corner of the net. Kettering supporters cheered, fair-minded "Heathens" said "Well played," and again the teams were at it "hammer and tongs." The Kettering defence had a lively period, but beyond a fruitless corner nothing tangible occurred. For some time the "Reds" [their opponents were possibly in a strip of white shirts and blue shorts] played splendidly, and the Newton defence was severely tried. It stood proof against all attacks, however, and a free kick against the "Reds" sent them near to their own goal. The ball was dropped well in front, and although Draper and Wallis made a game effort to get the ball away, Donaldson equalised with a low shot. End to end play followed for some time, the defence on either side being remarkably good. The home team appeared to be much more at home on the frozen ground than the "Reds," and their clever forward play, supported by the ever resourceful Jenkyns at centre half, was a source of considerable anxiety to the visitors' defence. The extreme men on either wing appeared to have too much liberty from the opposing half backs, neither Atherton nor Pell, the former especially, covering Bryant and Cassidy sufficiently. The result was many dangerous centres from these players, which it took all the skill of Draper, Wallis, and Perkins to divert from scoring. However, the breathing space arrived at last, with the scores equal, and there certainly seemed a possible chance for Kettering, considering that they now had the advantage of the breeze. Mr. Tomlinson allowed a lengthy interval, and on resuming the "Reds" at once took up the running. Graham and Whitehouse forced a corner, but the home backs came to the rescue and placed their forwards in possession. Bryant got well away, but found a stumbling block in the Kettering skipper, whose men returned to the attack. As time drew on, however,

THE FORWARD PLAY OF THE VISITORS

fell off, partly owing to Ball having received an injury, and Whitehouse being completely off colour. The half backs made strenuous exertions to make up for the shortcomings of the forwards, of whom Dixon appeared the only one able to maintain his equilibrium, but their strength fell before the vigour of the homesters' attacks. Gillespie and Cassidy were a terrible handful for Pell, and it was from this side that the danger was most to be feared. After a lot of manoeuvring round the Kettering goal, Perkins only partly saved from Gillespie, with the result that Bryant dashed up and gave the "Heathens" the lead. This was bad, with our forwards practically helpless, but worse was to follow. Within less than five minutes Cassidy had scored two more goals, thus putting the issue beyond doubt, to the jubilation of the "Heathens'" supporters. Before the finish the score had been made 5-1, Donaldson putting on the last point close on time. Perkins was at fault with at least two of the goals, although at times he saved

IN A MASTERLY MANNER.

Neither Draper nor Wallis were seen at their best, the terrible state of the ground evidently troubling the Kettering skipper considerably. Heskin struck me as being the best of the halves, both Pell and Atherton having masterly wings to oppose. Dixon was by far the best forward, and should have been fed more. Miller, Ball, and Graham worked hard, but Whitehouse, in the second half especially, was practically useless. For the winners Cassidy deserves the palm of the praise, whilst the backs were at all times a match for the opposing forwards. Just a word as to Cesar Jenkyns. If ever a player had a bad name and an unenviable notoriety for rough and violent play, surely that man is Cesar Jenkyns, late of Woolwich Arsenal. Such being the case, it is due to him to say that he played the most gentlemanly game on Saturday. He did not charge unnecessarily, whilst his exhibition was almost perfect football. Well, we lost, and lost easily, but we have our consolation, poor though it be, and that is that we advanced further than any other club in the county in the competition, and again had the satisfaction of beating Leicester Fosse. The trippers mostly spent the evening in viewing the sights of Cottonopolis, and leaving again at 11.30, Kettering was safely reached in the small hours of Sunday morning. [The match was played on 30 January 1897.]

The club was again undefeated at North Park during the Midland League campaign, but the away record of ten loses in fourteen games ensured a disappointing fifth place finish, with Doncaster Rovers taking the title.

Kettering fared even less well in the United League, finishing sixth – two places off the bottom. It was during one of the club's United League fixtures that tragedy struck when, on Monday, 23 November 1896, Woolwich Arsenal made their first competitive visit to the town (their very first appearance in Kettering had been for a friendly at Eldred's Field in 1892, six years after the club's formation by a group of workers at the Royal Arsenal armaments factory in Woolwich). Originally called Dial Square (after a section of the factory), the name was quickly changed to Royal Arsenal, followed by Woolwich Arsenal when they turned professional in 1891. The 'Woolwich' part of the title would become redundant after their move to Highbury in North London in 1913, but the club's humble beginnings are still remembered today in its nickname the 'Gunners'.

Just after half-time in the fateful match, which was settled by a single goal in Arsenal's favour, the visitors' full-back, Joe Powell, fell heavily and broke his left arm. On Friday, 4 December, the *Kettering Leader & Observer* conveyed the sad news that Powell had passed away the previous Sunday:

SAD DEATH OF A FOOTBALLER.

Result of an Accident at Kettering.

We are sorry to announce that the accident reported in our last issue to Joseph Powell, the Woolwich Arsenal back player, has had a fatal termination, the unfortunate player passing away on Sunday last.

The coroner's inquiry into the death was held at the Invicta Hall, Plumstead, on Wednesday evening, before Mr. Wood... – Mr. James Crone, of 48, Mount-street, Charlton, an engineer, who went to Kettering with the team on the same day, gave evidence. About half-past three deceased went to kick the ball, which was a good distance from the ground, but within his reach. He lifted his left foot in the air and it lighted on one of the Kettering player's shoulders. He lost his balance and fell backwards, and broke his left arm in the fall. – The Coroner: You consider it was an accident? Oh yes, quite. There was no rough play. Every care was taken of deceased. At Kettering a doctor set deceased's arm. – The Coroner: How did he bear it? Capital, and, under the circumstances, exceedingly well. No one expected a fatal result. – Mr. George Henry Porter, another director of the [Arsenal] club, said the Kettering ground had a "dip." Powell, when in the act of kicking the ball, tipped over in consequence. – George Buist, who played in the match, said the Kettering centre-forward was in the act of "heading" the ball, which was in the air. Powell went to kick it, and fell with great force, having lost his balance. – Dr. R. Williams, of Woolwich, said deceased had had several accidents lately – one to his left foot, and one to the same arm that was broken [Powell had already earned the sobriquet 'Unfortunate Joe']. On the night of the 23rd ult. witness saw deceased. He suffered from a fracture of the radius and a compound fracture of the left arm. The arm had been properly set. Deceased continued to improve until Friday, when he complained of stiffness of the jaws – an indication of tetanus. Witness took steps to prevent the growth of lockjaw, and on the Saturday called in Dr. Symonds, of Guy's Hospital, who suggested the amputation of the arm as a last resource. Witness continued to inject large doses of anti-toxin, and had great difficulty in getting supplies. The operation was performed, but deceased died at a quarter to one on Sunday morning [29 November, six days after the game] from tetanus, caused by dirt introduced into the wound at Kettering... – The Coroner said it was a terrible thing to see a young man die like that. Football seemed as bad as actual warfare, as Powell had already met with other accidents. He was glad to find there was no blame attaching to anyone. – The jury returned a verdict of "Death from tetanus, caused by an injury received whilst playing football on 23rd November." The jury expressed their admiration of Dr. Williams' conduct.

The funeral took place yesterday, in the new cemetery at Plumstead, the coffin being borne on the shoulders of six of his late fellow-players... The Kettering club was represented by its treasurer (Mr. Sidney Gibson), and he conveyed the wreath sent by the club, which was a lovely floral token, consisting of white roses, camelias, eucharis, and chrysanthemums.

The *Morning Leader* has opened a fund for the benefit of the widow and child.

UNITED LEAGUE.

KETTERING v. WOOLWICH ARSENAL.

INJURY TO A PLAYER.

The return match between Kettering and Woolwich Arsenal was played on the North Park, Kettering, on Monday.—Both teams were well represented, Pell being absent from the Kettering team through a family bereavement, T. Miller taking his place, and a noticeable absentee of the visitors was Crawford. A good deal of interest was manifested in the match, there being nearly 2,000 persons present. Mr. T. Hotson, of Birmingham, was the referee, and the teams lined up as under :–

Kettering.– Perkins, goal; Wallis and Draper, backs; T. Miller, Ball, and Atherton, half-backs; Whitehouse and Panter, right wing; E. Wright, centre ; Miller and Dixon, left wing.

Woolwich Arsenal.– Fairclough, goal; Buist and Powell, backs; Shrewsbury, Boyle, and Boylan, half-backs; Brock and Heywood, right wing; Boyd, centre ; Russell and McAvoy, left wing.

The visitors in the first half kicked from the entrance end, and the Arsenal gave a good exhibition of dashing play, their forwards especially showing up well. On several occasions the Ketts lost the easiest of chances. The ball was sent right across the mouth of goal, and no less than three players missed it when they had only the goalkeeper to beat. The match continued to be evenly fought, but neither side could score, and the interval came with the game standing –

Kettering 0
Woolwich Arsenal 0

Soon after restarting a most unfortunate and deplorable accident occurred. Powell, the visitors' right back, who had been playing magnificently, made a high jump to clear from an invasion by the opposing forwards and caught one of his legs on Wright's shoulders, and fell to the ground on his left arm, causing a compound fracture near to the wrist. He was at once taken off the field, and was afterwards attended to at Mr. Dryland's surgery. A collection was soon made on the ground, and a good sum was collected. With only ten men the Arsenal played up pluckily, and there was little to choose between the two teams. Just after came the only goal of the match. Russell essayed a run, and, eluding Wallis, centred to Boyd. Perkins saved the shot he sent in by throwing himself full length at it. The ball went out to Brock, and he returning it to Boyd, that player had no difficulty in scoring. After this Kettering made strenuous but unsuccessful efforts to score, and when the whistle blew the score stood –

WOOLWICH ARSENAL 1
KETTERING 0

During the early part of the day rain fell heavily so the ground was in a slippery condition. The rain abated before the match, but the clouds were threatening, and very few spectators assembled, there being less than fifty present when the match commenced. Play was even from the commencement, but it was affected by the rain which fell in torrents and rendered the ground worse than before. Some amusement was caused by the splashes and falls. It speaks a good deal for the enthusiasm which football engenders that a good proportion of the lookers-on, having brought their umbrellas into requisition, still remained in the enclosure. When Kettering conceded a corner, and the ball had been placed in good position from this, some exciting play was witnessed. Draper, however, headed away at a critical moment, and the right wing reversing Wright was seen to advantage, with the result that from a fine centre by Dixon, Panter netted the ball about seven minutes from the start. In the end to end play which followed both custodians were called upon though Draper put in some effective work, and before the game had been in progress another ten minutes Milliken had equalised. Play was still of an equal nature, and as the rain still continued the players and referee presented a sorry spectacle. At last, when a few minutes remained from half-time, the referee wisely decided to stop the play. The pools of water were thus the scenes of no more fun, and the players and referee left in a drenched condition. Some of the spectators, too, were not much better off.

Above: The Kettering Guardian's *report of the club's United League game against Tottenham Hotspur on 15 March 1897 – a contest that was abandoned just before half-time due to the weather.*

Opposite: The Kettering Leader & Observer's *report of the tragic Woolwich Arsenal encounter on 23 November 1896. Some 45 years later, Albert Toseland recalled the effect the incident had on Ernest Wright – the Kettering player involved: "I don't think "Ern" ever played again for the Town. He took it very much to heart, yet it was not his fault at all, but a pure accident."*

It was later reported that Powell's death was the first recorded fatality in British professional football. Irrespective of whether or not he was indeed the first *professional* to pass on as a result of an injury sustained whilst plying his trade, there is no doubting that football in Victorian times could be a downright dangerous sport (some sources indicate that around 100 men died during the 1890s playing football of one code or another).

Another team making their first visit to North Park was Tottenham Hotspur. Formed in 1882 simply as Hotspur FC, their title became a little grander two years later when they became known as Tottenham Hotspur Football & Athletic Club. Turning professional as late as 1895 and having been elected to the Southern League only this season, Tottenham's rise up the ranks would be rapid. They would move to White Hart Lane (from Northumberland Park) in 1899, win the Southern League a year later and, a year after that, become the only truly non-League club to win the FA Cup. Election to the Football League would follow in 1908.

Whilst the Arsenal match resulted in tragedy, the Tottenham encounter ended in farce. Rain and hail greeted the North London club on their arrival in the town but the fixture went ahead despite the atrocious conditions. However, it soon became obvious to the few spectators in attendance that, although the spectacle was amusing, it was hardly football, and the abandonment came with the score standing at a goal apiece. The match was rearranged for 13 April 1897, when Kettering ran out easy winners by five goals to two. Despite the promise of a brighter future, Tottenham eventually finished bottom of the United League, 17 points adrift of champions Millwall.

The curtain came down on Kettering's season with a 2-0 victory over Wellingborough on Monday, 26 April, which proved to be the club's final game at North Park. After having spent just four seasons here, it was time once again to up-sticks and move on.

It is worth recording that, athough the senior team ended the campaign without winning silverware, Kettering's footballers did enjoy some success when the reserves entered the Northamptonshire League (established the previous season and later to be known as the United Counties League) and finished as champions. They also won the Northants Junior Cup, beating Rothwell Swifts by five goals to nil in the final.

Ten

Rockingham Road

1897 - 1899

"It must be considerable interest in the game that draws those who have two milestones to pass before reaching the ground. Then again, there is not the least shelter of any kind. Even the players had to dress in a barn, the dressing tent not having been erected. But there is no-one who has a worse time of it than the reporters. A lad is engaged to hold an umbrella; under this the reporter crouches as best he can, the rain blows on to his copy rendering it almost undecipherable in some places, and altogether obliterating some of the adjectives which he would not have used under more favourable circumstances."

The move from Eldred's Field to North Park had been short-lived. When the club relocated in 1897 it proved far more permanent. The site of Kettering's home for what is now well over a century first appears on an 1875 plan of land for sale, situated adjacent to the road (marked on the document as Turnpike Road) leading north out of town towards Rockingham. The plan shows an area belonging to John Turner Stockburn divided into lots, bordered approximately by what are now Charles Street, Bath Road, Kingsley Avenue and Cowper Street (none of which existed at the time). The land to the north is owned by Viscountess Hood, and to the south by William Toller. Between what would become Cowper Street and Rockingham Road is a field detached from Stockburn's lots, recorded as being in the ownership of the trustees of the late James Bailey. Today, the majority of that field is the site of Kettering Town's (leased) Rockingham Road ground, a car park, a bowling alley and a few properties on Kingsley Avenue.

The town's senior club was not the first to play football here. On 20 January 1933, the *Kettering Leader* printed a photograph of Kettering Fuller Juniors and a snippet of information: "This photo was taken nearly 40 years ago, the club became Kettering Victorias. They used to play in Hale's meadow but then moved to Bob Hall's field on the Rockingham road, now used by Kettering Town, only that the pitch was across the top, instead of up the slope." And on 2 September 1960, writing in the *Northamptonshire Advertiser*, Jack Dainty (who would sign for Kettering in 1898) recalls that in February 1896 he played for Geddington Stars against Kettering Athletic in the vicinity of present-day Kingsley Avenue – the northern boundary of the field in which the club's ground would rise: "We changed in a hovel on farm premises. I remember the ploughman came in with his horses when we were changing after the match."

When the Reds arrived at their new home for the start of the 1897-98 season, the ground was still little more than a field sloping down towards Rockingham Road, and the amenities were extremely basic, as noted in the *Kettering Guardian* after the club's first match here – a Midland League encounter with Ilkeston on Saturday, 4 September:

> This year Kettering have said good-bye to the North Park, and have taken a field off the Rockingham road. This site is certainly not so level as the other. A few days ago it did not look very favourable for football but since then "Tommy Dodd" has been over it, and the ground is now in very fair condition. It is, however, a pity that a more central site could not have been secured. The field is perhaps not quite so far as the North Park from the centre of town, though there is very little in it, and the north part

of the town is that most interested in the game. But what a long way from the railway station! [Most visiting teams would have arrived via the railway, as would many spectators from the surrounding towns and villages.] It must be considerable interest in the game that draws those who have two milestones to pass before reaching the ground. Then again, there is not the least shelter of any kind. Even the players had to dress in a barn, the dressing tent not having been erected. But there is no-one who has a worse time of it than the reporters. A lad is engaged to hold an umbrella; under this the reporter crouches as best he can, the rain blows on to his copy rendering it almost undecipherable in some places, and altogether obliterating some of the adjectives which he would not have used under more favourable circumstances. How will it be in the depth of winter? Surely something could be done to remedy this state of affairs. The absence of shelter must affect the attendance considerably. This was apparent to the full on Saturday [the crowd at the commencement of the match was estimated at 1,000 – a figure that doubled after the rain abated]. The "standing slats" have been removed from the North Park it is true, but a structure of some kind, sufficient to screen spectators from the elements, would not be very expensive in comparison with the benefits, and the cost would most likely be recouped in a little time.

KETTERING FOOTBALL CLUB.

OPENING OF NEW GROUND, ROCKINGHAM ROAD.

Grand Match
KETTERING v. ILKESTON,
TO-MORROW, SATURDAY, SEPT. 4TH.

A de Sales Turland, Esq., President of the club, has kindly consented to kick off at 3 o'clock.

The Kettering Town Silver Band have generously given their services, and will parade the town and play a selection at the interval.

Admission, 6d. and 1s.

The advert for Kettering's first game at Rockingham Road as it appeared in the local press on Friday, 3 September 1897.

If the weather and facilities off the pitch were less than might have been hoped for, it was even worse on it, as Kettering, playing the majority of the game with ten men after Everard Lawrence was forced to retire through injury, went down by three goals to nil. A result that ended a run of 33 Midland League home games without defeat stretching back to 23 February 1895. Quite an anticlimax!

A fortnight later, the next visitors to experience the sloping pitch were the previous season's champions, Doncaster Rovers. This time Kettering ran out 1-0 winners – G. York being credited as the scorer of the club's first goal at Rockingham Road. It was, according to the *Kettering Guardian*'s hapless correspondent, another foul afternoon with regards to the weather:

> Just before the game started a heavy downpour sent the players running to the dressing tent and the supporters to the surrounding hedges. Hundreds of umbrellas were brought into requisition but the strong wind rendered them of little service. The rain continued for two thirds of the match. It is not surprising that some supporters are talking about "DONCATHTER" with accent that tells that the usual concomitants for a cold have not had the desired effect. Surely enthusiasm for football goes a long way when it is watched under such conditions.

Overall, the club's league results were disappointing, not helped by players like Alf Ball, Alf Heskin and Jack Whitehouse departing at the end of the previous season. And the loss of these men was compounded by some poor replacements. Of the non-local signings, only Jack Brearley from Notts County took part in a significant number of games. However, there was some light at the end of the tunnel; Heskin returned to the club for the latter stages of the campaign, whilst a Geddington lad by the name of Herbert Dainty, and James Garfield of Finedon, both made their mark (although the latter, who played in every game to the end of January, would be suspended for two months after failing to agree terms with the committee).

Dainty had been spotted by club officials Charles Robinson and Charles Bullock the previous season as they watched the conclusion of the Kettering & District Football Combination – The Champions (Geddington Stars) versus The Rest of the League. They had been so impressed with the 16-year-old that they signed him there and then.

A paltry 19 goals in 22 matches (ten different players were tried in the centre-forward position) ensured the Reds would finish no higher than seventh in the Midland League this time around, just below mid-table.

Kettering fared slightly better in the United League, attaining fourth place (nine clubs entered), just two points shy of Tottenham Hotspur and Woolwich Arsenal, but some way behind champions Luton Town. Tottenham made their first visit to Rockingham Road on Monday, 10 January 1898. Once again, judging by a report in a late edition of the *Evening Telegraph* (a daily publication that had appeared on the streets just a few months earlier), the weather was far from perfect:

KETTERING V. TOTTENHAM HOTSPUR.

The third meeting this season between these clubs took place at Kettering to-day. The first time was very early in the season. This match, which was a League match, ended in a pleasurable surprise, the Ketts succeeding in making a draw [1-1]. The play of the visitors met with much approval, and a few weeks ago the clubs again opposed each other on the Spurs ground in a friendly. This game was also keenly fought, and the home team won by the narrow margin of two to one. As since then Kettering have improved, it was not too much to expect that they would have the best of the encounter on the Rockingham-road Ground this afternoon. Still, the Spurs team, which possesses several ex-First Division League men, is not one to be despised wherever they may be met, and it was evident that the "reds" would have to continue the good form they have shown of late if they were to win. The Kettering team was the same as has performed in the last several matches. The 'Spurs' team was the same as took to the field against Rushden on Saturday. The teams were, therefore, as follows:–

Kettering.– Perkins, goal; Wallis and Draper, backs; Pell, Dainty, and Atherton, half-backs; Garfield and Panter, right wing; Brearley, centre; Miller and Dixon, left wing.

Tottenham.– Cullen, goal; Knowles and Montgomery, backs; Hall, Jones, and Stormont, half-backs; Hartley and Davidson, right wing; Joyce, centre; Madden and Black, left wing.

Referee: Mr. Fuller.

A fog hung over the ground, and it was uncertain prior to the match whether it would lift sufficiently to allow of a good view of the game being obtained. Tottenham won the toss, and Kettering were set to kick uphill. Dixon was pulled up for being off-side, although the decision was a doubtful one... The teams took some time to warm to their work, the opening movements being of a dilatory nature. Kettering were awarded a free well in, and Panter hooked on to the net. The leather being kept in the visiting half, it was not removed until the Tottenham left gained possession. They were then soon pulled up for fouling, but returning Perkins had to deal with a swift low shot. Matters brightened up after this, and Atherton sent by. Pell sent in a flyer, but Cullen saved. The home left and centre were conspicuous, and Panter grazed the upright. The 'Spurs' backs cleared finely on several occasions, and the goalkeeper got away splendidly a shot from Brearley, following some smart play by the centre. But the ball was not removed far away, and a series of shots from short range were sent in. The goal, however, escaped in a surprising manner. The match was now being fought at a rapid rate. Davidson missed a good chance by wild shooting. Kettering were pulled up for off-side as they were getting dangerous. Black forced a corner, and being well placed, the ball was shot through a forest of legs into the net, the visitors thus scoring. Soon after the re-start the visitors were awarded a free near the Kettering goal, and owing to the Reds being very slow on the ball the Kettering goal was again threatened. The home forwards broke away, and Brearley had a go. The ball, however, went wide of the mark, and Kettering were placed on the defensive. End to end play followed. The home right worked the ball up, and although Dixon headed through the referee instead of allowing the Ketts a goal gave the left winger off-side. The passing of the visitors was good, and Wallis well checked one of the rushes in excellent style. The visitors were penalised for unfair tactics, and a corner ensued. Brearley made a grand run and all but got through, but he was hampered too much, and Dainty sent over. Brearley passed out well to Dixon, who failed to take advantage of a good opening. Draper kicked away a shot from the left, and a centre by Dixon was not improved upon. The first half – of which one team had had as much of the play as the other – came to a close with the score –

Tottenham 1

Kettering 0

Kettering started in the second half as though they meant business, and a free fell to them. Tottenham fouled again, and from the resultant kick Brearley headed through amidst much cheering. The game, when this success was attained, had only been in progress a few minutes. Even play followed for a minute or two, but then Kettering again commenced to attack, and Miller ran through with the ball, thus giving Kettering the lead. Two goals were thus scored by the Reds in less than ten minutes, and the spectators were naturally immensely pleased. The Ketts were now monopolising the game, and the visitors, not at all liking the sudden change in their fortunes, showed it by committing a foul or two on their opponents. The worst being that in which Brearley, who had almost forced his way through unaided, was the victim. The Kettering goal was, however, jeopardised owing to Wallis giving a corner. The visitors did not improve on it, and by the aid of another foul Kettering again gave the 'Spurs' defence trouble. The Tottenham right broke away, and in consequence of Draper falling it looked as if they had a good chance. But the Ketts fouled, and the free did not avail the southerners much. Just afterwards, however, Perkins had some trouble in getting the ball away, and in the visiting half Cullen had just as much difficulty in getting rid while surrounded by a number of players. Between them Panter and Brearley came within an ace of scoring. The latter finished up with a swift low shot, which must have scored had not the leather come into contact accidentally with one of the backs. As it was a corner resulted, and from this Kettering gained a third goal, this point coming after a short scrimmage underneath the cross-bar. The 'Spurs' failed in their efforts to get away, and the Ketts were soon back again. They were pulled up for being off-side. Dixon put in a good run, and a corner accrued. This was unproductive. Still the Ketts for the greater part kept in the Tottenham half. On one occasion they got uncomfortably close, and for Joyce being held Tottenham were given a penalty. The visitors' centre took it, and Perkins, who did not come out, was beaten with a shot that went into the corner of the net, making the score three to two in favour of Kettering. The first noticeable bit of play after the ball had been kicked off from the centre was a very good try by Miller to run through. He just failed, and the Kettering goal was hard put to. The Tottenham goal also narrowly escaped. Towards the close both teams struggled desperately, and Miller put the issue beyond doubt by scoring a fourth goal with a fairly long shot. It now only wanted two or three minutes to time, and the game ended with the score –

KETTERING 4

TOTTENHAM HOTSPUR 2

A third-qualifying-round 1-0 home defeat at the hands of Wellingborough ensured there would be no repeat of the Manchester trips in the FA Cup. Kettering and their county rivals would lock horns on no less than eight occasions before the season ended. The Reds beating their neighbours 9-0 in a benefit match arranged for Harry Dixon, as well as winning all four Midland League and United League fixtures, but Wellingborough held sway in the cup games, winning two of the three played, including the final of the Wellingborough Charity Cup.

En route to the final, which Wellingborough won 1-0, Kettering encountered Northampton Town, a club that had only been formed the previous March. Kettering won the match, played at Rockingham Road on 29 January, by two goals to nil – exactly one week after the Red's reserve side had gone to Northampton and beaten them 3-2 (the county town's first competitive defeat on home soil). Kettering's second team and Northampton's first were both playing in Division One of the Northamptonshire League. Kettering Reserves ended the season as champions for the second year running, as well as lifting the Northants Junior Cup, also for the second successive year.

And there was silverware for the club's senior team, too. In fact two cups were won: the Senior Cup, which was played for on a round robin basis (an attempt by the county FA to revive dwindling interest in its competition) – the Reds beating Finedon Revellers and Wellingborough and drawing with Rushden; and the Kettering Charity Cup, in which wins over Burton Wanderers and Wolverton set up what was to be the highlight of the season on Monday, 25 April, when Rushden visited Rockingham Road for the final. The 'Holy Friar', the *Evening Telegraph*'s unashamedly pro-Kettering correspondent, takes up the story:

Kettering 7, Rushden 0.

There's something to feast your eyes upon, my worthies. Would you have thought it possible? No – rather impossible. But that was the number by which Kettering yesterday wiped the Russians off the face of the earth. At any rate, if the team that were annihilated yesterday do not hide themselves from the scornful looks of their own kith and kin for a short time to come, they will display more pluck than they did in the memorable match yesterday.

For it truly was a remarkable game. Rushden are an eccentric team, and they did nothing to tarnish their reputation yesterday. Still, it is not against Kettering that they accomplish anything very wonderful. They either just win or lose. But yesterday they did not just lose – they were completely conquered, and ground under the heels of Kettering in a way they have perhaps never experienced before.

The five or six thousand people could hardly believe their own eyes. What came they out for to see? Rushden give up seven goals to their rivals? Not likely. But that was what they did witness, and their surprise was great. Nobody could have grudged their entrance money – excepting, of course, the supporters of the team that were going through such a terrible time of it. It was slow torture to the Rushdenites.

And what was Kettering's victory due to? Well, first of all, it was due to the continued improvement shown by the forwards more particularly, and that of the whole team in general. The Rushden defence could not hold the front rank, who showed that their exhibition on Saturday [when Kettering beat Southampton 2-1] was no fluke. Their play was hardly so pretty, but it was quite, if not more, effective, and Rushden did not know how to deal with their intelligent runs, their dash near goal, and their shots that did not lack steam.

Every man did finely, and a special word is due to Teddy Panter for scoring the best two goals of the day. One was obtained by a very good individual effort. Three goals were scored in the first half, and four in the second, and when Kettering scored their second goal there were no signs of the approaching storm. But people looked amazed when Kettering scored a third, and in the second half – well, Rushden were both in for it.

Instead of making leeway they were like a ship without a rudder cast in troublesome waters. Kettering simply walked round them, and ... scored four more goals, one of which came from a long shot taken by Draper within the Kettering half. It seemed an act of mercy to Rushden to blow the final whistle for time.

One or two words can be said in mitigation of their overwhelming defeat. First they had to contend with a team who undoubtedly played a fine game. In the second place they were not three goals behind Kettering in the first half. But no excuse can be offered for their total collapse in the other "45," and there is not the slightest doubt but that they were right down-hearted.

It was truly a great victory, and one that will not be forgotten for some time to come. What I sincerely hope now is that they will treat Wellingborough to a somewhat similar dose. "Hock" have not yet finished bragging and boasting about beating us by the very big margin of one goal the other week, and if the team are in the same humour as yesterday and Saturday we will pay that one goal – which they will never forget – back with interest. There should be a tremendous gate to see this other local club be made to know who their masters really are. They have lost their heads because they have won a few home matches lately. [Kettering went on to beat Wellingborough 2-1 in the last game of the season.]

The Friar's report concluded: "The games on Saturday and Monday were played with one of the pneumatic balls, and it appeared to give every satisfaction." Likely to be firmer and therefore more 'lively' than the balls that preceded it, this was a step in the gradual transition from an inflated bladder encased in a laced-up stitched-leather outer, which quickly absorbed water and became progressively heavier, to the modern-day relatively smooth weatherproof football.

Overleaf: Rockingham Road as it would appear from the air in the mid-1920s, followed by a section of the 1900 Ordnance Survey Map of Kettering.

Comparing the two images, it is possible to visualise the layout of the ground in the late 1890s. The central of the three stands in the photograph dates from circa 1898 (the other two from the 1910s and 20s); the barn (?) located to the rear of the stands, at the bottom of what is now the car park, also appears on the map; as does a structure between the Rockingham Road goal and the road itself – more than likely belonging to the Athletic Club – which has later been replaced by the more substantial buildings revealed in the photograph. Otherwise, at the end of the 19th century, there were few landmarks close to the ground.

What the photograph does not convey is the slope of the pitch. This is best described in a Portsmouth Football Mail article written in 1902, following the visit of Portsmouth for a Southern League fixture: "One of the trickiest and almost unfair pitches in the country. From end to end there is a fall of over twelve feet and the dip is most pronounced near the lower [Rockingham Road] goal, where it shelves off at such an angle as to completely upset the calculations of players accustomed to a level stretch of turf."

And the pitch markings were different prior to 1905. The halfway-line and centre-circle were already in use, but instead of penalty areas there would have been a line right across the pitch 12 yards from each goal-line, and 6-yard semicircles centred on each goalpost.

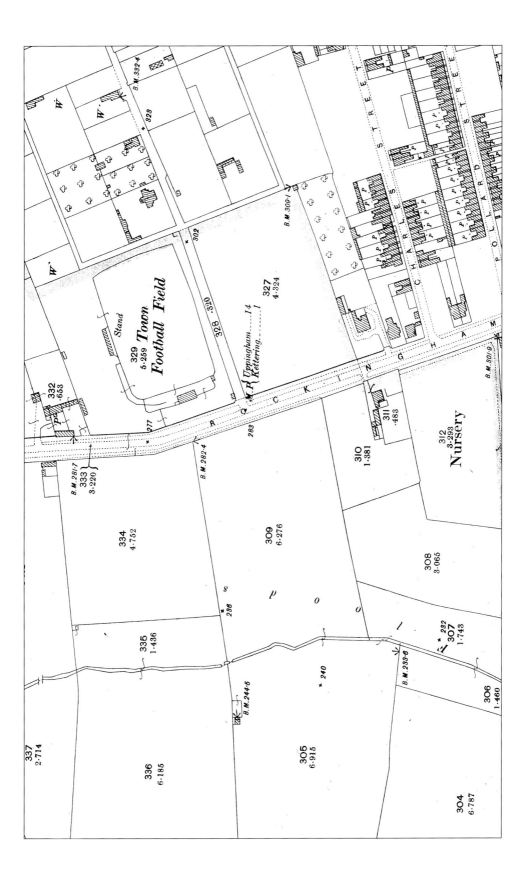

William 'Scotcher' Perkins.

William Perkins' career as a goalkeeper began at Burton Latimer Temperance. In 1895 he signed for Kettering, and during his first season was part of the side that won the Midland League, the Kettering Charity Cup and the Northants Senior Cup. In 1898 he moved to Luton Town, and less than a year later was transferred to Liverpool for £200. He played over 100 games for the Merseyside club – and was an ever-present in the team that secured their first Football League title in 1901. He returned south in 1903 to play for (and later captain) Northampton Town.

After his retirement from professional football in 1906, Perkins, like most of his contempories, still had to earn a living, and he can be found in the centre of the above image (captured circa 1930), surrounded by his fellow shoe workers at Buckby Bros. in Burton Latimer. A world away from the lot of a top-flight footballer today!

Rushden goalkeeper Ernest Baldry – a direct replacement for the excellent William Perkins, who left the club for Luton Town – was one of a number of local signings that included Jack Dainty, brother of Herbert. Also on their way out were James Garfield and James Atherton, to Gravesend and Bristol City respectively, whilst from points north and west came John Beaver (Preston), James McArlie (Glasgow) and W. Woodward (Hereford).

After the club's opening fixture – a United League encounter with Rushden on 3 September 1898, which Kettering won 1-0 (only to be docked the points later for having fielded Northampton's Jimmy Raynor, a player who *did* sign for the Reds but presumably not in time to be eligible for the Rushden game) – the *Kettering Guardian* reported on some improvements that had been made to Rockingham Road (or the Athletic Ground, as it was also referred to) during the summer:

> The ropes around the ground for the first game of the season were thickly lined with an excited crowd, while the grand-stand was fully occupied. The new fencing at the [Rockingham] road-end behind the goal meets a long felt necessity, but the accommodation for the reporters ought to be improved upon. The turf was in splendid condition. During the past week it has been widened to meet the requirements of the F.A. as regards cup matches, the width having been increased by two yards on each side which made the taking of corner kicks in the bottom corner rather difficult.

It is just as well that the FA's requirements had been met because the *Football Telegraph*'s description of the club's FA Cup fifth-qualifying-round tie against Leicester Fosse, played at Rockingham Road on 10 December, was: "The most important Association match which has ever taken place in this county." Leicester were third in the Second Division, but Kettering had already accounted for Loughborough (another side from the second tier of English football) in the previous round.

The grandstand was reportedly packed to bursting, and elsewhere supporters stood four or five deep behind the ropes. Many wore badges in their hats or lapels to show their allegiance; red for the home team and white for the Fossils. Kettering's players were at the ground at one o'clock and Leicester's arrived from training stables at Rushton half an hour later. The game kicked off at just gone 2.20 p.m. in front of around 5,000 expectant spectators.

It ended all square at a goal apiece, with the general consensus being that Kettering were unlucky not to win. A view the *Evening Telegraph*'s Holy Friar had no trouble in upholding the following Monday:

"Good old Kett!" That was the expression that assailed the ear as much as anything else on Saturday. Indeed, it was "Good old Kett." It was the Kett we love to see – fearless, dashing, plucky Kett; the Kett that accounted for the Fosse two years in succession, and that deserved to account for them again.

It was the Kett who stand as much in awe of the Fosse as they do of a team of juvenile football enthusiasts up a back street; the Ketts who would play as long as they can stand; and the Ketts who, in an English Cup tie, and on their own ground, would give any team a real good time of it.

And we are all sorry that they did not win. Well, that was not their fault; it was their misfortune. One cannot fight against fate, and truly it was the fate of the Reds to only draw. It was not because the players did not play well enough – they played grandly. It was not because Leicester were too good – they were distinctly the inferior team. No, it was due to none of these reasons. It was due, and due only, to the fortunes of the game going Leicester's way and dead against Kettering.

Whilst perhaps not in total disagreement with the Friar's opinions, the *Leicester Daily Post* carried a rather more sober account of proceedings:

Fosse supporters have reason to shake hands with themselves upon the result (a draw of one goal each) of Saturday's English Cup tie at Kettering. From a Leicester point of view, the game was a far more anxious than enjoyable one, for Kettering had really four-fifths of the play.

Kettering have had all the best of the English cup-ties between the teams in recent meetings, and a fact like this tells. The Fosse are a good Second League team, and the style of play associated with this football is altogether different from that seen in a local cup-tie. Some teams always seem to rise to the occasion in a cup-tie, and Kettering are one of these. They worry their opponents the whole of the 90 minutes, and their pulverising methods prevent even a good team from settling down to their usual play. Kettering are admittedly better hands at the cup-tie business than the Fosse.

Speaking generally, Fosse did not show their true form, and Kettering eclipsed themselves in their own style of play, on their own mountainous slope, and before their inspiring supporters. That just describes the whole conditions of play.

The goal which gave Kettering the lead was, to the Leicester supporters, a painful affair, the Fosse defence at the time being undoubtedly loose, for the opening should not have been obtained, and it looked as if the final shot – a slow daisy cutter – would have been saved by the agile Leicester goal-keeper. The latter, when the shot left Panter's foot, was at the opposite end of the goal, and, thinking the ball would pass wide of the post, Beardsley made no effort to save.

The question of the re-played tie is now the chief topic of conversation amongst Fosse supporters. After the match at Kettering an interview took place between the officials of the two clubs as to the date of the replayed tie. Fosse were anxious to replay the match on Wednesday, in view of the important League engagement with Newton Heath on the Saturday at Leicester. Kettering, on the other hand, favoured Thursday, contending that a better gate would ensue at Leicester on the half-holiday. No decision was arrived at on Saturday night, and even up to late last night (Sunday) the date had not been definitely decided; but in all probability the match will take place at Leicester on Thursday afternoon. A new ruling of the English Association allows replayed ties to take place on the following Thursday in case clubs do not mutually arrange to play off before that day.

The replay did indeed take place at Filbert Street the following Thursday, 15 December and, despite Leicester opening the scoring in the tenth minute, Kettering won the match 2-1 in the 90th. So, for the third time in four seasons, the club was one of the last 32 left in the competition. The draw for the first round paired Kettering with Notts County at Trent Bridge (home of Nottinghamshire County Cricket Club). It was the first time a team from Northamptonshire had been handed the opportunity to go up against a First Division side in the FA Cup, and when the Reds arrived in Nottingham, it was to face a club sitting fourth in the Football League.

The Kettering side that ran out at Trent Bridge on 28 January 1899 was Ernest Baldry, William Clarke, William Draper (captain), William Pell, Charlie Farren, Herbert Dainty, Herbert Winterhalder, Alf Heskin, Teddy Panter, John Beaver and Harry Dixon.

The image on this John Player & Sons cigarette card (issued in 1930) is of the original FA Cup (which was stolen in 1895 but replaced by an exact replica). The 'modern' trophy that supporters will be familiar with was not made until 1911.

Notts County won the Cup in 1894, five seasons before they met Kettering in the same competition. The oldest of the Football League's founding members, County was a well known and respected club at the time – and they could boast at least two players with international experience in the team they put out to face Kettering: goalkeeper Toone (of England) and Calderhead (of Scotland).

The odds were stacked against Kettering from the start and County, who were in no mood to be embarrassed, put in a thoroughly professional performance to win by two goals to nil. Writing in the *Evening Telegraph* two days after the event, the Friar was left to reflect on a day that saw his side defeated, but unbowed:

It does not need a glance at the above to know that for this season we shall strut no more on the stage of the English Football Cup Competition. We have played our part while we have been on in grand style, and we can retire knowing that we have done honour to our county.

We had more than ordinary antagonists to contend with on Saturday, by whom it was no discredit to be thrown. It is more than probable that any other club in the country would have met with precisely the same fate had they opposed Notts instead of ourselves, and it was also very possible that they would have lost by just as many. If Notts are beaten on their own ground in the competition their supporters will be greatly surprised – and so will many others.

For Kettering therefore to be defeated by only a couple of goals was anything but a disgrace. It was something of which they may well be intensely proud, taking all things into consideration. Notts were at home, cheered on by six thousand of their most loyal ones [the actual gate was close to 8,000, with at least 1,050 fans travelling from Kettering in two special trains]. The team was the strongest that could possibly have been put in the field. The players worked as though they knew they had no "snip" on, and gave a fine display. And yet they were only able to conquer the plucky Midland League team by two goals.

We had to succumb, but the way we did was no disgrace. It was the very opposite, and we did what perhaps no other club will be able to do – keep the Notts forwards from scoring for 43 minutes. The County string of forwards is a brilliant one, and, next to that of the Villa, is perhaps the best in the country. They are all fast, clever as they make 'em, grand shots – and they include Maconnachie [who scored the first Notts goal]. Yes, they comprise little "Mac," one of the finest forwards within this sea-girt island. He was the leading actor in this match, and the game was worth seeing if only on account of him.

He is young and he is not very big, although he is sturdily built. On this occasion he was in his really A1 form, and we had the pleasure of seeing him at his best. The subtlety of his play is marvellous. His skill is of the most refined nature, and the player who tries to dispossess him is apt to cut a sorry figure. There are no tricks of the trade but what he knows, besides which he manufacturers a number of his own to use when they are needed. His passes are well worked for and well judged, and his shots combine accuracy and power. In short, he is a marvel, and it would not be rash to prophecy for him ere long international honours.

It was a good thing for Notts that his injury did not prevent him playing, and the home people were of the same opinion, and that they were surprised at the form shown by Kettering will be gathered from the following, which appeared in the "Nottingham Football News":– "Probably not a score of individuals of the several thousands of Notts followers who made their way to Trent Bridge this afternoon anticipated such a keen struggle as that which took place. There is an old saying that when a superior team is pitted against an eleven of less 'class' the former quickly descend to the level of the latter. It cannot, however, be honestly said that such a criticism would hold good to-day. Kettering fought stubbornly throughout; they had reached the competition proper by real hard work, and they did not mean to resign it without a struggle. Consequently Notts were rather taken aback in the first half, but their ultimate triumph was only a matter of time, and, in view of the difficulty which they had in opening the scoring, the crowd was not at all inclined to grumble at the result, while more than one remarked as he left the ground, 'It's just as well that Maconnachie played, after all.' And to that remark I beg to add my modest 'Hear, hear.' The ex-Derby man had quite a field day, and from start to finish he was the life and soul of the vanguard..."

There is no doubt that had "Mac" not played – as it was thought possible he would not owing his injury – it would have made a great deal of difference to the winners. As it was they were distinctly the superior eleven. "Class will tell" is an old saying, and although it is not always true in regard to cup tie football, there was no doubt that it did so on Saturday. There were all the essentials to Notts showing their superiority, and they did so. It is no use shutting your eyes to facts, and so it is no use denying that by far the greater part of the operations were fought out in the Kettering half, and that compared with the visiting defence the home rearguard had an easy time of it.

But if Notts' greater skill enabled them to prevent Kettering getting often dangerous, it must also be admitted that they did not show up to very great advantage forward. For them to do so much aggressive work and yet only score two goals speaks well for the opposing defence, and the utmost praise is due to the Kettering defence for the magnificent way it succeeded against so formidable an attack. Their reputation was not tarnished in any way; the contrary was the case. Their efforts were characterised with that dash and pluck which has gained for them praise from all quarters.

Never before has Baldry been so severely tested. He had numerous shots – some of them most difficult ones – and he dealt with them in a magnificent manner, being again and again loudly applauded. It was a fine exhibition of goalkeeping, and Ern. cannot be too highly complimented on his display. He was well supported by the backs. It was a trying match for so young and comparatively inexperienced a player as the ex-Saints' back [referring to William 'Dillon' Clarke who was signed at the beginning of the season from Kettering St Mary's]. At first he was rather unsteady, but he afterwards settled down, and acquitted himself admirably. As for the captain, it would have been surprising had not he played as he did, viz.: a grand defensive game. The way he headed out caused surprise to the home followers.

The halves had a rare time of it with a slippery lot of forwards, but they met with a good deal of success, and on the whole did remarkably well. The forwards were not lacking in energy, but were not able to make much headway against the home strong defence. Perhaps they would have done better had they played a more open game instead of confining themselves to the short passing. Notts are used to this, and unless it is performed in a very high state of perfection is not likely to make much impression against a team like Notts. It would have been better to have adopted tactics to which Notts were not so familiar, and which would have put them about a good deal more.

But although they were not successful in their attempts, they are all deserving of commendation for the way they stuck to their work, Winterhalder especially. He distinguished himself by fine spirited runs, notwithstanding that he was well watched.

Considering the Forest v. Villa match, a gate of 8,000 was very good [just down the road, Cup-holders Nottingham Forest were playing Aston Villa in front of 32,070 – by far the highest first round attendance anywhere in the country that Saturday], and Kettering were enabled to clear about £100 [total gate receipts were £235]. So altogether we have not done badly this season in our cup battles. On the contrary, we have done exceedingly well. We have defeated two Second Division teams, and been defeated to the extent of two goals only by the club that stands as good a chance as anybody of winning the cup. [Notts County would lose by a goal to nil at home to Southern League Southampton in the next round!]

In the Midland League, the club remained undefeated at home and went into the last two games – both against bottom side Mexborough Town – needing three points to secure the championship. Inexplicably, a draw at home and a defeat away left Kettering in third place, behind Doncaster Rovers and Ilkeston Town.

It was stated that the club did not take the United League very seriously after finishing two places off the bottom, but it was arguably the most competitive league Kettering had ever played in, even more so this campaign with the addition of strong Bristol City and Reading sides.

There was a 3-0 defeat at the hands of Rushden in the semi-final of the Wellingborough Charity Cup, but the Reds took their revenge in beating the Russians 2-1 at Rockingham Road in a replayed Kettering Charity Cup final. The eighth clash of the season between the two Northamptonshire clubs came on 27 April, in the final of the Rushden Charity Cup. Despite being away from home and under pressure for much of the game, the defence held out and Kettering won by two goals to nil.

But the era of the charity cups was coming to an end. The club's victory over Rushden on Monday, 17 April was the last time that Kettering's was played for. Between 1888 and 1899 the competition raised £780 for the local community, initially benefiting the Northampton Infirmary and Kettering Dispensary, and later the Kettering Hospital Fund (the General Hospital opened on 30 October 1897).

In December 1904, Mr H.T. Favell would call together the committee responsible for the running of the Kettering Charity Cup – of which Messrs J.W. Dryland and H.F. Henson had acted as president and treasurer respectively throughout its 11 years – to officially wind up the competition and dispose of the valuable cup that had reclined, wrapped in velvet in a bank since 1899. In actual fact there had been two cups; the first was kept by Grantham Rovers after they won it on three successive occasions, and a second, valued at £90, had to be purchased to replace it. (Rovers eventually sold back the original and it became the trophy for the Kettering & District Football Combination.)

Professional football had, in effect, turned its back on altruism; clubs were no longer willing to undertake journeys without being paid, and the number of entrants fell away sharply when the FA decreed that even more of the profits generated by these competitions must go to worthy causes. So much for charity!

Kettering FC, 1898-99.

Back row: J.T. Smith (club secretary), G. West (reserve trainer), Sammy Wallis, Sammy Julian, Ernest Baldry, William Draper (captain), Albert Toseland, George Campbell (trainer), Sidney Gibson (club treasurer). Middle row: William Pell, William Clarke, Charlie Farren, Jack Dainty, Herbert Dainty. Front row: Herbert Winterhalder, Alf Heskin, Teddy Panter, W. Woodward, John Beaver, Harry Dixon.

RUSHDEN CHARITY CUP.

FINAL.

RUSHDEN V. KETTERING.

These teams met at Rushden yesterday in the final of the above competition. Teams:–

Rushden.– Daw, goal; Hendry and Clarke, backs; Sale, Bailey, and Dunkley, half-backs; Denton and Cole, right wing; Hingerty, centre; Pendered and Mellor, left wing.

Kettering.– Baldry, goal; Wallis and Draper, backs; Pell, J. Dainty, and H. Dainty, half-backs; Winterhalder and Heskin, right wing; Panter, centre; Beaver and Dixon, left wing.

Kettering won the toss, and availed themselves of a slight breeze, playing into the entrance goal. The visitors were the first to press, and Clarke knocked Panter off the ball in the mouth of the goal. Pendered and Mellor then cantered down, and got dangerously close, but Wallis succeeded in clearing. Kettering in their turn pressed, but Hendry was on the premises, and cleared. A foul against Clarke in front of the Rushden goal looked dangerous, but it was kicked behind by Draper. Then Rushden put in some telling work, Hingerty testing Baldry with a long shot, but the ex-Russian custodian was safe. Sale put in a grand shot, which looked like going through, but Pendered headed the ball on to the cross-bar, and directly afterwards Cole got off-side and spoilt a good opening. Rushden compelled Draper to yield a corner. Mellor placed well, but Dunkley kicked high over the cross-bar. Dixon then came down, and procured a grand opening, but shot straight into Daw's hands. Rushden took up the running, and Bailey put in a long shot which Baldry saved. Hingerty shot blindly, and the leather went high over the cross-bar. Rushden were now having the best of the play, Hingerty missing the goal by inches only. Mellor centred well, and Denton shot. Pendered secured, and a scrimmage ensued, but the Rushden player was ruled offside. Kettering then came down, but never became dangerous, the Rushden defence being too good. A corner fell to Rushden, which Mellor took, but the ball was cleared. A corner directly afterwards fell to Kettering, but the leather was headed over. Denton sent in a grand shot, but Draper, who stood under the cross-bar, headed away. Half-time came with Rushden pressing, the game then standing –

> Kettering 0
> Rushden 0

Re-starting, Rushden were the first to get down, but a bye resulted. Continuing to press, Wallis and Draper both headed out, the ball being very close each time. Kettering went down, and a long shot was put in, which Daw fisted away. Dainty gave a corner at the other end, but Mellor placed behind. Rushden then swarmed round their oppo-nents' goal, but a foul relieved the pressure. Pendered centred, and Hingerty passed to Denton, who had a clear course, but shot over the bar. In preventing the ball from going over Dunkley let Winterhalder in, and Daw was compelled to yield a corner. This was well placed, but headed out. The ball travelled to the other end, where another corner fell to Rushden. Mellor placed grandly, and a scene of wild excitement followed, the ball being headed at least ten times into the mouth of the goal, only to be returned, Bailey terminating the siege by kicking behind. Hendry played a champion game, and repeatedly dropped the ball at the feet of the home forwards. Bailey tried a long shot, but it went too high. A foul for Rushden a yard outside the penalty line gave Rushden a grand chance, but Bailey shot wide. From a breakaway Heskin headed a grand goal, completely beating Daw. Rushden played up spiritedly after this, but the Kettering backs worked for all they were worth, and kept the Russians at bay. Sale was injured at this point, and had to retire. Bailey came down with the ball, and ran the whole length of the field, being deprived on the goal-line. From a free kick Heskin scored the second goal for Kettering amid cheers. Sale returned to the field limping. Rushden pressed hard towards the finish, but failed to score, and the final came with the score –

> KETTERING 2
> RUSHDEN 0

PRESENTATION OF THE CUP.

Mr. Fred Knight, J.P., said that before he presented the Cup he would like to express the hope that the charities for which that Cup was played would reap a very considerable benefit by those matches. He also wished to congratulate Kettering on winning the Cup. (Cheers.) He would also like to congratulate Kettering on the splendid position which they had gained in the Midland League. (Cheers.) He sympathised very considerably with the home team, who, although they had lost, fought a splendid game. (Cheers.) He hoped both teams would "summer" well, and would recommend them to take up cricket as a recreation. He had very much pleasure in presenting that splendid trophy to Mr. Draper, the captain of the Kettering team. (Loud cheers.) That was the fourth time the Cup had been played for. Rushden won it the first year, Leicester Fosse the second, Wellingborough the third, and Kettering the fourth. (Cheers.)

Mr. Draper, on receiving the Cup, was met with cries of "Good old Ducky!" He said: "I feel very pleased to take this Cup on behalf of the Kettering team. I hope we shall have it again, for it's all right." (Laughter and cheers.)

Mr. Sam Knight proposed a vote of thanks to Mr. F. Knight, which was heartily accorded.

The teams afterwards sat down to tea together at the Coffee Tavern.

The Evening Telegraph*'s account of the Rushden Charity Cup final, 27 April 1899.*

Eleven

Local Rivalries

1899 - 1900

"Monday saw us pitted against our near and dear rivals, the Blues from Wellingborough, in the championship match between the prospective champions and runners-up of the Midland League. The League officials discretely avoided distinguishing which were prospective champions and which runners-up, but after Monday's exhibition there could not be the shadow of a doubt in the mind of anyone who witnessed the game as to which team deserves championship honours."

With a new century on the horizon, a harsh reality had begun to dawn on football clubs – not least those within Northamptonshire's borders – that the coat must be cut according to the cloth. Past overspending had led to more than occasional penny-pinching. For some clubs it was now a bitter struggle for their very survival, and there was no longer the wholesale signing on of players about whom little or nothing was known.

Just three men travelled any distance to join the ranks at Rockingham Road this season: A.B. Carter from Notts County, Fred Mawson from Mexborough and Richard Pegg from Loughborough. But what signings they proved to be! Between them scoring 57 goals in a combined total of 111 competitive matches. Pegg alone would hit the net 29 times in 38 appearances – registering his first goal in the 89th minute of his debut on the ninth day of the ninth month of 1899, playing in what is now regarded as the number nine position (numbers would not actually make an appearance on the back of jerseys before 1928).

A more local addition to the team was John George Coleman, who also turned out to be a natural goal scorer. Affectionately known as 'Tiddy', and later 'Tim', Coleman was apparently a 'perfect little wonder' who stood out from the rest of the local youths in passing, shooting, dribbling and 'trickiness'. Born in Kettering and yet to turn 18 when he joined his home-town club, he was destined to entertain crowds in the Football League playing for Woolwich Arsenal, Everton, Sunderland, Fulham and Nottingham Forest. On 16 February 1907, during his last full season on Arsenal's books, Coleman would become the only Kettering-born association footballer to win an England cap, being part of the team that defeated Ireland by a goal to nil at Goodison Park.

It was just as well that new talent could be unearthed because Kettering had lost two very influential players. Harry Dixon, a hugely popular man who had plied his trade at outside-left (or left wing) for the past decade, retired in the summer; and Herbert Dainty, who, like Coleman, had a great career ahead of him, was now with Leicester Fosse – a move that led to the Fossils agreeing to play a friendly at Rockingham Road (providing their railway expenses were reimbursed) to compensate the Reds for no money having changed hands. The game, which took place on 11 September 1899, was ceremonially kicked off by Kettering's new president and Master of the Woodland Pytchley Hounds, Lord Southampton. Disappointingly, Leicester sent only their reserve side, which was soundly thrashed 5-1.

Something of a wanderer, Dainty would regularly move between clubs for the next few years – from Leicester to New Brighton Tower, back to the Fossils, then on to Northampton, Notts County and Southampton – eventually arriving at Dundee in

1905, where he settled and, five years later, was captain of the Dark Blues' Scottish Cup-winning side. Arguably one of the finest English footballers never to represent his country (at his peak he was with Dundee, and the FA did not select men playing for Scottish clubs), Dainty would later coach teams in Canada and Ecuador, before returning to Kettering in 1931 for a brief spell as manager.

For the first time, the 1899-1900 campaign brought together the senior clubs from the towns of Kettering, Northampton, Rushden and Wellingborough, as all four entered the Midland League – and the United League. In fact the United League was to be a wholly Northamptonshire affair, with Finedon Revellers, Desborough Unity and Rothwell Town Swifts replacing the likes of Brighton United, Bristol City, Luton Town, Millwall Athletic, Reading, Southampton, Tottenham Hotspur and Woolwich Arsenal, who had all resigned at the end of the previous season.

Local rivalries were brought to the fore through the columns of the *Evening Telegraph*, where the Holy Friar's totally biased views were juxtaposed with those of Northampton's 'Rambler', Rushden's 'Wandering Russian', and Wellingborough's 'Peter Piper'. It was generally acknowledged that Kettering and Wellingborough were the county's top sides, with Northampton – known as the 'Babies' or 'Shoemakers' – a young, up-and-coming club.

Two cigarette cards showing former Kettering players who went on to make a name for themselves in the football world. On the left is John Coleman (issued by Taddy & Co. in 1907) and on the right is Herbert Dainty (F. & J. Smith, 1908).

NOTES ON THE GAMES.

"HOLY FRIAR" AND WELLINGBOROUGH'S DOWNFALL.

It is strange to Wellingborough people that we should not have been particularly surprised about the Reds winning on Saturday. If bounce and brag count for anything Wellingborough ought to have won by a big margin – that is if "Peter Piper" correctly voices the opinion of the Blues' supporters.

He has tried to impress us with the idea that Wellingborough are the better team, and has been somewhat cut because we have slily winked the other eye. "Hock and Dough" now quite understand why we have accepted what they had to tell us with the proverbial grain of salt. Saturday's game convinced them that their team is not as yet equal to the Reds. It was about the most useful lesson it supplied.

Wellingborough are a hard-working, enthusiastic, and well-balanced combination, and it is not a cause for wonder that they should have done so well. A team of triers is worth more than an eleven comprising more brilliant but less conscientious men. But the Kettering players are not only, as a whole, more scientific, but show that they have the true interests of the club at heart, ample evidence of which is forthcoming when necessary. Man for man they are in front of Wellingborough, and they showed it in the match under notice.

Kettering had been stagnating somewhat until the Luton encounter. They then showed some of their best form, and what they were capable of, and those who were present on that occasion thought it did not need the possession of a wonderful prophetic vision to "tip" them for the match at Wellingborough. True, the encounter was on the Wellingborough ground, but it was considered the Blues would want more advantage than they could derive from playing at home to prevent their defeat.

So it proved. Kettering were admittedly the superior eleven, and never looked like losing. The only wonder was that they did not leave the field victors by several goals. They would have done so had their shooting been even moderate. Wellingborough, of course, had good reason to complain that they lost a goal through the idiocy of the rules. But they only suffered like Kettering did in Christmas week, and the Reds' loss was the greater inasmuch as the match then was a Midland League one.

Above and opposite: Two opinions of the same game – Kettering's 1-0 win at Wellingborough's Dog and Duck ground in the United League on 17 March 1900 – both published in the Evening Telegraph *two days later, and which serve to illustrate how different correspondents saw things from 'their' club's perspective.*

"PETER PIPER" THINKS WELLINGBOROUGH OUGHT TO HAVE WON.

I suppose it counts, but, really, if Kettering beat Wellingborough on Saturday, I never want to see another football match.

I will at once admit that our team did not play as well as they did against Northampton last Monday, nor so well as they have done on several occasions just recently. The forwards did not get on so well together, and opportunity after opportunity was lost, Marriott being especially unfortunate in this respect, and on the first half of the game it is quite true that our men did not show up quite so well as Kettering. But that is not saying that Kettering ought to have won.

As a matter of fact, on the actual play Wellingborough not only deserved to make a draw, but they ought to have been a goal ahead at the finish. The dash exhibited by our men during the last half-hour in the effort to draw level ought to have been rewarded time after time, but the decisions of the referee seemed to be against us. I never like to criticise the gentleman with the whistle – the position is difficult enough, in all conscience – but it must be said that some of Mr. Jones' rulings were open to question.

Wellingborough were robbed of what should have been the equaliser in very tantalising fashion. We had a penalty, Bennett took it and scored, but for some infringement of the rules or another – it is said that one of the Kettering players was over the line at the time the kick was taken – the referee ordered a second kick, and (tableaux!) the ball hit the post and went by. Then another certain goal was denied us when Marriott was deliberately fouled at a moment when it seemed that he must score. Really, how the referee could overlook that foul I cannot comprehend. I could forgive all his other mistakes but for the memory of that one. If anyone, up to that moment, had entertained the thought that the referee did not intend Wellingborough to win – and the demeanour of the crowd indicated that there were not a few – the opinion must have been confirmed.

Judging from what occurred at the close of the match, some of the spectators felt it keenly, a number of the more exuberant ones crowding round the referee as he approached the pavilion, and there was a prospect of a bit of hustling until a few of the club officials intervened. It was also contended that time had not been played within two minutes, and when this was being pointed out to the referee someone foolishly commenced throwing pieces of turf. The field, however, was quickly cleared, and the referee fortunately escaped further molestation. Of course there is no justification for interfering with the referee, but it must be said that some of his decisions were exasperating.

I guess the "Friar" will chuckle and put on one of those amiable grins that the redoubtable Draper exhibited when Bennett missed the second kick at the penalty, but for decency's sake I hope he will not give to Kettering any credit for the result. The most aggravating part of the business is that it enables Kettering to claim as many victories in our League engagements as we can, but everybody who knows the actual circumstances must be aware of the fact that we have really had the best of the bargain. If there is any luck about Kettering seem to get it.

The United League having been somewhat devalued, the Midland League title was more than ever considered top prize. Kettering drew first blood, beating Wellingborough 2-1 on the opening day of the season at Rockingham Road, followed by a goalless draw at Rushden. A 4-1 defeat at home to Lincoln City Reserves was a setback, but 18 goals in the next three games set the club up nicely for the visit to Northampton on Saturday, 21 October. The largest grandstand for miles around had just been completed and a record crowd, estimated at 4,000, filled the County Ground. That evening's *Football Telegraph* carried a full report of the encounter:

NORTHAMPTON V. KETTERING.
A CLOSE WIN FOR THE KETTS.

By far the most important match in this county to-day was the one in which Northampton and Kettering were the opposing forces. The match was of special interest to both clubs inasmuch as it was the first time they had opposed each other when the result was uncertain and the teams evenly matched. Northampton is the "baby" club of the county, but the infant has grown rapidly, and this season aspires to try conclusions with the other and much older combinations of the county, and to occupy a position almost equally prominent with them in the football world. The county team has already met Rushden and Wellingborough this season, and the performances accomplished are such as Northampton can well be proud of. But the game to-day was looked upon by the rising club's supporters as

EXCEEDING IN IMPORTANCE

any in which their team have played a part in. They were the opponents of the club which has carried far more laurels off than any other of the Northamptonshire clubs, and which, judged by its achievements, is well qualified to speak of itself as the principal one in the county. The Northampton team's initial combat with the Ketts – the tug of war between the new and the old – was thus keenly anticipated, and so well have both been doing this season that the issue was very uncertain. But on the whole Kettering have outstripped Northampton. In the Midland League Northampton have secured five points out of a possible ten, and Kettering nine out of a possible twelve. Against this, however, was to be set the fact that Northampton were playing on their own ground, and apart from these considerations was the further one that in these local encounters, where the rivalry is so great, any paper superiority is of little value. The games invariably are of too exciting a character for really scientific play, and consequently the weaker team has a

BETTER CHANCE

than otherwise would be the case. In respect to the match to-day, the followers of Northampton and Kettering both looked with favour upon their respective team's chances. The visitors were fully represented, Heskin reappearing at centre-half. The

Northampton team underwent alteration, Shortland and Brawn being left out to make room for a new player in the person of Stewart, late of Bedminster, and Randall, of the Reserves; whilst Whiting figured in goal, Bullimer having sprained his ankle whilst at practice on Wednesday. The teams lined up as follows:–

Northampton.– Whiting, goal; Byles and Hendry, backs; Foster, Randall, and R. Warner, half-backs; Handley and F. Warner, right wing; Stewart, centre; Miller and Dunkley, left wing.

Kettering.– Baldry, goal; Wallis and Draper, backs; Pell, Heskin, and Dainty, half-backs; Winterhalder and Carter, right wing; Pegg, centre; Coleman and Mawson, left wing.

Referee: Mr. T. Saywell.

About 1,500 supporters of the Kettering team accompanied the players, and the Northampton followers also turned up in large numbers. The gate was a record one, and football enthusiasts streamed into the ground some time before the match, and continued to do so until long after the game had been started. Northampton won the toss, and chose to kick with the sun behind them. In the first minute, from a smart bit of passing, Northampton got dangerous, and Baldry had to clear from the right. The Reds instantly returned, but were driven back, and operations for a time were confined to midfield until a pass to Winterhalder resulted in that player beating Hendry and shooting by. Play had opened in a fast and exciting way, and continued to be full of life. A corner accrued to the home eleven, but Miller headed wide. The Northampton forwards were displaying

GRAND SHORT PASSING,

and gave the visiting defence considerable trouble. Hard fought hostilities ensued chiefly in the centre of the ground, neither goalkeeper up to the present having been seriously troubled. But just afterwards, from a centre by Winterhalder, Coleman all but scored. Byles was prominent in repulsing attack, but eventually had to concede an abortive corner. Both sides were now showing good form, and there appeared to be little or no difference between the teams. A free came to Kettering, but Hendry relieved, only for the ball to be sent into the mouth of the Northampton goal, where a sharp tussle ensued, ending in favour of the county town lads. After a visit to the Kettering end, the rush being initiated by Handley, the Reds returned, and Winterhalder was fouled in the twelve yards line. The home team claimed that he was offside, but the referee allowed a penalty, from which

DRAPER SCORED

for Kettering. After this Whiting had two or three shots to stop, and Baldry also had to get rid of the ball, and then Warner put in a beautiful shot, which dropped on to the net. Draper was volleying for Kettering, and Northampton were not showing the same dash that they did previous to Kettering scoring. Although Kettering were doing slightly the most of the attacking, after a while Northampton pulled themselves together, and once more there was keen fighting, in which neither side could claim superiority. Two corners fell to Northampton, for whom Dunkley missed an opening, and a combined attack lacked finish. The Northampton goal had an escape from Mawson, who up to this point had been starved. The other wing was being fed by far the best, and made some fine runs, and Carter was heartily applauded from all parts of the field for

A FINE SHOT,

which just skimmed the bar. No further incident of interest occurred until, from a centre by Pegg, Coleman had a good opportunity, but shot over. Most of the play was in the Northampton half, and the Kettering forwards, who opened in rather disappointing fashion, frequently troubled the home defence. Northampton had to suffer the penalty for another foul, but the Reds were kept from converting, and eventually the home team took up the running for some time, but Roger Warner spoiled matters. On the whole the game was fought in a fair spirit, but the referee had occasionally to speak to two of the players during the first half, the interval coming with the score:–

Kettering 1

Northampton 0

The second half opened in rather desultory fashion, but matters livened up on Northampton gaining a fruitless corner... Kettering, however, were unable to get to close quarters until Winterhalder, receiving from Carter, shot just wide. The home defence now had more work to do than the visiting back line, and a second goal came to Kettering from a scrimmage, Winterhalder scoring, whilst Pegg had a good deal to do with the obtaining of it. From the kick-off a good run by the Kettering forwards nearly resulted in Pegg scoring. Heskin was very clever at centre half and did much to break up the attacks of the home players. The game was stopped owing to a "tiff" between Hendry and Winterhalder, but matters were satisfactorily settled by the players

SHAKING HANDS.

After some slow movements, and when it appeared as if they were being beaten, a run, commenced by F. Warner, ended in the ball going over to the left and a good opening presented itself, which Northampton did not fail to take advantage of, Dunkley scoring amid tremendous cheering. Northampton were now playing with considerable dash, and for a time looked very dangerous. A run by Dunkley was stopped by Draper, and the game at this point was most exciting. Hands accrued to Kettering, and afterwards a corner, the ball after a severe struggle going by. Kettering invaded, but Northampton were now trying their hardest, as it looked possible for them to draw level. Handley missed a likely opportunity, and Dunkley with

A GREAT EFFORT

shot over. Northampton were now playing gamely, but the Kettering defence was good. Whiting saved grandly from a brilliant attempt by Mawson. A corner was conceded, but was of no avail. Northampton made one or two more spirited attacks, as did also Kettering ... there was no more scoring, and the game, which had looked all over at one time, but which was now being keenly contested ended:–

KETTERING 2

NORTHAMPTON 1

The win at Northampton left the Reds top of the table, a point ahead of Lincoln's reserves and four points in front of third-placed Rushden, with Northampton and Wellingborough some way behind, although all of Kettering's county rivals had games in hand.

A week later, the club was brought crashing back down to earth with a disastrous 8-2 thumping at Second Division Burton Swifts in the third qualifying round of the FA Cup. This was one of only two cup ties played all season, the other being a 2-1 defeat to Rushden in the semi-final of the Wellingborough Charity Cup.

As usual, the Christmas period was a busy time for the club, with fixtures coming thick and fast. On 23 December, Northampton were beaten 2-0 at Rockingham Road, followed by a 2-1 victory over Doncaster at the same venue on Christmas Day (a Monday). There was a 2-0 defeat at Wellingborough on the 27th, and Northampton gained some revenge for Kettering's Midland League 'double' over them by winning a United League game 4-0 two days later. Finally, 24 hours after conceding those four goals at the County Ground, Kettering rounded off the week by scoring four themselves at home to Burton Wanderers.

A 2-2 draw at Newark on 17 February 1900 was, bizarrely, the club's last Midland League game until 7 April, with United League, (one) cup and friendly fixtures filling the void. Northampton seized their opportunity, going top of the Midland League on 10 March (a day when Kettering's footballers were involved in a first team versus reserves 'comic' fixture – during which the firsts played in ladies attire!) Two days later, the *Evening Telegraph*'s Northampton correspondent was in bullish mood:

"From victory unto victory." Such was the heading of the account of the Town match at Burton [Wanderers] on Saturday in the "Football Telegraph." And certainly no more appropriate quotation could be found. Nothing seems to stop the team from winning; whether at home or away, it makes no difference. True, we don't get home by such large margins when on foreign territory as when on our own midden, but the margins are quite sufficient to serve our purpose. Points we want and points we get, and points win championship honours.

The win at Burton on Saturday [Northampton won 3-2] not only gave us our thirteenth successive win, but also put us for the first time this season at the head of the League. How long we shall stay there is only a matter of opinion. I daren't broach the matter to my esteemed friend the "Holy Friar"; he might turn round and say, "Those 'Babies' are getting too perky." One thing, however, is certain – the Ketts will not have to make a slip in the competition, for on a glance at the table you will notice both Northampton and Wellingborough seem to have an "inside" chance of carrying off premier honours.

Who would have thought at the beginning of the season that the team from the county town would have dared to keep company with Kettering and Wellingborough at the head of the table? Well, we have been through the fire and proved our worth, and I say again Kettering must look out or the "Babies" might easily slip in and kill.

Just let us see for a moment where our chance of winning the League comes in. We have three more matches to play – two at home and one away. Of the two at home we feel confident of winning, but the match at Doncaster will no doubt prove a teaser. Of the five Kettering have to play three are away (this is the consolation to Northampton) and two at home... Of course if Kettering get the full ten points we are whacked into a "cocked hat," because, presuming we win the whole of our remaining matches, our total points will only reach 35. Therefore our only hope is in the Ketts failing in their out matches. Whether they will do this remains to be seen. You may bet your bottom dollar that the Kettering team won't give up the ghost to suit Northampton. However, I can assure the Ketts that Northampton will take a decided interest in their doings in the Midland League during the next few weeks.

But Northampton could not hold on to top spot, and April turned into a scrap for the championship between Kettering and Wellingborough. The Reds went to Burton Wanderers on the 7th and returned with both points after a 2-0 win. A week later they picked up another point, drawing 0-0 away to Derby County Reserves. The following Monday – with the destiny of the title still undecided – the Midland League Championship Match took place at Rockingham Road between the top two clubs, at the conclusion of which the Holy Friar was only restrained in his glee by an enforced reduction in the column inches usually afforded him:

My jottings to-day must be short and sweet, not that the doings of the team do not deserve extended notice, but the big blue pencil of the editor is always busy on an Easter Tuesday trying in vain to squeeze three days' doings into one day's paper...

Monday [16 April] saw us pitted against our near and dear rivals, the Blues from Wellingborough, in the championship match between the prospective champions and runners-up of the Midland League. The League officials discretely avoided distinguishing which were prospective champions and which runners-up, but after Monday's exhibition there could not be the shadow of a doubt in the mind of anyone who witnessed the game as to which team deserves championship honours.

Under Mr. Kingscott, the able and popular secretary of the Midland League, the teams lined up as follows:–

Kettering.– Baldry, goal; Clarke and Draper, backs; Pell, Panter, and Dainty, half-backs; Barnett and Winterhalder, right wing; Carter, centre; Pegg and Mawson, left wing.

Wellingborough.– Cook, goal; Bennett and Martin, backs; Toseland, Heapy, and Cobley, half-backs; Walker and Davies, right wing; Hulme, centre; Busby and Marriott, left wing.

The possession of the wind on a day like Monday meant a good deal, and having got the gale at their backs the Ketts made things a bit lively during the first "45." Only ten minutes had elapsed when Pegg smartly headed our first point; Winterhalder, with a low, clean shot, quickly gave us another to keep that company, whilst before half an hour had elapsed a smart shot from Pegg realised the third goal. The fourth came from Carter; Pell from the half-back line successfully negotiated a fifth, whilst just before the interval the level half-dozen was reached as the result of a dash in by Pegg, in which "Dicky" sustained a nasty knock in the "bellows" which compelled him to leave play until the second half.

We were all pleasurably surprised in the second moiety to see that the Ketts were by no means confined to defensive tactics. In fact, though facing the "zephyr breezes," they had far more of the game than the Blues. The latter, however, scored their one and only goal in this half, a fine run up the wing by Walker enabling Marriott to convert his centre. Directly afterwards Carter enabled Winterhalder to put through, but the referee promptly disallowed the goal as offside. And so ended the championship game.

6-1 was a comprehensive victory, and Kettering went on to end the season in style, winning their next three home games – 2-0 against Barnsley Reserves, 4-0 against Rushden and 8-0 against Finedon Revellers (the club's final United League match) – before undertaking the short journey north for the club's last-ever Midland League fixture – a 3-0 triumph over Leicester Fosse Reserves that clinched the title by a single point.

Both Kettering and Wellingborough had won 16 of their 24 matches in the competition, but Kettering had lost just three – to Wellingborough's four. Northampton finished third and Rushden third from bottom. At the league's AGM in Nottingham on 19 May, Kettering would be declared Midland League Champions for a second time, and awarded a championship flag (valued at three guineas) and medals to present to the players.

In the United League, the top two positions were reversed as Kettering finished runners-up to Wellingborough. Northampton cemented their place as the county's third club and Rushden came in fourth (although it should be noted that just one point separated them all!)

On 4 May, the *Kettering Leader & Observer* carried a review of the club's championship-winning season:

Now the hurly burly's done;

Now the battle's lost and won.

And, on the whole, Kettering need by no means be ashamed of the figure they
have cut in the football world this season. In fact, it is, perhaps, not too much to say
that the season which concluded on Monday [30 April] has been as successful as any
in the history of the club. True, the team did not make the mark in the English Cup
competition which has characterised some previous seasons, but they have pulled off
the championship of the Midland League, and finished second in the United League,
and this is a record few other clubs can point to. Unlike the season preceding it, this
– the last football season of the century – has witnessed very few changes in the
personell of

THE TEAM.

At the commencement of the season Pegg, of Loughborough; Carter, of Notts County;
and Mawson, of Mexborough, were the only three players from "abroad" signed on
by the club. All these played among the forwards, which, during the preceding season
had been the palpably weak line of the team. Their advent undoubtedly wrought a
marvelous improvement in the Kettering attack, and all three have been consistently
good goal getters. "Tiddy" Colemen, a local lad, was also given a trial on the front
line, and has more than justified the good opinions formed of him earlier in the season.
Herbert Winterhalder, a true Ketteringite bred and born, was the only old player retained
in the forwards, and it was a serious blow to the club when, in the Midland League
fixture at Wellingborough on December 27th, he had the misfortune to break his collar
bone, from the effects of which it is feared he has even yet not altogether recovered.
During his absence from the team Barnett, a Woodford lad, was played on the right,
and has lately developed exceedingly well. In the earlier part of the season Pell, Heskin,
and Dainty constituted the half-back line, and a formidable trio they were. In December,
however, Alf. Heskin was taken ill, and has gradually got worse, until it is now feared
he will never again rise from his bed. As a center-half he had few equals in the Midland
League, and his absence was keenly felt in the team. To fill the vacancy Panter fell
back from among the forwards, and has taken to the position like a duck to water. The
three worked together admirably, and could scarcely be improved upon. Of the backs
Captain Draper has played throughout the season in inimitable form. What more can
be said of old "Ducky" than has been said over and over again? He is, as he always
has been, the backbone of the team. Respected by friends and enimies alike, it will be
a sorry day for Kettering when William deems it time he retired into private life. His
partner during the first part of the season was Wallis, but latterly Clarke has figured
on the captain's right. In goal Baldry has been the custodian throughout the season,
and has served the club well. So much for the team. Coming to their performances,

THE MIDLAND LEAGUE

tourney claims first attention. It was reserved for the last match of the season to provide

Kettering with the points necessary to constitute them champions of the Midland League, a position which they last occupied at the conclusion of the 1895-6 season. That season was probably the most brilliant in the history of the Kettering club, the team only being defeated three times in the Midland League, in which they finished five points in front of Gainsborough Trinity, who, it is interesting to note, were the next season admitted as members of the Second Division of the English League. The season concluded on Monday with a 3-0 victory over Leicester Fosse Reserves, which left the Ketts champions of the League by a margin of a single point over Wellingborough... The greatest win registered by the team in the Midland League was against Leicester Fosse Reserves, who were defeated at Kettering by 7-1, whilst the worst defeat sustained by Kettering was at the hands of Lincoln City [Reserves], who on that occasion played several first team men and won by 4-1, this being the only time the Reds have been defeated in the League on their own ground. The

UNITED LEAGUE

has been a bit of a "white elephant," and it is a moot point whether membership does not mean more expenditure than income. The matches have certainly proved far from "draws," and players and spectators have manifested little interest in the competition. By Kettering's 8-0 victory over Finedon on Saturday last they finish second on the chart, the sweets of the championship falling to Wellingborough by a margin of a single point. The League has never caught on at Kettering, and since the secession of the Southerners interest in it has dropped to a very low point. Still, we have the satisfaction of knowing that the club finish higher on the chart than in any other season.

A meeting of the committee had been held back in February to discuss the advisability of the club applying for election to the Football League at the end of the season; and the club duly did just that once the Midland League was won.

In 1900 the Second Division (there would only be two divisions until 1920) consisted of 18 clubs, and those finishing in the bottom three places – Barnsley, Luton and Loughborough – were obliged to seek re-election to the Football League, whilst non-League clubs were invited to put themselves forward as an alternative. And so it was that Kettering's name appeared alongside those of fellow hopefuls Blackpool, Doncaster Rovers, Stalybridge Rovers and Stockport County.

When the counting was done, Barnsley had polled 29 votes, Stockport 28, Blackpool 24, Doncaster 5, Loughborough 3, Kettering 2 and Stalybridge 1 (other sources credit Kettering with as many as 12 votes, but even this would still only have been half the number required). Luton, who Kettering had beaten 10-1 in a friendly back in March, declined to seek re-election and they, along with Loughborough, were replaced in the League by Stockport and Blackpool. Not for the last time, Kettering's supporters were left to reflect on what might have been.

L A W S   O F   T H E   G A M E.

REVISED JUNE, 1899.

—————

1.– The game should be played by 11 players on each side. The dimensions of the field of play shall be – maximum length, 130 yards; minimum length, 100 yards; maximum breadth, 100 yards; minimum breadth, 50 yards. The field of play shall be marked by boundary lines. The lines at each end are the goal-lines, and the lines at the sides are the touch-lines. The touch-lines shall be drawn at right angles with the goal-lines. A flag with a staff not less than 5ft. high shall be placed at each corner. Lines defining 12 yards from the goal-lines and a half-way line shall be marked out, also semi-circles defining 6 yards from each goal post. The centre of the field of play shall be indicated by a suitable mark, and a circle with a 10 yards radius shall be made round it. The goals shall be upright posts fixed on the goal-lines equi-distant from the corner flag-staffs, 8 yards apart, with a bar across them, 8 feet from the ground. The maximum width of the goal posts and the maximum depth of the cross-bar shall be 5 inches. The circumference of the ball shall be not less than 27 inches, nor more than 28 inches. In International matches, the dimensions of the field of play shall be – maximum length, 120 yards; minimum length, 110 yards; maximum breadth, 80 yards; minimum breadth, 70 yards; and at the commencement of the game the weight of the ball shall be from 13 to 15 ounces.

2.– The duration of the game shall be 90 minutes, unless otherwise mutually agreed upon. The winners of the toss shall have the option of kick-off or choice of goals. The game shall be commenced by a place-kick from the centre of the field of play in the direction of the opponents' goal-line; the opponents shall not approach within 10 yards of the ball until it is kicked off, nor shall any player on either side pass the centre of the ground in the direction of his opponents' goal until the ball is kicked off.

3.– Ends shall only be changed at half-time. The interval at half-time shall not exceed five minutes, except by consent of the Referee. After a goal is scored the losing side shall kick off, and after the change of ends at half-time the ball shall be kicked off by the opposite side from that which originally did so; and always as provided in Law 2.

4.– A goal shall be scored when the ball has passed between the goal-posts under the bar, not being thrown, knocked on, nor carried by any player of the attacking side. If from any cause during the progress of the game the bar is displaced, the Referee shall have power to award a goal if in his opinion the ball would have passed under the bar if it had not been displaced. The ball is in play if it rebounds from a goal-post, cross-bar, or a corner flag-staff into the field of play. The ball is in play if it touches the Referee or a Linesman when in the field of play. The ball crossing the goal-lines or touch-lines, either on the ground or in the air, is out of play.

5.– When the ball is in touch, a player of the opposite side to that which played it out shall throw it in from the point on the touch-line where it left the field of play. The player throwing the ball must stand on the touch-line facing the field of play, and shall throw the ball in over his head with both hands in any direction, and it shall be in play when thrown in. A goal shall not be scored from a throw in, and the thrower shall not again play until the ball has been played by another player. (NOTE.– This law is complied with if the player has any part of both feet on the line when he throws the ball in).

6.– When a player plays the ball, or throws it in from touch, any player of the same side who at such moment of playing or throwing-in is nearer to his opponents' goal-line is out of play, and may not touch the ball himself, nor in any way whatever interfere with an opponent, until the ball has been played, unless there are at such moment of playing or throwing-in at least three of his opponents nearer their own goal-line. A player is not out of play in the case of a corner-kick, or when the ball is kicked off from goal, or when it has been last played by an opponent.

7.– When the ball is played behind the goal-line by a player of the opposite side, it shall be kicked off by any one of the players behind whose goal-line it went, within 6 yards of the goal-post nearest the point where the ball left the field of play; but, if played behind by any one of the side whose goal-line it is, a player of the opposite side shall kick it from within 1 yard of the nearest corner flag-staff. In either case an opponent shall not be allowed within 6 yards of the ball until it is kicked off.

8.– A player shall not intentionally handle the ball under any pretence whatever, except in the case of the goalkeeper, who, within his own half of the field of play, shall be allowed to use his hands in defence of his goal, but not by carrying the ball. The goalkeeper may be changed during the game, but notice of such change must first be given to the Referee.

Above and opposite: The 17 laws of association football as they appeared in the 1899-1900 edition of the Athletic News Football Annual.

The FA's game had come a long way since it was formalised in 1863. A bit rougher than we are used to today, and with pitch markings that might appear somewhat quirky, but by the dawn of the 20th century the foundations of the modern game were in place.

9.– In no case shall any goal be scored from any free kick (except as provided in Law 14), nor shall the ball be again played by the kicker until it has been played by another player. The kick-off, corner-kick, and goal-kick, shall be free kicks within the meaning of this law.

10.– Neither tripping, kicking, nor jumping at a player shall be allowed. A player shall not use his hands to hold or push an opponent, or play in any manner likely to cause injury. A player shall not be charged from behind unless he is facing his own goal and is also intentionally impeding an opponent. The goalkeeper shall not be charged except when he is holding the ball or obstructing an opponent.

11.– A player shall not wear any nails, except such as have their heads driven in flush with the leather, or metal plates or projections, or gutta percha, on his boots, or on his shin guards. If bars or studs on the soles or heels of the boots are used, they shall not project more than half an inch, and shall have all their fastenings driven in flush with the leather. Bars shall be transverse and flat, not less than half an inch in width, and shall extend from side to side of boot. Studs shall be round in plan, not less than half an inch in diameter, and in no case conical or pointed. Any player discovered infringing this law shall be prohibited from taking further part in the match. The Referee shall, if required, examine the players' boots before the commencement of a match.

12.– A Referee shall be appointed, whose duties shall be to enforce the laws and decide all disputed points; and his decision on points of fact connected with the play shall be final. He shall also keep a record of the game and act as timekeeper. In the event of any ungentlemanly behaviour on the part of any of the players, the offender or offenders shall be cautioned, and if the offence is repeated, or in case of violent conduct without any previous caution, the Referee shall have power to order the offending player or players off the field of play, and shall transmit the name or names of such player or players to his or their (National) Association, who shall deal with the matter. The Referee shall have power to allow for time wasted, to suspend the game when he thinks fit, and to terminate the game whenever by reason of darkness, interference by spectators, or other cause, he may deem necessary; but in all cases in which a game is so terminated he shall report the same to the Association under whose jurisdiction the game was played, who shall have full power to deal with the matter. The Referee shall have power to award a free kick in any case in which he thinks the conduct of a player dangerous, or likely to prove dangerous, but not sufficiently so as to justify him in putting in force the greater powers vested in him. The power of the Referee extends to offences committed when the play has been temporarily suspended, or the ball is out of play.

13.– Two linesmen shall be appointed, whose duty (subject to the decision of the Referee) shall be to decide when the ball is out of play, and which side is entitled to the corner-kick, goal-kick, or throw-in, and to assist the Referee in carrying out the game in accordance with the laws. Any undue interference by a linesman shall be reported by the Referee to the National Association having jurisdiction over him, who shall deal with the matter.

14.– If any player shall intentionally trip, charge from behind, push, or hold an opponent, or intentionally handle the ball, within 12 yards from his own goal-line, the Referee shall award the opponents a penalty kick, which shall be taken from any point 12 yards from the goal-line, under the following conditions: All players with the exception of the player taking the penalty kick and the opponents' goalkeeper (who shall not advance more than 6 yards from the goal-line) shall stand at least six yards behind the ball. The ball must be kicked forward. The ball shall be in play when the kick is taken, and a goal may be scored from a penalty kick; but the ball shall not be again played by the kicker until it has been played by another player. If necessary, time of play shall be extended to admit of the penalty kick being taken.

15.– In the event of a supposed infringement of the laws, the ball shall be in play until a decision has been given.

16.– In the event of any temporary suspension of play from any cause, the ball not having gone into touch, or behind the goal-line, the game shall be re-started by the Referee throwing up the ball where play was suspended. The players on either side shall not play the ball until it has touched the ground.

17.– In the event of any infringement of Laws 2, 5, 6, 8, 9, 10, or 16 a free kick shall be awarded to the opposite side, from the place where the infringement occurred.

DEFINITION OF TERMS.

1.– A Place Kick is a kick at the ball while it is on the ground in the centre of the field of play.

2.– A Free Kick is a kick at the ball in any direction the player pleases, when it is lying on the ground, none of the kicker's opponents being allowed within 6 yards of the ball, unless they be standing on their own goal-line. The ball must at least be rolled over before it shall be considered played; i.e., it must make a complete circuit or travel the distance of its circumference. A place kick or a free kick must not be taken until the Referee has given a signal for the same.

3.– Carrying by the goalkeeper is taking more than two steps while holding the ball, or bouncing it on the hand.

4.– Knocking-on is when a player strikes or propels the ball with his hands or arms.

5.– Handling is intentionally playing the ball with the hand or arm, and Tripping is intentionally throwing, or attempting to throw, an opponent by the use of the legs, or by stooping in front of or behind him. Unless, in the opinion of the Referee, handling or tripping is intentional, no punishment shall be imposed; thus, within the 12 yards line, a Referee must enforce Law 14, and has no power to mitigate the penalty.

6.– Holding includes the obstruction of a player by the hand or any part of the arm extending from the body.

7.– Touch is that part of the ground on either side of the field of play.

The summer of 1900 fell in the last full year of Queen Victoria's reign. At home there was canvassing ahead of a general election that would see Winston Churchill become an MP for the first time and the recently-formed Labour Party secure its first two seats in the House of Commons (it would be almost another two decades and a World War before it was accepted that women had the right to vote); across the Channel there was a celebration of the previous century's achievements and a vision of the future at the World's Fair in Paris – a city where Picasso would soon embark on works that would take 'modern' art to another level; in South Africa there was fighting, as Britain continued its struggle with the Boers; and across the Atlantic the Wright brothers were developing a 'heavier-than-air' craft that would, within a few years, open up the skies.

Aston Villa was recognised as the best football club in England, having just secured a fifth First Division championship in seven seasons. At Kettering, new challenges were around the corner. Having failed to gain a place in the Football League for the 1900-01 season, the club looked instead to the Southern League, which at the time was arguably as strong as the Second Division, counting amongst its members the likes of Portsmouth, Queens Park Rangers, Reading, Southampton (1900 FA Cup finalists), Tottenham Hotspur (who would go on to win the Cup in 1901), Watford and West Ham United.

Almost 28 years after George Roughton had led his Kettering team on to George Eldred's field on a wet December afternoon in 1872, Portsmouth arrived at a packed Rockingham Road on the first day of September 1900, heralding the start of a new season.

The next chapter in the history of the club that had first adopted Uppingham School's code of football and then excelled at rugby union before settling on the FA's game was about to unfold...

Football had not only come to Kettering – it had taken root and was flourishing.

Opposite: A collectors card issued by John Baines of Manningham, Bradford. Baines first produced cards with sporting images in the late 1880s, and continued to do so for about 40 years. It is not known when the Kettering card was issued, but by the end of the 19th century the club had achieved more than enough to warrant the accolade of 'WELL PLAYED'.

Appendix A

Players: 1872 - 1892

Appendix A is an attempt to list everyone who played a first team game for Kettering FC between seasons 1872-3 and 1891-2, the vast majority of which were friendly fixtures. (In 1892 the club would join the Midland League, and all senior players who joined the ranks after this point can be found in Appendix B – a record of participants in competitive games up to 1900.)

Some of those listed in Appendix A played only rugby, others only association football (possibly a minority only ever played under Uppingham rules), and some would have participated in two or more codes. A few may only have 'guested' from another club for a one-off match, whilst others wore the colours for more than a decade.

The task of researching names is made difficult by a number of factors. Some seasons are poorly covered in contemporary newspapers, and even when coverage is good there are mistakes; some players had nicknames, and others went by a different Christian name to that given at birth. And then there is the matter of distinguishing between what might be considered first and second team games.

There are doubtless omissions from the list, as well as errors amongst those individuals contained within it. But it is at least a starting point for anyone who wishes to discover more about the players who represented the club during its formative years.

ABRAHAMS A.	1886 - 88	**EAST** FRED	1872 - 78
ABRAHAMS R.	1886 - 89	**EAST** WALTER C.	1873 - 75
ALLEN	1889 - 90	**EAYRES** JACK	1872 - 75
ALTHORPE J.	1880 - 82	**EVANS**	1888 - 89
ASHER G.	1886 - 87	**EVANS** W.	1891 - 92
ASHMOLE	1888 - 89		
		FAREY G.	1887 - 88
BAILEY A.	1889 - 90	**FERRIL** H.J.	1888 - 89
BAILEY HARRY	1877 - 80	**FOSTER** H.D.	1888 - 91
BALL HARRY	1890 - 92	**FOULDS** ARTHUR J.	1877 - 82
BATES GEORGE	1887 - 92	**FREEMAN** LEVI	1891 - 92
BAYES A.	1879 - 80		
BAYES CHARLES	1872 - 85	**GOTCH** D.	1872 - 73
BAYES HARRY	1874 - 85	**GOTCH** HARRY G.	1874 - 76
BELL SAM	1877 - 78		
BELLAMY A.	1889 - 90	**HANGER** CHARLIE	1877 - 80
BENFORD A.	1890 - 91	**HANGER** FRED	1880 - 85
BIDDLE J.	1885 - 88	**HANGER** HARRY	1872 - 78
BIESIEGAL P. KARL	1888 - 89	**HANGER** JOHN	1872 - 73
BLOOMFIELD J.	1888 - 89	**HARRIS** WRIGHT	1889 - 91
BRADLEY A. 'JOE'	1890 - 91	**HARRISON** T.	1889 - 90
BRAINS GEORGE	1882 - 84	**HART** J. WILLIAM	1883 - 88
BREWER M.H.	1888 - 91	**HAWKES** GEORGE	1874 - 75
BRIDGEMAN	1891 - 92	**HAWTHORNE** J.	1884 - 89
BRIGSTOCK G.	1886 - 89	**HENSON** ALEXANDER	1874 - 78
BRIGSTOCK H.	1891 - 92	**HENSON** CHARLES	1874 - 78
BURGESS W.	1888 - 89	**HENSON** FRANK B.	1874 - 76
		HENSON FRED	1874 - 76
CAMPBELL GEORGE	1883 - 85	**HOOPER** H.	1888 - 89
CASHMORE W.R.	1891 - 92	**HOUGHTON** E.	1883 - 85
CATTELL WILLIAM 'BILL'	1873 - 84	**HUMPHRIES** H.	1887 - 88
CHAMBERLAIN T.	1883 - 85	**HUTCHEN** JACK	1883 - 90
CHETTLE	1888 - 89		
CLARKE D. 'GOSS'	1874 - 81	**JAMES** E.	1887 - 88
COLEMAN JOSH	1884 - 86	**JAMES** H.A.	1888 - 89
COLES T.	1890 - 91	**JAMES** W.	1878 - 81
COLTMAN A.	1886 - 88	**JENKINS** ARTHUR J.	1887 - 91
COLTMAN G.W. 'BILLY'	1886 - 90	**JOYCE** W.	1886 - 89
COOCH C.	1879 - 82		
CRANE W.	1884 - 87	**KNIGHT** WALTER	1888 - 91
CURTIS HARRY 'NOBBY'	1890 - 92		
		LAMB F.	1872 - 73
DARKER T.	1886 - 87	**LAMBERT** A.K.	1888 - 89
DAVIES GEORGE	1891 - 93	**LAMBERT** H.S.	1888 - 89
DENTON CHARLES	1877 - 85	**LANGFORD** JACK	1888 - 92
DIXON CHARLIE 'HAP'ORTH'	1874 - 91	**LAWRENCE** J.	1890 - 91
DIXON F.	1880 - 81	**LETTS** A.	1886 - 87
DIXON HARRY	1889 - 99	**LEWIS** J.	1886 - 89
DIXON HORACE	1890 - 91	**LILLEY** J.	1888 - 89
DIXON J.C.	1879 - 82	**LILLEY** W. 'FESSOR'	1886 - 94
(a) **DRAPER** WILLIAM 'DUCKY'	1889 - 04	**LINDSAY** HARRY M.	1873 - 74
DRISCALL J. JAMES	1877 - 82	**LINDSAY** L.J. 'LEW'	1882 - 85
DYER S.	1874 - 76	**LINDSAY** R.H.	1883 - 85
		LOASBY A.	1877 - 80
(a) Draper spent seasons 1893-94 and 1894-95 at		**LOASBY** F.W.	1882 - 88
Burton Wanderers.		**LUDLAM** G.	1874 - 75

MABBOTT C.	1891 - 92	**RAY** W.B.	1888 - 89
MABLESTONE WILLIAM 'SMILER'	1891 - 96	**RHODES**	1888 - 89
MARRIOTT J.	1888 - 89	**ROBINSON** CHARLES 'CHING'	1884 - 94
MARSH S.L.	1880 - 85	**ROBINSON** JAMES P.	1872 - 75
MARSHAM Rev. JOHN	1873 - 74	**ROUGHTON** A.	1872 - 73
MARTIN O.	1884 - 89	**ROUGHTON** GEORGE W.	1872 - 74
MASON C.A.	1888 - 89	**ROUGHTON** HENRY S.	1872 - 73
MASON G.S.	1888 - 89	**ROUGHTON** HUGH	1887 - 90
MASON G.T.	1890 - 91	**ROUGHTON** JAMES W.	1872 - 73
MAYCOCK CHARLIE	1872 - 73	**ROUGHTON** JOHN	1884 - 85
MAYCOCK TOMMY	1884 - 90		
McBIRNIE G.	1891 - 92	**SADDINGTON** JOHN	1873 - 76
McDONALD G.	1888 - 89	**SCULTHORPE** W.	1873 - 75
MEAD F.F.	1888 - 89	**SEDDON** J.	1888 - 89
MERCELL A.R.	1886 - 87	**SHORTLAND** J.	1888 - 89
MITTEN B.	1889 - 90	**SHRIVES** W.	1872 - 74
MITTON A.	1880 - 88	**SLOW** WILLIAM	1880 - 85
MOBBS CHARLIE F.	1874 - 83	**SMITH** A.L.	1882 - 83
MOBBS FRANK	1872 - 78	**SMITH** CHARLIE	1872 - 85
MOBBS GEORGE	1877 - 80	**SMITH** EDWARD 'TEDDY'	1873 - 76
MOBBS HARRY W.	1874 - 87	**SMITH** W.	1888 - 89
MOBBS J.	1873 - 74	**SPENCE** GEORGE W.	1877 - 85
MOBBS SEPTIMUS G.	1877 - 87	**SPENCE** JOE	1874 - 75
		SPENCE OWEN	1874 - 75
NEWMAN C.	1872 - 73	**SPENCE** R.	1882 - 83
NEWMAN F.	1882 - 88	**SPENCE** WILLIAM 'BUFF'	1882 - 88
(b) **NEWMAN** HARRY	1886 - 94	**SPENCER** TOM	1874 - 80
NEWMAN NAT	1872 - 75	**St. JOHN** Rev. E.T.	1873 - 75
(b) **NEWMAN** T.	1890 - 91	**STARR** JACKIE T.	1891 - 95
NEWMAN W.	1887 - 88	**SUMPTER** J.	1889 - 90
NEWMAN WALTER 'TROOBY'	1873 - 85	**SUTTERBY** A.	1873 - 74
NOBLE G.	1890 - 91		
NOBLE M.	1873 - 75	**TEBBUTT** C.A.	1889 - 90
NORMAN W.	1885 - 89	**THOMPSON** ERNEST G.	1882 - 84
		THURSTON Rev. GEORGE	1879 - 84
(b) These are possibly the same person.		**TILLEY** J.	1887 - 88
		TOSELAND H.	1887 - 90
OWEN G.	1886 - 88	**TUNNICLIFFE** GEORGE	1884 - 89
		TURNER P.	1888 - 89
PALMER FRED A.	1887 - 90		
PANTER AVERY B. 'JUMMY'	1885 - 97	**WEST** GEORGE	1889 - 93
PANTHER G.	1887 - 89	**WESTLEY** J.	1885 - 89
PARISH H.	1882 - 83	**WILLIAMS** J.	1888 - 89
PARKER C.	1872 - 73	**WILSON** GEORGE 'TUG'	1885 - 90
PARKER WILLIAM H. 'BILLY'	1873 - 85	**WILSON** GEORGE I.	1872 - 73
PATRICK F.	1873 - 74	**WILSON** THOMAS 'MILLER'	1872 - 75
PAYNE J.	1886 - 89	**WOOD** ARTHUR 'BENNY'	1889 - 91
PETERS ALBERT	1891 - 94	**WOODROW** G.	1888 - 89
PHILLIPS J.	1886 - 87	**WOOLSTON** EDWARD 'TEDDY'	1873 - 80
PIGGOTT CHARLIE	1886 - 90	**WOOLSTON** JACK	1878 - 89
PIGGOTT J.	1888 - 89	**WRIGHT** C.	1872 - 75
PINNOCK H.	1888 - 89	**WRIGHT** E.	1888 - 89
PLATT A.E.	1885 - 86	**WRIGHT** GEORGE 'TAFF'	1887 - 91
		WRIGHT H.	1883 - 84
QUINCEY EDWARD R.	1874 - 85	**WYKES** H. 'ALF'	1872 - 75
QUINCEY TOM	1874 - 75		
		YORK FRANK	1882 - 83

Appendix B

Players: Competitive Games 1881 - 1900

Appendix B is a record of everyone who played a competitive first team game for Kettering FC between seasons 1881-82 and 1899-1900, with details of appearances and goals scored in each competition (there are still a number of goals unaccounted for). Goals being 'rushed through' may refer to a body of players forcing the ball over the line, or perhaps a goalkeeper being bundled into the goal clutching the ball.

The difficulties in extracting data from contemporary sources has already been spelled out in Appendix A. An added complication when compiling Appendix B (and C and D) is that of not knowing which account of a particular match is correct – it is not unusual to find two reports of the same game with goals credited to different players.

The club's first competitive game under Association rules, in what is now known as the Northants (Hillier) Senior Cup – the county FA's competition – took place in October 1883. Prior to this, Kettering played two competitive games of rugby union, both in the Midland Counties Football Union Challenge Cup, and were represented by:

1881-82

ALTHORPE J., **BAYES** CHARLES, **BAYES** HARRY, **COOCH** C., **DIXON** CHARLIE 'HAP'ORTH', **HANGER** FRED, **MARSH** S.L., **MITTON** A., **MOBBS** HARRY W., **NEWMAN** WALTER 'TROOBY', **PARKER** WILLIAM H. 'BILLY', **SLOW** WILLIAM, **SMITH** CHARLIE, **SPENCE** GEORGE W., **WOOLSTON** JACK. (1 game each, 0 goals scored.)

1882-83

BAYES CHARLES, **BRAINS** GEORGE (1 goal), **DIXON** CHARLIE 'HAP'ORTH', **HANGER** FRED, **LOASBY** F.W., **MARSH** S.L., **MITTON** A., **MOBBS** HARRY W., **MOBBS** SEPTIMUS G., **NEWMAN** WALTER 'TROOBY', **SLOW** WILLIAM, **SMITH** CHARLIE, **SPENCE** GEORGE W., **SPENCE** R., **WOOLSTON** JACK. (1 game each, 1 goal scored – see note, Appendix C.)

1883-84	Northants Senior Cup	
	games	goals
1 **BAYES** HARRY	3	
2 **DIXON** CHARLIE 'HAP'ORTH'	4	(1)
3 **HART** J. WILLIAM	3	
4 **HOUGHTON** E.	1	
5 **LINDSAY** L.J. 'LEW'	4	(1)
6 **LINDSAY** R.H.	3	
7 **MOBBS** HARRY W.	3	
8 **MOBBS** SEPTIMUS G.	4	
9 **NEWMAN** WALTER 'TROOBY'	3	
10 **PARKER** WILLIAM H. 'BILLY'	4	(2)
11 **SPENCE** WILLIAM 'BUFF'	4	
12 **THOMPSON** ERNEST G.	1	
13 **THURSTON** Rev. GEORGE	3	(1)
14 **WOOLSTON** JACK	4	(2)
maximum possible appearances	4	
own goals		(1)
total goals scored		(8)

1884-85	Northants Senior Cup	
	games	goals
1 **BAYES** HARRY	2	
2 **CAMPBELL** GEORGE	2	
3 **DIXON** CHARLIE 'HAP'ORTH'	2	
4 **HART** J. WILLIAM	2	
5 **HOUGHTON** E.	2	
6 **LINDSAY** L.J. 'LEW'	1	
7 **MARTIN** O.	1	
8 **MAYCOCK** TOMMY	1	
9 **PARKER** WILLIAM H. 'BILLY'	2	(1)
10 **ROUGHTON** JOHN	1	
11 **SPENCE** WILLIAM 'BUFF'	2	
12 **TUNNICLIFFE** GEORGE	2	
13 **WOOLSTON** JACK	2	(1)
maximum possible appearances	2	
total goals scored		(2)

1885-86	Northants Senior Cup	
	games	goals
1 **BIDDLE** J.	1	
2 **COLEMAN** JOSH	1	
3 **DIXON** CHARLIE 'HAP'ORTH'	2	
4 **HART** J. WILLIAM	2	
5 **HUTCHEN** JACK	1	
6 **MAYCOCK** TOMMY	2	
7 **PANTER** AVERY B. 'JUMMY'	1	
8 **PLATT** A.E.	2	
9 **SPENCE** WILLIAM 'BUFF'	2	
10 **TUNNICLIFFE** GEORGE	2	
11 **WESTLEY** J.	2	
12 **WILSON** GEORGE 'TUG'	2	
13 **WOOLSTON** JACK	2	
maximum possible appearances	2	
goals unaccounted for		(7)
total goals scored		(7)

1886-87	Northants Senior Cup	
	games	goals
1 **COLTMAN** A.	1	
2 **DIXON** CHARLIE 'HAP'ORTH'	1	
3 **HART** J. WILLIAM	1	
4 **NORMAN** W.	1	
5 **PANTER** AVERY B. 'JUMMY'	1	
6 **PIGGOTT** CHARLIE	1	(2)
7 **SPENCE** WILLIAM 'BUFF'	1	
8 **TUNNICLIFFE** GEORGE	1	
9 **WESTLEY** J.	1	
10 **WILSON** GEORGE 'TUG'	1	
11 **WOOLSTON** JACK	1	
maximum possible appearances	1	
total goals scored		(2)

1887-88	Northants Senior Cup	
	games	goals
1 **BATES** GEORGE	1	
2 **DIXON** CHARLIE 'HAP'ORTH'	1	
3 **JAMES** E.	1	(1)
4 **JENKINS** ARTHUR J.	1	
5 **LILLEY** W. 'FESSOR'	1	
6 **MAYCOCK** TOMMY	1	(1)
7 **NEWMAN** W.	1	
8 **PIGGOTT** CHARLIE	1	
9 **SPENCE** WILLIAM 'BUFF'	1	
10 **TUNNICLIFFE** GEORGE	1	
11 **WILSON** GEORGE 'TUG'	1	
maximum possible appearances	1	
total goals scored		(2)

1888-89	F.A. Cup		Kettering Charity Cup		TOTALS	
					games	goals
1 **BATES** GEORGE	1		2		3	
2 **BREWER** M.H.	1				1	
3 **DIXON** CHARLIE 'HAP'ORTH'	1		1	(1)	2	(1)
4 **FOSTER** H.D.			2		2	
5 **JAMES** H.A.			1		1	
6 **JENKINS** ARTHUR J.	1	(1)	1		2	(1)
7 **LANGFORD** JACK	1		2		3	
8 **LILLEY** W. 'FESSOR'			2		2	
9 **NEWMAN** HARRY			1		1	
10 **PALMER** FRED A.	1		2		3	
11 **PANTER** AVERY B. 'JUMMY'			2		2	
12 **PIGGOTT** CHARLIE	1	(1)	2	(2)	3	(3)
13 **ROUGHTON** HUGH	1				1	
14 **TUNNICLIFFE** GEORGE	1				1	
15 **WILSON** GEORGE 'TUG'	1	(1)	2		3	(1)
16 **WRIGHT** GEORGE 'TAFF'	1		2		3	
maximum possible appearances	1		2		3	
total goals scored		(3)		(3)		(6)

1889-90	Kettering Charity Cup	
	games	goals
1 **ALLEN**	1	(2)
2 **BATES** GEORGE	3	(5)
3 **COLTMAN** G.W. 'BILLY'	1	
4 **DIXON** CHARLIE 'HAP'ORTH'	2	
5 **DRAPER** WILLIAM 'DUCKY'	4	
6 **FOSTER** H.D.	4	
7 **HUTCHEN** JACK	1	(1)
8 **KNIGHT** WALTER	4	(2)
9 **LANGFORD** JACK	4	
10 **LILLEY** W. 'FESSOR'	4	(1)
11 **NEWMAN** HARRY	1	(1)
12 **PALMER** FRED A.	2	
13 **PANTER** AVERY B. 'JUMMY'	3	
14 **WEST** GEORGE	3	(1)
15 **WILSON** GEORGE 'TUG'	4	
16 **WRIGHT** GEORGE 'TAFF'	3	
maximum possible appearances	4	
goals rushed through		(4)
total goals scored		(17)

1890-91	F.A. Cup	Grantham Charity Cup		Kettering Charity Cup		Luton Charity Cup		TOTALS games	goals
1 **BALL** HARRY	1					3	(1)	4	(1)
2 **BATES** GEORGE	1							1	
3 **BENFORD** A.		1						1	
4 **BRADLEY** A. 'JOE'		1		1		4	(4)	6	(4)
5 **CURTIS** HARRY 'NOBBY'						3	(1)	3	(1)
6 **DIXON** CHARLIE 'HAP'ORTH'	1	2				4	(4)	7	(4)
7 **DIXON** HARRY	1	2		1	(1)	4	(3)	8	(4)
8 **DRAPER** WILLIAM 'DUCKY'	1	2		1		4		8	
9 **FOSTER** H.D.		1						1	
10 **HARRIS** WRIGHT	1							1	
11 **LANGFORD** JACK	1	2		1		3		7	
12 **LAWRENCE** J.				1				1	
13 **LILLEY** W. 'FESSOR'	1	2		1		4		8	
14 **MASON** G.T.		2	(1)	1		1	(1)	4	(2)
15 **NEWMAN** T.						3		3	
16 **PANTER** AVERY B. 'JUMMY'	1	2	(1)	1		4	(8)	8	(9)
17 **ROBINSON** CHARLES 'CHING'				1		1		2	
18 **WEST** GEORGE	1	2		1		2		6	
19 **WOOD** ARTHUR 'BENNY'		1				3	(1)	4	(1)
20 **WRIGHT** GEORGE 'TAFF'	1	2		1		1		5	
maximum possible appearances	1	2		1		4		8	
goals rushed through				(1)		(1)		(2)	
total goals scored	(0)	(2)		(2)		(24)		(28)	

1891-92	Grantham Charity Cup	Kettering Charity Cup	Luton Charity Cup	TOTALS games	goals
1 **BATES** GEORGE			1	1	
2 **DAVIES** GEORGE	3	4	4	11	
3 **DIXON** HARRY	3	4 (3)	4 (1)	11	(4)
4 **DRAPER** WILLIAM 'DUCKY'	2	4	3	9	
5 **EVANS** W.	3	3	4 (3)	10	(3)
6 **FREEMAN** LEVI	3 (2)	4 (1)	3 (1)	10	(4)
7 **LILLEY** W. 'FESSOR'	3	4	4	11	
8 **MABBOTT** C.		1	1	2	
9 **MABLESTONE** WILLIAM 'SMILER'	3	4	4	11	
10 **McBIRNIE** G.	3	4	3	10	
11 **PANTER** AVERY B. 'JUMMY'	3	4 (1)	4 (1)	11	(2)
12 **PETERS** ALBERT	3	4 (1)	4	11	(1)
13 **STARR** JACKIE T.	3 (3)	4 (1)	4 (1)	11	(5)
14 **WEST** GEORGE	1		1	2	
maximum possible appearances	3	4	4	11	
goals rushed through			(1)		(1)
goals unaccounted for		(11)			(11)
total goals scored	(5)	(18)	(8)		(31)

1892-93	Midland League	F.A. Cup	TOTALS games	goals
1 **COWPER** G.	1		1	
2 **DAVIES** GEORGE	6	2	8	
3 **DIXON** HARRY	24 (6)	3 (2)	27	(8)
4 **DRAPER** WILLIAM 'DUCKY'	23	3	26	
5 **GARFIELD** BENNY W.	18 (9)		18	(9)
6 **GOODE** T.	10 (2)		10	(2)
7 **HOPEWELL** BOB	20	3	23	
8 **LILLEY** W. 'FESSOR'	11		11	
9 **MABLESTONE** WILLIAM 'SMILER'	24 (3)	3	27	(3)
10 **MARSHALL** R.	1		1	
11 **McGAHEY** C.	1		1	
12 **McURICH** C.	24 (10)	3 (1)	27	(11)
13 **NEWMAN** HARRY	2		2	
14 **PANTER** AVERY B. 'JUMMY'	10 (2)	3 (4)	13	(6)
15 **PETERS** ALBERT	21 (1)	3	24	(1)
16 **PHILLIPS** HENRY		1	1	
17 **ROBERTS** EVAN	12	3	15	
18 **STARR** JACKIE T.	24 (11)	3 (1)	27	(12)
19 **STOTT** JIMMY	13 (1)	3 (2)	16	(3)
20 **WALLIS** SAMMY	17		17	
21 **WEST** GEORGE	2		2	
maximum possible appearances	24	3	27	
own goals	(1)		(1)	
goals unaccounted for	(2)		(2)	
total goals scored	(48)	(10)	(58)	

1893-94	Midland League	F.A. Cup	Northants Senior Cup	Kettering Charity Cup	TOTALS games	goals
1 BARKER	2				2	
2 (a) BELLAMY	1				1	
3 BODDINGTON W.	1			1	2	
4 BROOKES	1				1	
5 DIXON HARRY	18 (5)	1	1	2 (1)	22	(6)
6 ELSON				1	1	
7 FREEMAN W.			1		1	
8 GOODE T.	5 (2)			2	7	(2)
9 (a) HALFPENNY	1				1	
10 HITCHCOCK IKE	19 (4)	1	1	2	23	(4)
11 HOWE A.	1				1	
12 LILLEY J.	2			1	3	
13 LILLEY W. 'FESSOR'	1				1	
14 LITCHFIELD T.	1				1	
15 MABLESTONE WILLIAM 'SMILER'	19	1	1	2 (3)	23	(3)
16 McDERMOTT JACK	10 (2)				10	(2)
17 McLEAN TOMMY	4				4	
18 McURICH C.	13 (1)	1	1 (2)	1 (1)	16	(4)
19 MEECHAM JIMMY	9				9	
20 NEWMAN HARRY	4		1		5	
21 PACK GEORGE	10			1	11	
22 PANTER AVERY B. 'JUMMY'	11	1	1	1	14	
23 PARKER H.	1				1	
24 PETERS ALBERT	17 (2)	1 (1)		2	20	(3)
25 PHILLIPS HENRY	5	1	1		7	
26 ROBERTS EVAN	2				2	
27 ROBINSON CHARLES 'CHING'				1	1	
28 ROWBOTHAM W.	3	1	1	1	6	
29 STARR JACKIE T.	15 (3)	1	1 (2)	2 (1)	19	(6)
30 TAFFS	1				1	
31 THORBURN	1				1	
32 TOSELAND ALBERT	19	1	1	1	22	
33 WALKER	1				1	
34 WALLIS SAMMY	12			1	13	
35 WHITTICK	9 (3)	1			10	(3)
maximum possible appearances	20	1	1	2	24	
own goals	(4)					(4)
total goals scored	(26)	(1)	(4)	(6)		(37)

(a) Kettering played a Midland League match at Long Eaton Rangers on 6 January with ten men, including two 'lent' by Long Eaton. These were possibly Bellamy and Halfpenny.

1894-95	Midland League	F.A. Cup	Kettering Charity Cup	TOTALS games	goals
1 **ASHWORTH** JACK	16 (6)		1	17	(6)
2 **BAKER** JOHN	7			7	
3 **BALL** ALF	24 (1)	1	1	26	(1)
4 **BATES** G.	1			1	
5 **CHAPMAN** E.	1			1	
6 **DIXON** HARRY	24 (6)	1	1	26	(6)
7 **DIXON** HORACE	1			1	
8 **FALL** G.	12		1	13	
9 **HITCHCOCK** IKE	6	1		7	
10 **MABLESTONE** WILLIAM 'SMILER'	23 (2)		1	24	(2)
11 **McDERMOTT** JACK	1			1	
12 **PACK** GEORGE	13	1		14	
13 **PALMER** J.	6			6	
14 **PANTER** AVERY B. 'JUMMY'	6	1		7	
15 **PANTER** E. 'TEDDY'	2			2	
16 **PELL** WILLIAM 'BILL'	24	1	1	26	
17 **ROBINSON** CHARLES	19 (9)		1	20	(9)
18 **ROSE** CHARLES	10 (2)	1		11	(2)
19 **STARR** JACKIE T.	2			2	
20 **THORPE** JACK	25 (13)	1	1	27	(13)
21 **TOSELAND** ALBERT	17 (1)	1	1	19	(1)
22 **TOWELL** W.	1			1	
23 **WALLIS** SAMMY	17	1	1	19	
24 **WHITEHOUSE** JACKIE	24 (9)	1	1	26	(9)
25 **YOUDES**	4			4	
maximum possible appearances	26	1	1	28	
own goals	(2)				(2)
goals rushed through			(1)		(1)
goals unaccounted for	(8)				(8)
total goals scored	(59)	(0)	(1)		(60)

175

1895-96	Midland League	Midland League Champ. Match	F.A. Cup	Northants Senior Cup	Kettering Charity Cup	Luton Charity Cup	Wellingborough Charity Cup	TOTALS games goals
1 ASHWORTH JACK	9 (5)		4 (3)			1 (1)		14 (9)
2 BABES	3 (1)							3 (1)
3 BALL ALF	13		4		1	2 (1)	1	21 (1)
4 DIXON HARRY	26 (5)	1	5 (1)	3 (1)	4	3	2 (1)	44 (8)
5 DRAPER WILLIAM 'DUCKY'	28 (1)	1	5	3	4	3 (1)	2 (1)	46 (3)
6 FARREN CHARLIE	1							1
7 HESKIN ALF	11 (4)		3			2 (2)		16 (6)
8 HITCHCOCK IKE	2		1			1		4
9 HOLLOWELL	1							1
10 MABLESTONE WILLIAM 'SM LER'	24 (3)	1	3	3	4 (1)	2 (1)	2	39 (5)
11 MASLIP	1							1
12 McMAIN JOE	24 (17)	1 (1)	5 (5)	3	4	3 (4)	2 (1)	42 (28)
13 MILLER WILLIAM 'TOUT'	27 (8)	1	5	3 (1)	4 (4)	3 (2)	2 (1)	45 (16)
14 PANTER AVERY B. 'JUMMY'	12 (1)	1		3 (3)	3 (1)		1	20 (5)
15 PANTER E. 'TEDDY'	15 (9)	1	1	3 (2)	4	2	2	28 (11)
16 PELL WILLIAM 'BILL'	28 (2)	1	5 (1)	3	4	3	2	46 (3)
17 PERKINS WILLIAM H.	28	1	5	3	4	3	2	46
18 SIMPSON	2							2
19 TOSELAND ALBERT	13		3					16
20 WALLIS SAMMY	13	1	2	3	4	3 (1)	2	28 (1)
21 WHITEHOUSE JACKIE	27 (5)	1	4 (1)	3 (2)	4	2 (2)	2 (1)	43 (11)
maximum possible appearances	28		5	3	4	3	2	46
goals rushed through		(1)	(1)					(2)
goals unaccounted for	(13)							(14)
total goals scored	(74)	(2)	(13)	(9)	(6)	(15)	(5)	(124)

1896-97	Midland League	United League	F.A. Cup	Northants Senior Cup	Kettering Charity Cup	TOTALS games	goals
1 ALLEN J.	10 (4)	4 (1)				14	(5)
2 ATHERTON JAMES	27 (1)	10	4	1	1	43	(1)
3 BALL ALF	19 (5)	10 (2)	4 (1)	1	1	35	(8)
4 BANKS RICHARD	5 (1)	3				8	(1)
5 COWAN	10 (1)	4 (1)				14	(2)
6 DAINTY HERBERT C.	2	2				4	
7 DIXON HARRY	25 (6)	11 (4)	4 (2)	1	1	42	(12)
8 DRAPER WILLIAM 'DUCKY'	26	12	4	1	1	44	
9 DUGDALE		1				1	
10 FISH W.	1					1	
11 GRAHAM	3 (1)	1	1			5	(1)
12 GREEN THOMAS	9 (3)	6 (1)				16	(4)
13 HESKIN ALF	13 (6)	6 (5)	3 (1)	1	1	23	(12)
14 McMAIN JOE	9 (3)	3				12	(3)
15 MILLER THOMAS		1				1	
16 MILLER WILLIAM 'TOUT'	26 (5)	14 (4)	4	1	1	46	(9)
17 PANTER AVERY B. 'JUMMY'		1				1	
18 PANTER E. 'TEDDY'	17 (5)	10 (1)	3 (2)	1	1	32	(8)
19 PARKER W.A. 'TOMMY'	3 (1)	3 (1)				6	(2)
20 PELL WILLIAM 'BILL'	28 (1)	14 (1)	4	1	1	48	(2)
21 PERKINS WILLIAM H.	28	14	4	1	1	48	
22 TOSELAND ALBERT	3	4				8	
23 WALLIS SAMMY	27 (1)	11	4	1	1	43	(1)
24 WHITEHOUSE JACKIE	15 (3)	6 (1)	4	1	1 (1)	27	(5)
25 WINTERHALDER HERBERT	2 (1)					2	(1)
26 WRIGHT ERNEST		1	1	1	1	4	
maximum possible appearances	28	14	4	1	1	48	
own goals	(1)						(1)
goals unaccounted for	(3)						(3)
total goals scored	(51)	(23)	(6)	(0)	(1)		(81)

1897-98

1897-98	Midland League	United League	F.A. Cup	Northants Senior Cup	Kettering Charity Cup	Wellingborough Charity Cup	TOTALS games	goals
1 ATHERTON JAMES	21 (2)	13	1	3	2	3	43	(2)
2 BELLFIELD F.	3	3	1				7	
3 BREARLEY JACK	12 (3)	9 (3)		2	2 (2)	3 (1)	28	(9)
4 DAINTY HERBERT C.	14	12		3 (1)	2	3	34	(1)
5 DENTON L.						1	1	
6 DIXON ERNEST	1 (1)	1					2	(1)
7 DIXON HARRY	21	16 (5)	1	3 (1)	3	3 (1)	47	(7)
8 DIXON HORACE					1		1	
9 DRAPER WILLIAM 'DUCKY'	21 (1)	15 (1)	1	3	3 (1)	3	46	(3)
10 FARREN CHARLIE	1	4			1 (1)		6	(1)
11 GARFIELD JAMES	14 (3)	7 (1)	1	1 (1)	2 (1)	1	26	(6)
12 GREEN CHARLIE	8	4 (1)	1	1			14	(1)
13 HESKIN ALF	3	5 (2)			2	2	12	(2)
14 HITCHCOCK IKE	4	5 (1)					9	(1)
15 INGRAM CHARLES	2	1		2 (1)			5	(1)
16 LAWRENCE EVERARD	2	1 (1)					3	(1)
17 MILLER WILLIAM 'TOUT'	19 (1)	14 (4)	1	3 (1)	3 (5)	3 (3)	43	(14)
18 OAKEY		1					1	
19 PANTER E. 'TEDDY'	20 (6)	15 (3)	1	3 (1)	3 (2)	3	44	(12)
20 PARKER W.A. 'TOMMY'	1						1	
21 PELL WILLIAM 'BILL'	21	16 (2)	1	3 (3)	3	3	47	(5)
22 PERKINS WILLIAM H.	22	15	1	3	2	3	46	
23 TOSELAND ALBERT	3	4			1	1	9	
24 WALLIS SAMMY	20	12	1	3	3	1	40	
25 WHEATCROFT		1					1	
26 WINTERHALDER HERBERT	2	1	1				4	
27 WRIGHT ERNEST	2						2	
28 YORK G.	5 (2)	1					6	(2)
maximum possible appearances	22	16	1	3	3	3	48	
own goals	(1)	(1)						(1)
goals unaccounted for	(3)	(3)						(3)
total goals scored	(19)	(28)	(0)	(9)	(12)	(5)		(73)

1898-99	Midland League	United League	F.A. Cup	Kettering Charity Cup	Rushden Charity Cup	Wellingborough Charity Cup	TOTALS games	goals
1 **BALDRY** ERNEST	20	15	5	3	3	1	47	
2 **BEAVER** JOHN	24 (6)	19 (3)	5 (2)	3 (1)	3 (1)	1	55	(13)
3 **CARVEL**		1					1	
4 **CLARKE** WILLIAM H. 'DILLON'	9	4	1	2	1	1	18	
5 **DAINTY** HERBERT C.	25 (2)	18	5	3	3	1	55	(2)
6 **DAINTY** JACK	2	4		1	2		9	
7 **DIXON** HARRY	20 (9)	13 (1)	3	3	3 (1)		42	(11)
8 **DRAPER** WILLIAM 'DUCKY'	19 (4)	15 (4)	4 (1)	2	2	1	43	(9)
9 **FARREN** CHARLIE	15 (1)	9	5			1	30	(1)
10 **HARRIS**	1						1	
11 **HESKIN** ALF	17	16 (1)	4 (1)	2	2 (2)	1	42	(4)
12 **INGRAM** CHARLES	4 (1)	3					7	(1)
13 **JULIAN** A. 'SAMMY'	6	4					10	
14 **McARLIE** JAMES	3	5 (2)					8	(2)
15 **MILLER** WILLIAM 'TOUT'	8 (2)	9 (1)	3				20	(3)
16 **PANTER** E. 'TEDDY'	21 (5)	14 (2)	5 (1)	3	3	1	47	(8)
17 **PELL** WILLIAM 'BILL'	24 (1)	17	5	2 (1)	2	1	51	(2)
18 **RAYNOR** JIMMY	9	11	2		1 (1)		23	(1)
19 **SMITH** J.	3	2					5	
20 **TOSELAND** ALBERT	1	2			1		4	
21 **WALLIS** SAMMY	15	10	2	3	3		33	
22 **WEST** T.	1						1	
23 **WINTERHALDER** HERBERT	25 (8)	13	5 (1)	3	3	1	50	(9)
24 **WOODWARD** W.	14 (5)	16 (7)	1	3 (2)	1	1	36	(14)
maximum possible appearances	26	20	5	3	3	1	58	
own goals	(1)							(1)
goals rushed through	(1)							(1)
goals unaccounted for	(1)							(1)
total goals scored	(47)	(21)	(6)	(4)	(5)	(0)		(83)

1899-1900	Midland League	Midland League Champ. Match	United League	F.A. Cup	Wellingborough Charity Cup	TOTALS games	goals
1 **BALDRY** ERNEST	21	1	12		1	35	
2 **BARNETT** W.	9 (1)	1	10		1	21	(1)
3 **CARTER** A.B.	22 (7)	1 (1)	10 (7)	1	1	35	(15)
4 **CLARKE** WILLIAM H. 'DILLON'	5	1	7		1	14	
5 **COLEMAN** JOHN G. 'TIDDY'	20 (8)		11 (4)	1 (1)	1 (1)	33	(14)
6 **DAINTY** JACK	24	1	12	1	1	39	
7 **DRAPER** WILLIAM 'DUCKY'	24 (8)	1	12 (1)	1		38	(9)
8 **HESKIN** ALF	8 (3)		2			10	(3)
9 **JULIAN** A. 'SAMMY'	1		1	1		3	
10 **LEATON** A.			1			1	
11 **MAWSON** FRED	24 (9)	1	11 (4)	1	1	38	(13)
12 **PANTER** E. 'TEDDY'	16	1	9			26	
13 **PARKER** W.H.	1		3	1	1	6	
14 **PEGG** RICHARD	24 (17)	1 (3)	11 (8)	1 (1)	1	38	(29)
15 **PELL** WILLIAM 'BILL'	23 (1)	1 (1)	10 (1)	1	1	36	(3)
16 **ROBINSON** ARTHUR	2					2	
17 **TAYLOR** ARTHUR			1			1	
18 **WALLIS** SAMMY	20		6	1		27	
19 **WILLIAMS** T.	1					1	
20 **WINTERHALDER** HERBERT	19 (4)	1 (1)	3 (4)	1	1	25	(9)
maximum possible appearances	24	1	12	1	1	39	
goals unaccounted for			(2)				(2)
total goals scored	(58)	(6)	(31)	(2)	(1)		(98)

Appendix C

Results: Cup Ties 1881 - 1900

Appendix C is a record of Kettering FC's first team cup-tie results between seasons 1881-82 and 1899-1900; including (where known) the date the match was played, opponents, round, venue (H – home, A – away), result (Kettering's score first), scorers (in alphabetical order) and attendance (which was based on gate receipts or an estimate, rather than an accurate count).

Not until 1888-89 did the club participate in more than one knockout competition. In the five seasons prior to this – the transition from rugby union to association football – Kettering's only competitive games were in the Northants Senior Cup. The advent of the Kettering Charity Cup in 1888 led to a number of similar competitions, and Kettering entered Grantham's, Luton's, Wellingborough's and Rushden's before the turn of the century. But it was in the FA Cup that the club really made a name for itself, reaching the last 32 of the competition three times during the 1890s.

As noted in Appendix B, in the two seasons prior to entering the Senior Cup, Kettering played two competitive games of rugby union in the Midland Counties Football Union Challenge Cup. The results of these ties were:

1881-82

Oct 22, MOSELEY HARRIERS, 1st round, away, lost by 4 goals to nil.

1882-83

Oct 21, LEAMINGTON ROVERS, 1st round, home, won by 1 goal (Brains) to nil.

Note: The tie was subsequently declared void and awarded to Leamington.

date	opponents	round	venue	result	scorers	crowd
				1883-84		
Oct 20	WELLINGBORO' REVELLERS	1	H	2-0	L. Lindsay, Woolston	
Mar 22	HIGHAM FERRERS	semi	W	1-1	Parker	
Mar 29	HIGHAM FERRERS	replay	W	3-0	Parker, Woolston, 1 own goal	
Apr 5	WELLINGBOROUGH TOWN	final	A	2-1	Dixon, Rev. Thurston	
				1884-85		
Nov 1	WELLINGBORO' REVELLERS	1	A	2-1	Parker, Woolston	
Dec 27	RUSHDEN WANDERERS	semi	W	0-2		
				1885-86		
Dec 26	NORTHAMPTON ASSOCIATION	2	H	7-0	7 goals unaccounted for	700
Feb 20	RUSHDEN WANDERERS	semi	W	0-2		
				1886-87		
Dec 4	WELLINGBOROUGH TOWN	1	H	2-4	Piggott (2)	
				1887-88		
Jan 21	RUSHDEN WANDERERS	1	A	2-4	James, Maycock	
				1893-94		
Dec 11	WELLINGBOROUGH TOWN	1	A	4-1	McUrich (2), Starr (2)	
Feb 24	RUSHDEN TOWN	semi	W	(a)		

(a) Kettering forfeited the match because it clashed with a Midland League fixture.

date	opponents	round	venue	result	scorers	crowd
				1894-95		
Mar 23	RUSHDEN TOWN	final	W	1-4	(b)	

(b) Not classed as a first team match. Kettering fielded a 'third' team, mostly assembled from other clubs around the town.

date	opponents	round	venue	result	scorers	crowd
				1895-96		
Feb 17	WELLINGBOROUGH TOWN	semi	A	6-0	Dixon, Miller, A. Panter (2), Whitehouse (2)	
Apr 13	RUSHDEN TOWN	final	W	0-0		600
Apr 23	RUSHDEN TOWN	replay	W	3-0	A. Panter, E. Panter (2)	800
				1896-97		
Feb 22	WELLINGBOROUGH TOWN	semi	A	0-1		1,200
				1897-98		
Nov 22	FINEDON REVELLERS	(c)	H	5-1	Garfield, Miller, Pell (3)	
Feb 7	RUSHDEN TOWN	(c)	A	1-1	Panter	
Mar 7	WELLINGBOROUGH TOWN	(c)	A (d)	3-1	Dainty, Harry Dixon, Ingram	

(c) This season the Northants Senior Cup, won by Kettering, was contested on a league basis.

(d) Other sources indicate the match was played at home.

Where the venue is marked W, the match was played on a neutral ground in Wellingborough.

F.A. CUP

date	opponents	round	venue	result	scorers	crowd
1888-89						
Oct 6	NEWARK	1 qual	H	3-4 (a)	Jenkins, Piggott, Wilson	1,000

(a) At full time the score stood at 2-2. Instead of replaying the match, both teams agreed to 30 minutes extra time.

date	opponents	round	venue	result	scorers	crowd
1889-90						
Oct 26	GAINSBOROUGH TRINITY	2 qual	A	(b)		

(b) Kettering forfeited the match rather than travel such a distance (and played a Kettering Charity Cup match instead).

date	opponents	round	venue	result	scorers	crowd
1890-91						
Oct 4	LANGLEY GREEN VICTORIA	1 qual	A	0-5		

date	opponents	round	venue	result	scorers	crowd
1891-92						
Oct 3	HEREFORD	1 qual	A	(c)		

(c) Kettering forfeited the match to aviod the cost of travelling (and played a friendly instead).

date	opponents	round	venue	result	scorers	crowd
1892-93						
Oct 15	LANGLEY MILL RANGERS	1 qual	H	3-1	Panter, Stott (2)	
Oct 29	BEESTON	2 qual	H	6-1	Dixon (2), McUrich, Panter (2), Starr	2,000
Nov 19	LOUGHBOROUGH TOWN	3 qual	H	1-2	Panter	2,000

date	opponents	round	venue	result	scorers	crowd
1893-94						
Oct 14	LOUGHBOROUGH TOWN	1 qual	A	1-4	Peters	1,500

date	opponents	round	venue	result	scorers	crowd
1894-95						
Oct 13	LOUGHBOROUGH TOWN	1 qual	A	0-4		

date	opponents	round	venue	result	scorers	crowd
1895-96						
Oct 12	GEDLING GROVE	1 qual	H	4-0	Ashworth (2), McMain (2)	
Nov 2	COALVILLE TOWN	2 qual	A	4-0	Dixon, McMain, 1 goal rushed through, 1 goal unaccounted for	
Nov 23	LOUGHBOROUGH TOWN	3 qual	H	2-1	McMain (2)	
Dec 14	LEICESTER FOSSE	4 qual	A	2-1	Ashworth, Whitehouse	6,000
Feb 1	NEWTON HEATH	1	A	1-2	Pell	6,000

date	opponents	round	venue	result	scorers	crowd
1896-97						
Nov 21	RUSHDEN TOWN	3 qual	A	2-0	E. Panter (2)	2,500
Dec 12	MANSFIELD	4 qual	A	1-0	Heskin	
Jan 2	LEICESTER FOSSE	5 qual	H	2-1	Ball, Dixon	5,000
Jan 30	NEWTON HEATH	1	A	1-5	Dixon	4,000

date	opponents	round	venue	result	scorers	crowd
1897-98						
Oct 30	WELLINGBOROUGH TOWN	3 qual	H	0-1		4,000

date	opponents	round	venue	result	scorers	crowd
1898-99						
Oct 29	HUCKNALL St. JOHN'S	3 qual	A	(d)		
Nov 3	HUCKNALL St. JOHN'S	replay	H	1-0	Winterhalder (e)	1,000
Nov 19	LOUGHBOROUGH TOWN	4 qual	H	2-1	Beaver, Heskin	3,000
Dec 10	LEICESTER FOSSE	5 qual	H	1-1	Panter	5,000
Dec 15	LEICESTER FOSSE	replay	A	2-1	Beaver, Draper	3,500
Jan 28	NOTTS COUNTY	1	A	0-2		8,000

(d) Match abandoned after 78 minutes because of bad light. Kettering were winning 2-0.

(e) Other sources credit the goal to Miller.

date	opponents	round	venue	result	scorers	crowd
1899-1900						
Oct 28	BURTON SWIFTS	3 qual	A	2-8	Coleman, Pegg	5,000

KETTERING CHARITY CUP

date	opponents	round	venue	result	scorers	crowd
				1888-89		
Dec 22	WELLINGBOROUGH TOWN	1	H	3-1	Dixon, Piggott (2)	
Feb 2	LOUGHBOROUGH TOWN	2	H	0-2		
				1889-90		
Oct 26	HIGHAM FERRERS	1	H	5-2	Bates, Lilley, West, 2 goals rushed through	
Nov 30	BEDFORD	2	H	8-1	Allen (2), Hutchen, Knight (2), Newman, 2 goals rushed through	
Feb 8	LEICESTER FOSSE	3	H	3-1	Bates (3)	1,500
Mar 8	LUTON TOWN	semi	H	1-2	Bates	2,000
				1890-91		
Feb 2	FINEDON REVELLERS	2	H	2-3	H. Dixon, 1 goal rushed through	
				1891-92		
Dec 12	LEICESTER FOSSE	2	H	5-0	Dixon (2), Freeman, Panter, Starr	
Jan 23	KETTERING ANCHOR	3	H	12-0	Dixon, 11 goals unaccounted for	
Feb 20	FINEDON REVELLERS	semi	H	(a)		
Mar 26	GRANTHAM ROVERS	final	H	1-1	Peters	5,500
Apr 23	GRANTHAM ROVERS	replay	H	0-1		

(a) Finedon Revellers forfeited the match after the death of a player the previous day.

date	opponents	round	venue	result	scorers	crowd
				1893-94		
Dec 4	KETTERING HAWKS	2	H	6-1	Dixon, Mablestone (3), McUrich, Starr	
Dec 30	LEICESTER FOSSE	semi	A	0-8		
				1894-95		
Feb 11	LEICESTER FOSSE	2	A	1-6	1 goal rushed through	1,500
				1895-96		
Dec 24	RUSHDEN TOWN	1	H	3-0	Mablestone, Miller (2)	
Mar 16	NOTTINGHAM FOREST	semi	H	1-0	Miller	
Apr 20	BURTON WANDERERS	final	H	0-0		4,000
Apr 29	BURTON WANDERERS	replay	H	2-0	Miller, A. Panter	3,500
				1896-97		
Feb 1	LUTON TOWN	1	A	1-4	Whitehouse	
				1897-98		
Nov 27	BURTON WANDERERS	1	H	(b)		
Dec 28	BURTON WANDERERS	replay	H	2-0	Brearley, Miller	
Mar 21	WOLVERTON	semi	H	3-0	Brearley, Miller (2)	
Apr 25	RUSHDEN TOWN	final	H	7-0	Draper, Farren, Garfield, Miller (2), Panter (2)	5,500

(b) Match abandoned after 83 minutes because of bad light. Kettering were winning 2-1.

date	opponents	round	venue	result	scorers	crowd
				1898-99		
Mar 6	LOUGHBOROUGH TOWN	semi	H	2-0	Beaver, Woodward (c)	1,000
Apr 10	RUSHDEN TOWN	final	H	0-0		1,500
Apr 17	RUSHDEN TOWN	replay	H	2-1	Pell, Woodward	2,500

(c) Other sources credit both goals to Beaver.

GRANTHAM CHARITY CUP

date	opponents	round	venue	result	scorers	crowd
				1890-91		
Dec 6	GRANTHAM TOWN	2	H	2-0	Mason, Panter	
Jan 17	GRANTHAM ROVERS	3	H	0-4		
				1891-92		
Dec 5	GRANTHAM ROVERS	2	H	2-0	Starr (2)	3,000
Feb 27	LINCOLN CITY SWIFTS	semi	G	3-1	Freeman (2), Starr	
Apr 2	DERBY COUNTY WANDERERS	final	G	0-1		

Where the venue is marked G, the match was played on a neutral ground in Grantham.

LUTON CHARITY CUP

date	opponents	round	venue	result	scorers	crowd
				1890-91		
Jan 24	IRTHLINGBORO' REVELLERS	2	H	10-0 (a)	Bradley, C. Dixon (2), H. Dixon (2), Mason, Panter (4)	
Mar 9	RUSHDEN TOWN	3	H	3-0	Ball, Wood, 1 goal rushed through	1,500
Mar 28	BEDFORD	semi	L	6-1	Curtis, H. Dixon, Panter (4)	
Apr 18	WINDSOR PHEONIX	final	L	5-1	Bradley (3), C. Dixon (2) (b)	3,500

(a) Irthlingborough Revellers 'retired' when Kettering scored their tenth goal early in the second half. The result stood.
(b) Other sources credit one of Bradley's goals to H. Dixon.

date	opponents	round	venue	result	scorers	crowd
				1891-92		
Nov 7	FINEDON REVELLERS	1	H	1-0	1 goal rushed through	4,000
Dec 19	RUSHDEN TOWN	2	A	2-0	Evans, Panter	2,000
Feb 6	WOLVERTON	3	H	5-0	Dixon, Evans (2), Freeman, Starr	
Mar 12	MILLWALL ATHLETIC	semi	L	0-1		3,000
				1895-96		
Jan 11	COLDSTREAM GUARDS	2	H	11-0	Ball, Draper, Heskin (2), McMain (2), Miller (2), Wallis, Whitehouse (2)	
Mar 2	RUSHDEN TOWN	semi	L	4-1	Ashworth, Mablestone, McMain (2)	1,500
Mar 30	LUTON TOWN	final	A	0-3		4,000

Where the venue is marked L, the match was played on a neutral ground in Luton.

WELLINGBOROUGH CHARITY CUP

date	opponents	round	venue	result	scorers	crowd
				1895-96		
Jan 27	FINEDON REVELLERS	1	H	5-0	Dixon, Draper, McMain, Miller, Whitehouse	
Mar 23	WALSALL	semi	W	0-2		3,000
				1897-98		
Jan 29	NORTHAMPTON TOWN	1	H	2-0	Miller (2)	
Mar 14	READING	semi	W	3-0	Brearley, Harry Dixon, Miller	
Apr 12	WELLINGBOROUGH TOWN	final	A	0-1		
				1898-99		
Jan 30	RUSHDEN TOWN	semi	W	0-3		
				1899-1900		
Apr 2	RUSHDEN TOWN	semi	W	1-2	Coleman	

Where the venue is marked W, the match was played on a neutral ground in Wellingborough.

RUSHDEN CHARITY CUP

date	opponents	round	venue	result	scorers	crowd
				1895-96		
Mar 30	LEICESTER FOSSE RES.	semi	R	2-5	(a)	

(a) Not classed as a first team match. Kettering fielded a reserve side because it clashed with the final of the Luton Charity Cup.

date	opponents	round	venue	result	scorers	crowd
				1898-99		
Apr 12	WELLINGBOROUGH TOWN	semi	R	0-0		
Apr 25	WELLINGBOROUGH TOWN	replay	R	3-0	Beaver, Dixon, Raynor	
Apr 27	RUSHDEN TOWN	final	A	2-0	Heskin (2)	

Where the venue is marked R, the match was played on a neutral ground in Rushden.

Appendix D

Results & Tables: League Matches 1892 - 1900

Appendix D is a record of Kettering FC's first team league results between seasons 1892-93 and 1899-1900; including (where known) the date the match was played, opponents, venue, result, scorers and attendance (comments made on these points in Appendix C also apply to Appendix D). Abandoned games, or those which were initially designated league fixtures but completed as friendlies, have not been included. However, the Midland League Championship Matches, played in 1896 and 1900 are included.

The club joined the Midland League in 1892 and the United League in 1896. Both were based on the Football League (established in 1888) format of teams playing each other on a home and away basis.

Appendix D is also a record of the final league tables for each season (United League tables in particular can vary according to which source is consulted). It should be noted that throughout this period it was two points for a win, one for a draw and none for a defeat in league competitions. Teams level on points are separated by 'goal average' – the number of goals scored divided by the number conceded – rather than 'goal difference', which is the norm today.

MIDLAND LEAGUE
1892-93

date	opponents	venue	result	scorers	crowd
Sep 17	DERBY JUNCTION	H	2-2	Garfield, McUrich	
24	WEDNESBURY OLD ATHLETIC	H	2-4	Mablestone, Starr	
Oct 1	GRANTHAM ROVERS	A	1-2	Garfield	
8	LEICESTER FOSSE	H	0-4		
22	NEWARK	H	3-0	Dixon, McUrich, Stott	
Nov 5	DONCASTER ROVERS	A	2-2	Panter (2)	1,400
Dec 17	ROTHERHAM TOWN	H	4-0	McUrich (2), Starr (2)	
24	NEWARK	A	2-3	Dixon, 1 goal unaccounted for	
28	GAINSBOROUGH TRINITY	A	1-7	1 goal unaccounted for	
Jan 14	GRANTHAM ROVERS	H	0-0		
21	LONG EATON RANGERS	A	5-2	Garfield, Mablestone, Peters, Starr, 1 own goal	
28	ROTHERHAM TOWN	A	0-4		
Feb 4	LONG EATON RANGERS	H	3-0	Garfield, McUrich, Starr	
11	MANSFIELD TOWN	A	1-0	Mablestone	
18	BURTON WANDERERS	A	1-2	Starr	
Mar 11	LOUGHBOROUGH TOWN	A	0-2		
31	DERBY JUNCTION	A	5-1	Dixon (2), McUrich, Starr (2)	
Apr 1	BURTON WANDERERS	H	3-0	Dixon, Goode, Starr	1,500
4	MANSFIELD TOWN	H	3-0	Garfield, McUrich (2)	
8	LEICESTER FOSSE	A	1-3	Garfield	
15	GAINSBOROUGH TRINITY	H	2-0	Dixon, Goode	1,000
22	LOUGHBOROUGH TOWN	H	1-3	McUrich	1,500
26	WEDNESBURY OLD ATHLETIC	A	3-0	Garfield (2), McUrich	
29	DONCASTER ROVERS	H	3-0	Garfield, Starr (2)	1,000

FINAL TABLE

	played	won	drawn	lost	for	against	points
1 ROTHERHAM TOWN	24	19	3	2	80	28	41
2 BURTON WANDERERS	24	15	4	5	49	33	34
3 LOUGHBOROUGH TOWN	24	15	3	6	64	30	33
4 LEICESTER FOSSE	24	12	3	9	50	37	27
5 DONCASTER ROVERS	24	11	4	9	47	44	26
6 GAINSBOROUGH TRINITY	24	12	1	11	51	34	25
7 KETTERING	**24**	**11**	**3**	**10**	**48**	**41**	**25**
8 GRANTHAM ROVERS	24	10	2	12	46	43	22
9 WEDNESBURY OLD ATHLETIC	24	8	3	13	41	51	19
10 LONG EATON RANGERS	24	6	6	12	34	53	18
11 MANSFIELD TOWN	24	7	2	15	26	70	16
12 NEWARK	24	6	3	15	34	62	15
13 DERBY JUNCTION	24	3	5	16	32	76	11

MIDLAND LEAGUE
1893-94

date	opponents	venue	result	scorers	crowd
Sep 9	NEWARK	A	1-6	Starr	
30	DONCASTER ROVERS	H	0-0		
Oct 7	NEWARK	H	2-1	Hitchcock, Whittick	
21	GRANTHAM ROVERS	A	0-4		1,500
28	LOUGHBOROUGH TOWN	A	1-1	Dixon	
Nov 11	MANSFIELD GREENHALGH'S	H	3-6	Goode (2), Whittick	850
Dec 2	MANSFIELD TOWN	H	3-1	Hitchcock, Starr, Whittick	
9	BURTON WANDERERS	H	2-4	McUrich, 1 own goal (a)	
23	DONCASTER ROVERS	A	1-2	1 own goal (b)	
Jan 6	LONG EATON RANGERS	A	1-12	Hitchcock	
27	MANSFIELD TOWN	A	1-1	1 own goal	
Feb 10	LONG EATON RANGERS	H	3-0	McDermott (2), 1 own goal	1,000
24	LEICESTER FOSSE	A	0-4		3,000
Mar 3	GAINSBOROUGH TRINITY	A	0-1		
23	LOUGHBOROUGH TOWN	H	1-1	Dixon	1,200
24	LEICESTER FOSSE	H	1-1	Dixon	2,000
31	MANSFIELD GREENHALGH'S	A	1-2	Dixon (c)	100
Apr 14	GAINSBOROUGH TRINITY	H	3-1	Dixon, Hitchcock, Starr	1,000
21	GRANTHAM ROVERS	H	2-3	Peters (2)	1,400
28	BURTON WANDERERS	A	0-8		

(a) Other sources credit the own goal to Starr.

(b) Other sources credit the goal to Hitchcock.

(c) Other sources credit the goal to McUrich.

FINAL TABLE

		played	won	drawn	lost	for	against	points
1	BURTON WANDERERS	20	17	3	0	82	12	35 (d)
2	LEICESTER FOSSE	20	15	2	3	49	13	32
3	LOUGHBOROUGH TOWN	20	12	6	2	52	22	30
4	GRANTHAM ROVERS	20	9	4	7	35	33	22
5	MANSFIELD GREENHALGH'S	20	9	3	8	43	54	21
6	LONG EATON RANGERS	20	7	4	9	43	44	18
7	DONCASTER ROVERS	20	5	4	11	27	48	14
8	NEWARK	20	6	2	12	28	55	14
9	**KETTERING**	**20**	**4**	**5**	**11**	**26**	**59**	**13**
10	GAINSBOROUGH TRINITY	20	5	1	14	28	46	11
11	MANSFIELD TOWN	20	2	4	14	27	54	8

(d) Burton Wanderers were docked two points for fielding an ineligible player.

MIDLAND LEAGUE
1894-95

date	opponents	venue	result	scorers	crowd
Sep 1	GRANTHAM ROVERS	A	1-0	Thorpe	
15	LOUGHBOROUGH TOWN	A	2-2	Mablestone, Thorpe	2,500
22	LONG EATON RANGERS	H	2-2	Thorpe (2)	2,000
24	RUSHDEN TOWN	A	1-2	Harry Dixon	4,000
29	DONCASTER ROVERS	H	2-1	2 own goals (a)	2,000
Oct 6	NEWARK	H	2-1	Harry Dixon (2)	1,500
27	MANSFIELD	A	0-2		
Nov 3	DERBY COUNTY RESERVES	A	1-3	Rose	
10	HEANOR TOWN	H	2-1	Thorpe, Whitehouse	1,500
17	LONG EATON RANGERS	A	1-2	Rose	
Dec 1	DERBY COUNTY RESERVES	H	2-2	Thorpe (2)	
8	HEANOR TOWN	A	3-3	Ashworth, Robinson, Thorpe	
15	GAINSBOROUGH TRINITY	A	2-4	2 goals unaccounted for	
25	STOKE SWIFTS	H	2-2	Robinson, Whitehouse	2,500
Jan 5	MATLOCK	A	2-1	Robinson, Whitehouse	
12	MANSFIELD	H	4-1	Ashworth (2), Harry Dixon, Robinson	
Feb 9	STOKE SWIFTS	A	3-2	Ball, 2 goals unaccounted for	
16	NEWARK	A	4-2	Thorpe, 3 goals unaccounted for	
23	LOUGHBOROUGH TOWN	H	1-4	Robinson	4,000
Mar 2	DONCASTER ROVERS	A	1-1	Thorpe	
9	MATLOCK	H	7-0 (b)	Ashworth, Harry Dixon, Mablestone, Toseland, Whitehouse (3)	
16	GRANTHAM ROVERS	H	4-2	Robinson, Whitehouse (3) (c)	
23	ILKESTON TOWN	A	2-4	Robinson, 1 goal unaccounted for (d)	
Apr 6	ILKESTON TOWN	H	4-0	Ashworth, Robinson, Thorpe (2)	
13	GAINSBOROUGH TRINITY	H	3-1	Harry Dixon, Robinson, Thorpe	
15	RUSHDEN TOWN	H	1-0	Ashworth	3,500

(a) Other sources credit the goals to Hitchcock and Thorpe.

(b) Other sources give the score as 7-1 (and the crowd as 300).

(c) Other sources credit Robinson with two goals whilst the other two are unaccounted for.

(d) Other sources credit both goals to Thorpe.

FINAL TABLE

		played	won	drawn	lost	for	against	points
1	LOUGHBOROUGH TOWN	26	19	4	3	84	25	42
2	STOKE SWIFTS	26	14	7	5	90	33	35
3	DERBY COUNTY RESERVES	26	12	8	6	46	27	32
4	GAINSBOROUGH TRINITY	26	14	4	8	55	36	32
5	**KETTERING**	26	13	6	7	59	45	32
6	ILKESTON TOWN	26	13	5	8	53	46	31
7	MANSFIELD	26	12	5	9	46	37	29
8	HEANOR TOWN	26	9	5	12	49	48	23
9	RUSHDEN TOWN	26	10	3	13	47	70	23
10	LONG EATON RANGERS	26	7	5	14	41	55	19
11	NEWARK	26	6	6	14	37	63	18
12	DONCASTER ROVERS	26	6	6	14	35	70	18
13	GRANTHAM ROVERS	26	6	5	15	27	59	17
14	MATLOCK	26	3	7	16	37	92	13

MIDLAND LEAGUE
1895-96

date		opponents	venue	result	scorers	crowd
Sep	7	GRANTHAM ROVERS	A	2-0	Babes, Heskin	
	14	HEANOR TOWN	H	1-1	Ashworth	
	21	LONG EATON RANGERS	H	1-1	Mablestone	
	23	RUSHDEN TOWN	A	4-3	Heskin, McMain, Miller, Whitehouse	4,500
	28	BARNSLEY St. PETER'S	A	2-1	Ashworth, McMain	4,000
Oct	19	MATLOCK	H	7-1	Ashworth (2), Dixon (2), Heskin (2), Miller	
	26	MANSFIELD	A	0-0		
	28	WELLINGBOROUGH TOWN	A	3-1	Ashworth, Pell, Whitehouse (a)	3,000
Nov	9	WALSALL	H	5-2	McMain (4), Miller	3,000
	16	ILKESTON TOWN	A	2-0	Dixon, McMain	
	30	MANSFIELD	H	5-0	McMain, E. Panter (2), Pell, Whitehouse (b)	
Dec	7	NEWARK	A	2-1	2 goals unaccounted for	
Jan	4	ILKESTON TOWN	H	2-0	McMain, Miller	
	25	GAINSBOROUGH TRINITY	A	0-2		2,500
Feb	8	DONCASTER ROVERS	A	3-1	McMain, 2 goals unaccounted for	
	10	DRESDEN UNITED	H	3-1	McMain (2), E. Panter	
	15	NEWARK	H	7-0	Draper, Mablestone, Miller, E. Panter (3), Whitehouse	1,500
	22	LONG EATON RANGERS	A	2-1	Miller, E. Panter	
	29	WALSALL	A	2-5	2 goals unaccounted for	
Mar	14	DONCASTER ROVERS	H	3-0	Miller, A. Panter, Whitehouse	
	21	MATLOCK	A	4-0	4 goals unaccounted for	
	28	BARNSLEY St. PETER'S	H	3-0	Dixon, McMain, Miller	
Apr	4	WELLINGBOROUGH TOWN	H	2-0	McMain (2)	
	6	RUSHDEN TOWN	H	3-1	Dixon, McMain, E. Panter	5,000
	8	HEANOR TOWN	A	1-1	1 goal unaccounted for	
	18	GAINSBOROUGH TRINITY	H	1-1	Mablestone	3,000
	25	DRESDEN UNITED	A	0-1		1,000
	30	GRANTHAM ROVERS	H	4-3	Mc Main, E. Panter, 2 goals unaccounted for	

(a) Other sources credit Whitehouse's goal to Dixon.
(b) Other sources credit both of E. Panter's goals to A. Panter.

MIDLAND LEAGUE CHAMPIONSHIP MATCH

Apr	3	REST OF THE MIDLAND LEAGUE	H	2-2	McMain, 1 goal rushed through (c)	2,500

(c) Other sources credit both goals to McMain.

FINAL TABLE

		played	won	drawn	lost	for	against	points
1	**KETTERING**	**28**	**20**	**5**	**3**	**74**	**28**	**45**
2	GAINSBOROUGH TRINITY	28	17	6	5	59	26	40
3	WALSALL	28	17	6	5	91	47	40
4	LONG EATON RANGERS	28	18	3	7	68	39	39
5	RUSHDEN TOWN	28	14	4	10	61	46	32
6	HEANOR TOWN	28	12	7	9	70	45	31
7	ILKESTON TOWN	28	14	2	12	62	41	30
8	BARNSLEY St. PETER'S	28	13	3	12	62	52	29
9	GRANTHAM ROVERS	28	11	5	12	64	47	27
10	DONCASTER ROVERS	28	10	6	12	44	56	26
11	DRESDEN UNITED	28	9	6	13	44	49	24
12	WELLINGBOROUGH TOWN	28	10	4	14	44	71	24
13	MANSFIELD	28	9	2	17	35	68	20
14	NEWARK	28	6	1	21	36	78	13
15	MATLOCK	28	0	0	28	9	130	0

MIDLAND LEAGUE
1896-97

date	opponents	venue	result	scorers	crowd
Sep 5	ILKESTON TOWN	H	1-1	Green	2,000
12	BARNSLEY St. PETER'S	A	0-4		2,000
19	LONG EATON RANGERS	H	2-0	Dixon, Green	
21	RUSHDEN TOWN	A	0-2		
26	HEANOR TOWN	A	2-1	McMain, Pell	
Oct 3	DONCASTER ROVERS	H	5-1	Dixon, Green, McMain (2), Whitehouse (a)	
17	MEXBOROUGH TOWN	A	1-2	Banks	
22	ILKESTON TOWN	A	3-0	3 goals unaccounted for	
24	WELLINGBOROUGH TOWN	H	2-1	Dixon, Whitehouse	4,500
Nov 7	WORKSOP TOWN	A	1-0	1 own goal (b)	
14	DRESDEN UNITED	A	1-3	Whitehouse	
28	LONG EATON RANGERS	A	1-2	Dixon	
Dec 5	GLOSSOP NORTH END	A	0-7		
19	GRANTHAM ROVERS	H	3-0	Ball, E. Panter, Wallis	800
25	GLOSSOP NORTH END	H	4-1	Ball (3), Graham	
Jan 9	BURSLEM PORT VALE	A	1-2	W. Miller	
Feb 6	GRANTHAM ROVERS	A	1-2	W. Miller	
13	BURSLEM PORT VALE	H	2-2	Ball, Heskin	
Mar 6	MEXBOROUGH TOWN	H	4-0	Allen, Dixon, W. Miller (2) (c)	
13	WORKSOP TOWN	H	2-0	E. Panter (2)	
20	CHESTERFIELD	A	0-3		
27	WELLINGBOROUGH TOWN	A	1-1	E. Panter	
Apr 3	BARNSLEY St. PETER'S	H	6-1	Allen, Atherton, Heskin (2), W. Miller, E. Panter	700
5	HEANOR TOWN	H	4-0	Allen (2), Dixon, Heskin (d)	
10	DONCASTER ROVERS	A	0-1		2,000
19	RUSHDEN TOWN	H	2-2	Heskin, Parker	4,000
20	DRESDEN UNITED	H	1-1	Heskin	1,000
24	CHESTERFIELD	H	1-0	Cowan	

(a) Other sources credit Dixon with two goals and McMain with one.

(b) Other sources credit the goal to Dixon.

(c) Other sources credit Dixon with two goals and W. Miller with one.

(d) Other sources credit one of Allen's goals to E. Panter.

FINAL TABLE

	played	won	drawn	lost	for	against	points
1 DONCASTER ROVERS	28	17	5	6	77	40	39
2 GLOSSOP NORTH END	27 (e)	15	4	8	67	39	36
3 LONG EATON RANGERS	28	15	2	11	55	39	32
4 CHESTERFIELD	28	13	6	9	74	53	32
5 **KETTERING**	28	13	5	10	51	40	31
6 WELLINGBOROUGH TOWN	28	12	7	9	52	46	31
7 BURSLEM PORT VALE	28	14	3	11	62	56	31
8 HEANOR TOWN	28	12	6	10	55	47	30
9 ILKESTON TOWN	28	11	7	10	60	57	29
10 DRESDEN UNITED	28	12	5	11	48	63	29
11 BARNSLEY St. PETER'S	28	10	4	14	57	71	24
12 RUSHDEN TOWN	28	9	5	14	43	53	23
13 MEXBOROUGH TOWN	28	7	7	14	39	50	21
14 WORKSOP TOWN	28	6	5	17	27	63	17
15 GRANTHAM ROVERS	27 (e)	6	3	18	26	76	15

(e) Glossop North End v Grantham Rovers was not played. Glossop were awarded two points.

UNITED LEAGUE
1896-97

date	opponents	venue	result	scorers	crowd
Sep 1	WELLINGBOROUGH TOWN	A	3-3	Ball, W. Miller (2)	4,500
16	LOUGHBOROUGH TOWN	A	2-2	Pell, Winterhalder	
Oct 12	LOUGHBOROUGH TOWN	H	2-0	Dixon, W. Miller	400
Nov 2	WOOLWICH ARSENAL	A	1-1	Whitehouse	1,000
16	RUSHDEN TOWN	H	2-3	Ball, Dixon	2,000
23	WOOLWICH ARSENAL	H	0-1		2,000
Jan 16	RUSHDEN TOWN	A	1-2	Dixon	800
Feb 8	MILLWALL ATHLETIC	H	2-3	Heskin, W. Miller (a)	
20	MILLWALL ATHLETIC	A	1-3	Green	2,000
27	LUTON TOWN	A	0-3		
Apr 12	LUTON TOWN	H	1-0	Heskin	
13	TOTTENHAM HOTSPUR	H	5-2	Allen, Cowan, Heskin (2), Parker	
17	TOTTENHAM HOTSPUR	A	1-1	Heskin	200
26	WELLINGBOROUGH TOWN	H	2-0	Dixon, E. Panter	2,000

(a) Other sources credit Heskin's goal to Green.

FINAL TABLE

		played	won	drawn	lost	for	against	points
1	MILLWALL ATHLETIC	14	11	1	2	43	22	23
2	LUTON TOWN	14	10	1	3	52	16	21
3	WOOLWICH ARSENAL	14	6	3	5	28	34	15
4	LOUGHBOROUGH TOWN	14	6	1	7	29	31	13
5	RUSHDEN TOWN	14	6	1	7	25	42	13
6	**KETTERING**	**14**	**4**	**4**	**6**	**23**	**24**	**12**
7	WELLINGBOROUGH TOWN	14	3	3	8	17	39	9
8	TOTTENHAM HOTSPUR	14	1	4	9	25	34	6

MIDLAND LEAGUE
1897-98

date	opponents	venue	result	scorers	crowd
Sep 4	ILKESTON TOWN	H	0-3		2,000
11	BURTON WANDERERS	A	0-0		1,500
18	DONCASTER ROVERS	H	1-0	York	
25	BURSLEM PORT VALE	A	0-4		2,000
27	RUSHDEN TOWN	A	0-1		6,500
Oct 2	BURTON WANDERERS	H	4-0	Panter (3), York	
16	WELLINGBOROUGH TOWN	H	2-1	E. Dixon, Miller	3,000
21	ILKESTON TOWN	A	0-0		
Nov 6	CHESTERFIELD	A	0-3		2,000
13	MEXBOROUGH TOWN	H	1-3	Garfield (a)	
Dec 4	CHESTERFIELD	H	0-0		
18	LONG EATON RANGERS	A	1-2	Panter	
25	WELLINGBOROUGH TOWN	A	1-0	Brearley	
27	BURSLEM PORT VALE	H	4-1	Atherton, Brearley, Garfield (2)	3,000
Jan 1	DONCASTER ROVERS	A	1-1	Panter	3,000
22	GLOSSOP NORTH END	H	1-0	Atherton	2,000
Feb 5	LONG EATON RANGERS	H	1-0	Brearley	
12	GLOSSOP NORTH END	A	1-2	Panter	
19	BARNSLEY St. PETER'S	H	0-1		2,000
26	MEXBOROUGH TOWN	A	0-3		
Mar 26	BARNSLEY St. PETER'S	A	0-2		800
Apr 11	RUSHDEN TOWN	H	1-1	Draper	4,000

(a) Other sources credit the goal to Miller.

FINAL TABLE

	played	won	drawn	lost	for	against	points
1 MEXBOROUGH TOWN	22	15	3	4	53	30	33
2 BARNSLEY St. PETER'S	22	14	3	5	47	29	31
3 CHESTERFIELD	22	11	7	4	54	23	29
4 ILKESTON TOWN	22	9	6	7	37	39	24
5 BURSLEM PORT VALE	22	10	3	9	46	32	23
6 RUSHDEN TOWN	22	9	5	8	35	44	23
7 KETTERING	**22**	**7**	**5**	**10**	**19**	**28**	**19**
8 LONG EATON RANGERS	22	7	5	10	26	44	19
9 GLOSSOP NORTH END	22	8	2	12	41	47	18
10 DONCASTER ROVERS	22	5	6	11	33	35	16
11 BURTON WANDERERS	22	5	6	11	31	44	16
12 WELLINGBOROUGH TOWN	22	5	3	14	21	48	13

UNITED LEAGUE
1897-98

date	opponents	venue	result	scorers	crowd
Sep 1	WELLINGBOROUGH TOWN	A	5-3	Harry Dixon, Green, Lawrence, Pell, 1 goal unaccounted for	
16	TOTTENHAM HOTSPUR	A	1-1	1 goal unaccounted for	
Oct 4	WOOLWICH ARSENAL	A	0-4		1,000
18	LUTON TOWN	A	1-3	Harry Dixon (a)	1,000
Nov 1	MILLWALL ATHLETIC	H	3-1	Harry Dixon, Panter (2)	
Dec 13	LUTON TOWN	H	1-0	Miller (b)	
Jan 10	TOTTENHAM HOTSPUR	H	4-2	Brearley, Miller (2), 1 goal unaccounted for	
Feb 28	MILLWALL ATHLETIC	A	0-1		
Mar 5	RUSHDEN TOWN	H	1-0	Hitchcock	3,000
12	LOUGHBOROUGH TOWN	A	0-2		
19	RUSHDEN TOWN	A	3-1	Brearley, Harry Dixon, Heskin	
Apr 2	LOUGHBOROUGH TOWN	H	3-0	Brearley, Miller, Panter	
4	WOOLWICH ARSENAL	H	1-2	Harry Dixon	1,000
9	SOUTHAMPTON	A	1-2	Draper	
23	SOUTHAMPTON	H	2-1	Garfield, Heskin	
30	WELLINGBOROUGH TOWN	H	2-1	Pell, 1 own goal (c)	

(a) Other sources credit the goal to Miller.
(b) Other sources credit the goal to Harry Dixon.
(c) Other sources credit both goals to Pell.

FINAL TABLE

		played	won	drawn	lost	for	against	points
1	LUTON TOWN	16	13	2	1	49	11	28
2	TOTTENHAM HOTSPUR	16	8	5	3	40	27	21
3	WOOLWICH ARSENAL	16	8	5	3	35	24	21
4	**KETTERING**	**16**	**9**	**1**	**6**	**28**	**24**	**19**
5	RUSHDEN TOWN	16	7	1	8	24	26	15
6	SOUTHAMPTON	16	6	3	7	23	28	15 (d)
7	MILLWALL ATHLETIC	16	4	4	8	27	27	12
8	WELLINGBOROUGH TOWN	16	3	3	10	17	42	9
9	LOUGHBOROUGH TOWN	16	1	2	13	8	42	4

(d) Other sources indicate Southampton were docked two points for fielding an ineligible player.

MIDLAND LEAGUE
1898-99

date	opponents	venue	result	scorers	crowd
Sep 17	HEANOR TOWN	H	3-1	Miller, Pell, Winterhalder	1,000
24	LEICESTER FOSSE RESERVES	A	0-3		1,500
26	RUSHDEN TOWN	A	0-1		3,500
Oct 1	DERBY COUNTY RESERVES	H	3-3	Beaver, Winterhalder (2)	
8	CHESTERFIELD	H	2-2	Winterhalder, Woodward	1,500
10	SHEFFIELD UNITED RESERVES	A	3-3	Beaver, Winterhalder, Woodward	
20	ILKESTON TOWN	A	0-2		1,000
22	LEICESTER FOSSE RESERVES	H	3-0	Winterhalder, Woodward, 1 own goal	
Nov 12	HEANOR TOWN	A	2-1	Panter, 1 goal rushed through	1,000
26	LONG EATON RANGERS	H	1-0	Panter	1,000
Dec 3	DERBY COUNTY RESERVES	A	2-0	Beaver, Panter	1,500
17	ILKESTON TOWN	H	4-1	Beaver, H. Dainty (2), Miller	2,000
26	DONCASTER ROVERS	H	2-1	Dixon, Farren	3,000
28	WELLINGBOROUGH TOWN	A	2-2	Dixon (2)	4,000
31	BURTON WANDERERS	A	1-1	Ingram	
Jan 2	CHESTERFIELD	A	1-2	Panter	3,000
14	THE WEDNESDAY RESERVES	H	2-0	Dixon, Draper	
Feb 4	SHEFFIELD UNITED RESERVES	H	1-0	Draper	1,000
25	LONG EATON RANGERS	A	7-0	Dixon (3), Draper, Winterhalder, Woodward, 1 goal unaccounted for	
Mar 11	WELLINGBOROUGH TOWN	H	0-0		3,500
18	BURTON WANDERERS	H	2-0	Beaver, Dixon	
25	THE WEDNESDAY RESERVES	A	1-2	Panter	
30	DONCASTER ROVERS	A	1-3	Dixon	
Apr 3	RUSHDEN TOWN	H	2-1	Beaver, Woodward (a)	5,000
8	MEXBOROUGH TOWN	H	1-1	Draper	
22	MEXBOROUGH TOWN	A	1-2	Winterhalder	2,000

(a) Other sources credit Woodward's goal to Winterhalder.

FINAL TABLE

		played	won	drawn	lost	for	against	points
1	DONCASTER ROVERS	26	14	5	7	56	47	33
2	ILKESTON TOWN	26	15	2	9	55	37	32
3	**KETTERING**	**26**	**12**	**7**	**7**	**47**	**32**	**31**
4	CHESTERFIELD	26	14	3	9	59	42	31
5	WELLINGBOROUGH TOWN	26	11	6	9	49	34	28
6	BURTON WANDERERS	26	11	5	10	49	38	27
7	RUSHDEN TOWN	26	12	3	11	44	42	27
8	DERBY COUNTY RESERVES	26	10	5	11	61	47	25
9	SHEFFIELD UNITED RESERVES	26	9	7	10	45	45	25
10	THE WEDNESDAY RESERVES	26	10	5	11	42	52	25
11	HEANOR TOWN	26	8	5	13	35	53	21
12	LEICESTER FOSSE RESERVES	26	9	2	15	34	58	20
13	LONG EATON RANGERS	26	9	2	15	37	65	20
14	MEXBOROUGH TOWN	26	8	3	15	33	54	19

UNITED LEAGUE
1898-99

date	opponents	venue	result	scorers	crowd
Sep 3	RUSHDEN TOWN	H	1-0	McArlie	
10	BRISTOL CITY	A	0-3		5,000
19	MILLWALL ATHLETIC	H	2-0	McArlie, Miller	1,000
Oct 5	SOUTHAMPTON	A	0-4		
24	WOOLWICH ARSENAL	H	2-1	Panter, Woodward	
26	READING	A	0-4		
31	MILLWALL ATHLETIC	A	0-1		
Nov 14	READING	H	1-1	Beaver	
21	LUTON TOWN	H	4-0	Beaver, Draper, Heskin, Panter	500
Dec 5	TOTTENHAM HOTSPUR	A	0-3		
24	BRIGHTON UNITED	A	0-2		
27	RUSHDEN TOWN	A	3-1	Draper, Woodward (2) (a)	
Feb 6	WOOLWICH ARSENAL	A	2-4	Woodward (2)	600
18	BRIGHTON UNITED	H	2-0	Draper, Woodward	
27	TOTTENHAM HOTSPUR	H	0-1		1,000
Mar 13	SOUTHAMPTON	H	1-2	Dixon	1,000
Apr 1	BRISTOL CITY	H	0-3		
15	WELLINGBOROUGH TOWN	A	0-2		
26	LUTON TOWN	A	2-1	Beaver, Woodward	
29	WELLINGBOROUGH TOWN	H	1-0	Draper	800

(a) Other sources credit Draper's goal as an own goal.

FINAL TABLE

	played	won	drawn	lost	for	against	points
1 MILLWALL ATHLETIC	20	14	3	3	42	19	31
2 SOUTHAMPTON	20	12	1	7	53	32	25
3 (b) TOTTENHAM HOTSPUR	20	11	2	7	36	25	24
4 (b) WOOLWICH ARSENAL	20	10	4	6	40	30	24
5 BRISTOL CITY	20	11	0	9	43	31	22
6 READING	20	8	5	7	36	25	21
7 BRIGHTON UNITED	20	10	1	9	41	42	21
8 WELLINGBOROUGH TOWN	20	7	1	12	32	40	15
9 KETTERING	**20**	**8**	**1**	**11**	**21**	**33**	**15** (c)
10 RUSHDEN TOWN	20	6	1	13	26	45	13
11 LUTON TOWN	20	2	3	15	24	71	7

(b) Other sources have Woolwich Arsenal third and Tottenham Hotspur fourth.

(c) Kettering were docked two points for fielding an ineligible player versus Rushden Town on 3 September.

MIDLAND LEAGUE
1899-1900

date	opponents	venue	result	scorers	crowd
Sep 9	WELLINGBOROUGH TOWN	H	2-1	Draper, Pegg	
25	RUSHDEN TOWN	A	0-0		
30	LINCOLN CITY RESERVES	H	1-4	Carter	
Oct 5	BARNSLEY RESERVES	A	6-3	Coleman, Heskin, Mawson, Pegg (2), Winterhalder	
7	NEWARK	H	5-1	Carter, Coleman (2), Draper, Winterhalder	
14	LEICESTER FOSSE RESERVES	H	7-1	Carter, Coleman (2), Mawson, Pegg (3)	
21	NORTHAMPTON TOWN	A	2-1	Draper, Winterhalder	4,000
Nov 4	ILKESTON TOWN	A	1-1	Draper	
11	HEANOR TOWN	H	2-1	Heskin, Mawson	
25	DONCASTER ROVERS	A	2-3	Heskin, Winterhalder	
Dec 16	HEANOR TOWN	A	2-1	Carter, Mawson	
23	NORTHAMPTON TOWN	H	2-0	Coleman, Draper	
25	DONCASTER ROVERS	H	2-1	Mawson, Pegg	
27	WELLINGBOROUGH TOWN	A	0-2		
30	BURTON WANDERERS	H	4-0	Barnett, Carter, Coleman, Pegg	
Jan 6	ILKESTON TOWN	H	4-1	Coleman, Draper (2), Pegg	
13	LINCOLN CITY RESERVES	A	0-0		
20	DERBY COUNTY RESERVES	H	3-1	Pegg (3)	
Feb 17	NEWARK	A	2-2	Pegg (2)	
Apr 7	BURTON WANDERERS	A	2-0	Mawson, Pegg	
14	DERBY COUNTY RESERVES	A	0-0		
18	BARNSLEY RESERVES	H	2-0	Carter, Pegg	
23	RUSHDEN TOWN	H	4-0	Carter, Draper, Mawson, Pell	
30	LEICESTER FOSSE RESERVES	A	3-0	Mawson (2), Pegg	

MIDLAND LEAGUE CHAMPIONSHIP MATCH

date	opponents	venue	result	scorers	crowd
Apr 16	WELLINGBOROUGH TOWN	H	6-1	Carter, Pegg (3), Pell, Winterhalder	

FINAL TABLE

	played	won	drawn	lost	for	against	points
1 KETTERING	**24**	**16**	**5**	**3**	**58**	**24**	**37**
2 WELLINGBOROUGH TOWN	24	16	4	4	64	38	36
3 NORTHAMPTON TOWN	24	16	2	6	66	36	34
4 DERBY COUNTY RESERVES	24	11	5	8	63	46	27
5 LINCOLN CITY RESERVES	24	11	3	10	45	46	25
6 HEANOR TOWN	24	9	7	8	31	36	25
7 DONCASTER ROVERS	24	9	6	9	51	42	24
8 ILKESTON TOWN	24	9	6	9	43	44	24
9 NEWARK	24	10	1	13	51	50	21
10 BURTON WANDERERS	24	6	6	12	40	62	18
11 RUSHDEN TOWN	24	7	2	15	38	56	16
12 BARNSLEY RESERVES	24	5	6	13	39	68	16
13 LEICESTER FOSSE RESERVES	24	3	3	18	34	74	9